# XPath and XPointer

# XPath and XPointer

*John E. Simpson*

O'REILLY®

Beijing · Cambridge · Farnham · Köln · Sebastopol · Tokyo

**XPath and XPointer**
by John E. Simpson

Published by O'Reilly & Associates, Inc., 1005 Gravenstein Highway North, Sebastopol, CA 95472.

O'Reilly & Associates books may be purchased for educational, business, or sales promotional use. Online editions are also available for most titles (*safari.oreilly.com*). For more information, contact our corporate/institutional sales department: (800) 998-9938 or *corporate@oreilly.com*.

| | |
|---|---|
| **Editor:** | Simon St.Laurent |
| **Production Editor:** | Linley Dolby |
| **Cover Designer:** | Ellie Volckhausen |
| **Interior Designer:** | David Futato |

**Printing History:**

| | |
|---|---|
| August 2002: | First Edition. |

ISBN: 978-0-596-00291-6
[LSI]

# Table of Contents

# Preface

XML documents contain regular but flexible structures. Developers can use those structures as a framework on which to build powerful transformative and reporting applications, as well as to establish connections between different parts of documents. XPath and XPointer are two W3C-created technologies that make these structures accessible to applications. XPath is used for locating XML content within an XML document; XPointer is the standard for addressing such content, once located. The two standards are not typically used in isolation but in support of two critical extensions to the core of XML: Extensible Stylesheet Language Transformations (XSLT) and XLink, respectively. They are also finding wide use in other applications that need to reference parts of documents. These two closely related technologies provide the underpinning of an enormous amount of XML processing.

## Who Should Read This Book?

Presumably, if you're browsing a book like this, you already know the rudiments of XML itself. You may have experimented with XSLT but, if so, haven't completely mastered it. (You can't do much in XSLT without first becoming comfortable with at least the basics of XPath.) Similarly, you may have experimented with XLinks; in this case, you've probably focused on linking to entire documents other than the one containing the link. XPointer will be your tool of choice for linking to portions of documents—external to or within the document where the XLink reference is made.

As support for XPath is integrated into the Document Object Model (DOM), DOM developers may also find XPath a convenient alternative to walking through document trees. Finally, developers interested in hypertext and other applications where references may have to cross node boundaries will find a thorough explanation of XPointer, the leading technology for creating those references.

You need not be an XML document author or developer to read this book. The XPath standard is fairly mature, and therefore is already incorporated in a number of high-level tools. XPointer, by contrast, is not yet a final standard; for this reason, the use of XPointers will probably be limited to experimental purposes in the short term.

Regardless of whether you're coming at the subject as primarily a document author or designer, or as a developer, *XPath and XPointer* can be revisited as often as you need it: for reference or as a refresher.

## Who Should Not Read This Book?

If you don't yet understand XML (including XML namespaces) and have never looked at XSLT, you probably need to start with an XML book. John E. Simpson's *Just XML* (Prentice-Hall PTR) and Erik Ray's *Learning XML* (O'Reilly & Associates) are both good places to start.

## Organization of the Book

Chapter 1, *Introducing XPath and XPointer*, introduces you to the foundations of XPath and XPointer, and where they're used.

Chapter 2, *XPath Basics*, gets you started with XPath's node tree model for documents and XPath syntax, as well as the set of node types accessible in XPath.

Chapter 3, *Location Steps and Paths*, moves deeper into XPath, detailing the use of XPath axes, node tests, and predicates.

Chapter 4, *XPath Functions and Numeric Operators*, explains the tools XPath offers for manipulating content once it has been located.

Chapter 5, *XPath in Action*, demonstrates XPath techniques with over 30 examples using a wide variety of XPath parts.

Chapter 6, *XPath 2.0*, examines the upcoming 2.0 version of XPath, including new features and interoperability issues.

Chapter 7, *XPointer Background*, explains XPointer's perspective on XML documents and how its use in URLs requires some changes from basic XPath.

Chapter 8, *XPointer Syntax*, explains the details of using XPointer syntax, including "bare names," child sequences, and interactions with namespaces.

Chapter 9, *XPointer Beyond XPath*, delves deeper into XPointer, exploring the techniques XPointer offers for referencing points and ranges of text, not just nodes.

## Conventions Used in This Book

The following font conventions are used throughout the book:

Constant width is used for:

- Code examples and fragments
- Anything that might appear in an XML document, including element names, tags, attribute values, entity references, and processing instructions

- Anything that might appear in a program, including keywords, operators, method names, class names, and literals

**Constant-width bold** is used for:

- User input
- Signifying emphasis in code statements

*Constant-width italic* is used for:

- Replaceable elements in code statements

*Italic* is used for:

- New terms where they are defined
- Pathnames, filenames, and program names
- Host and domain names (*www.xml.com*)
- URLs (*http://xmlhack.com/read.php?item=1721*)

 Theis icon indicates a tip, suggestion, or general note.

 This icon indicates a warning or caution.

Please note that XML (and therefore XPath and XPointer) is case sensitive. Therefore, a BATTLEINFO element would not be the same as a battleinfo or BattleInfo element.

## Comments and Questions

Please address comments and questions concerning this book to the publisher:

O'Reilly & Associates, Inc.
1005 Gravenstein Highway North
Sebastopol, CA 95472
(800) 998-9938 (in the United States or Canada)
(707) 829-0515 (international/local)
(707) 829-0104 (fax)

There is a web page for this book, which lists errata, examples, or any additional information. You can access this page at:

*http://www.oreilly.com/catalog/xpathpointer*

To comment or ask technical questions about this book, send email to:

*bookquestions@oreilly.com*

For more information about books, conferences, Resource Centers, and the O'Reilly Network, see the O'Reilly web site at:

*http://www.oreilly.com*

## Acknowledgments

It's almost laughable that any technical book has just a few names on the cover, if that many. Such books are always the product of many minds and talents being brought to bear on the problem at hand.

For their help with *XPath and XPointer*, I am especially indebted to a number of individuals. Simon St.Laurent, my editor, has for years been a personal hero; I was flattered that he asked me to write the book in the first place and am grateful for his patience and support during its development. I came to XPath in particular by way of XSLT, and for this reason I happily acknowledge the implicit contributions to this book from that standard's user community, especially (in alphabetical order): Oliver Becker, David Carlisle, James Clark, Bob DuCharme, Tony Graham, G. Ken Holman, Michael Kay, Evan Lenz, Steve Muench, Dave Pawson, Wendell Piez, Sebastian Rahtz, and Jeni Tennison. J. David Eisenberg, Evan Lenz, and Jeni Tennison served as technical reviewers during the book's final preproduction stage; words cannot express how grateful I am for their patience, thoroughness, and good humor. Acknowledging the (unwitting or explicit) help of all those people does not, of course, imply that they're in any way responsible for the content of this book; errors and omissions are mine and mine alone.

I am also grateful to my colleagues and superiors in the City of Tallahassee's Public Works and Information Systems Services departments for their support during the writing of *XPath and XPointer*. They have endured far more than their deserved share of blank, preoccupied stares from me over the last few months.

Finally, to my wife Toni: to paraphrase Don Marquis's dedication to his *Archie and Mehitabel*, thanks "for Toni knows what/and Toni knows why."

# CHAPTER 1

# Introducing XPath and XPointer

The XPath and XPointer specifications promulgated by the World Wide Web Consortium (W3C) aim to simplify the location of XML-based content. With software based on those two specs, you're freed of much of the tedium of finding out if something useful is in a document, so you can simply enjoy the excitement of *doing* something with it.

Before getting specifically into the details of XPath or XPointer, though, you should have a handle on some concepts and other background the two specs have in common. Don't worry, the details—and there are enough, it seems, to fill a phone directory (or this book, at least)—are coming.

## Why XPath and XPointer?

Detailed answers to the following questions are implicit throughout this book and explicit in a couple of spots:

Why should I care about XPath and XPointer? What do they even *do*?

To answer them briefly for now, consider even a simple XML document, such as this:

```
<house_pet_hazards>
   <hazard type="cleanup">
      <name>hairballs</name>
      <guilty_party species="cat">Dilly</guilty_party>
      <guilty_party species="cat">Nameless</guilty_party>
      <guilty_party species="cat">Katie</guilty_party>
   </hazard>
   <hazard type="cleanup">
      <name>miscellaneous post-ingestion surprises</name>
      <guilty_party species="cat">Dilly</guilty_party>
      <guilty_party species="cat">Katie</guilty_party>
      <guilty_party species="dog">Kianu</guilty_party>
      <guilty_party species="snake">Mephisto</guilty_party>
   </hazard>
```

```
<hazard type="phys_jeopardy">
   <name>underfoot instability</name>
   <guilty_party species="cat">Dilly</guilty_party>
   <guilty_party species="snake">Mephisto</guilty_party>
</hazard>
</house_pet_hazards>
```

Even so simple a document as this opens the door to dozens of potential questions, from the obvious ("Which pets have been guilty of tripping me up as I walked across the room?") to the non-obvious, even baroque ("Which species is most likely to cause a problem for me on a given day?" and "For hazards requiring cleanup, is there a correlation between the species and the number of letters in a given pet's name?"). For real-world XML applications—the ones inspiring you to research XPath/XPointer in the first place—the number of such practical questions might be in the thousands.

XPath provides you with a standard tool for locating the answers to real-world questions—answers contained in an XML document's content or hidden in its structure. For its part, XPointer (which in part is built on an XPath foundation) provides you with standard mechanisms for creating references to parts of XML documents and using them as addresses.

On a practical level, if you know and become comfortable with XPath, you'll have prepared yourself for easy use not only of XPointer but also of numerous other XML-related specifications, notably Extensible Stylesheet Language Transformations (XSLT) and XQuery. Knowing XPointer provides you with a key to a smaller castle (the XLink standard for advanced hyperlinking capabilities within or among portions of documents) but without that key the door is barred.

## Antecedents/History

An interesting portion of many W3C specs is the list of non-normative (or simply "other") references at the end. After wading through all the dry prose whose overarching purpose is the removal of ambiguity (sometimes at the expense of clarity and terseness), in this section you get to peek into the minds and personalities of the specs' authors. (The "non-normative" says, in effect, that the resources listed here aren't required reading—although they may have profoundly affected the authors' own thinking about the subject.)

The XPath specification's "other references," without exception, are other formally published standards from the W3C or other (quasi-)official institutions. But XPath, as you will see, is a full-blown standard (the W3C refers to these as "recommendations"). XPointer is still a bit ragged around the edges at the time of this writing, and its non-normative references (Appendix A.2 of the *XPointer xpointer() Scheme*) are consequently more revealing of the background. This is especially useful, because there is some overlap in the membership of the W3C Working Groups (WGs) that produced XPointer and XPath.

Following is a brief look at a few of the most influential historical antecedents for XPath and XPointer.

## DSSSL

The Document Style Semantics and Specification Language (DSSSL) was developed as a means of defining the presentation characteristics of SGML documents. Based syntactically on a programming language called Scheme, DSSSL does for SGML roughly what XSLT does for XML: it identifies for a DSSSL processor portions of the structure of an input document and how to behave once those portions are located.

Of particular interest in relation to this book's subject matter is DSSSL's *core query language*. This is the portion of a DSSSL instruction that locates content of a particular kind in an SGML document. For instance:

```
(element bottle
   [...instructions...])
```

tells the processor to follow the steps outlined in [...instructions...] for each occurrence of a bottle element in the source document. You can also navigate to various portions of the source document based on *context*. For example, the following starts with the current node (the portion of the source document with which the processor is currently working) to locate the nearest packaging ancestor:

```
(ancestor packaging (current-node)
   [...instructions...])
```

An *ancestor* is the parent of a given node, or that parent's parent, and so on up the tree of nodes to the document root. The concepts of a tree of nodes, ancestors, children, and the like all made their way eventually into XPath.

## XSL

In August 1997, even before XML 1.0 became a W3C Recommendation itself, the W3C received a first stab at a language for describing how an XML documents contents should be displayed, such as in a web browser. The initial proposal called for the creation of the Extensible Stylesheet Language (XSL). The W3C began work on its own version of XSL in mid-1998, and the complete XSL only reached Recommendation status in October 2001. Along the way, its editors recognized its complex nature: like DSSSL, XSL included both a language for locating content in a source document and a language for describing processor behavior upon locating that content.

The principal editor of the XSL specification was James Clark, who had previously developed the widely used Jade DSSSL processor. Unsurprisingly, then, XSL could be characterized as a DSSSL wolf in an XML sheep's clothing. Taken together, the specification of which portion of the source tree an instruction referred to, and the instruction itself, were referred to as *construction rules*. The implication of this term was that for a given bit of source tree content, the XSL stylesheet would construct a particular result. A simple XSL construction rule might look something like this:

```
<rule>
    <target-element type="bottle"/>
    <p font-size="12pt">
        <children/>
    </p>
</rule>
```

The XSL processor would, for each occurrence of a bottle element in the source tree, construct a resulting p element with the indicated type attribute, then the processor would proceed to handle any children of that p element. (Elsewhere in the stylesheet, presumably, would be construction rules describing what to do with these children.)

One problem with XSL, as you can see above, is that it indiscriminately mixed elements from its own vocabulary (such as rule, target-element, and children) with those from the resulting documents (p, in this example). This was a perfect case for the use of namespaces, which XSL integrated when that specification was ready.

XSL went through a couple of Working Draft iterations before a light bulb went on over the editors heads: the ability to locate content in an XML source tree fit a general-purpose need, not only for XSL transformations from source to result but also for other applications, such as XPointer and eventually XQuery. The W3C eventually split the original XSL project into XSLT and XSL-Formatting Objects (XSL-FO, covered in the main XSL specification), and XPath emerged as a separate entity from XSLT soon after. XSLT and XPath reached Recommendation status in late 1999, well ahead of the rest of XSL.

## TEI

The venerable and influential Text Encoding Initiative (TEI) first appeared in 1994 as a joint product of three professional/academic bodies: the Association for Computers and the Humanities (ACH), the Association for Computational Linguistics (ACL), and the Association for Literary and Linguistic Computing (ALLC).

 An authoritative list of references on the TEI is provided at *http://www.uic.edu/orgs/tei/p3*. As one of the resources there notes, the 1994 publication of "Guidelines for Text Encoding and Interchange" followed five years of work—venerable indeed.

TEI's main product was a series of several hundred "textual feature definitions" in the form of extensible SGML elements and attributes. With some exceptions, these SGML-based features are readily understandable by anyone familiar with XML DTDs. Among the supplementary tagsets provided is a group whose purpose is to establish links from one portion of an SGML document to another within the same document or from one SGML document to a completely separate one. (If this already sounds familiar, no surprise there: these concepts later were carried over not just to the relatively recent XPath and XPointer, but much earlier to HTML itself.)

Particularly important for XPath and XPointer was TEI's notion of *extended pointers*. A regular TEI link or cross-reference depended on such language features as the SGML equivalent of XML's ID- and IDREF-type attributes for its operation. Extended pointers went further, permitting you to locate content on the basis of the content's markup structure. As a TEI tutorial on "Cross-References and Links" (at *http://www.tei-c.org/Lite/U5-ptrs.html*) puts it:

> In this language, locations are defined as a series of steps, each one identifying some part of the document, often in terms of the locations identified by the previous step. For example, you would point to the third sentence of the second paragraph of chapter two by selecting chapter two in the first step, the second paragraph in the second step, and the third sentence in the last step. A step can be defined in terms of SGML concepts (such as parent, descendent, preceding, etc.) or, more loosely, in terms of text patterns, word, or character positions.

Without this essential concept, it's doubtful that XPath and XPointer would have emerged in the form they ultimately adopted.

Note that the most specific form of HTML linking possible depends on the presence of named targets in the resource to which you're linking. The smartest HTML link doesn't have any intelligence remotely like that described in the above quotation.

## Intermedia

Even before work began on the TEI Guidelines, various individuals at Brown University had been exploring the possibilities of what they called *hypertext*. (The term itself was coined in the 1960s by Ted Nelson, who by 1968 was an instructor at Brown.) In 1988, the group published "Intermedia: The Concept and the Construction of a Seamless Information Environment" in the professional journal *IEEE Computer*.

Intermedia was an ambitious research project that came, in time, to include such features as text and graphics editors, a timeline editor, and so on. One of its crucial features was dubbed the "Web view." (Remember, this was in the mid- to late 1980s. A capital-W Web existed in almost no one else's mind at the time.)

The thorny problem that Intermedia's Web view attempted to tackle was the possibility of becoming "lost in hyperspace." As the number of hypertext documents (and the points within them) multiplied, the number of possible links among them quickly grew out of control—to the point of unintelligibility.

The Web view's seminal contribution to the future of hypertext media—certainly as codified in XPath and XPointer—was its provision for considering only the local context. Instead of trying to deal with all possible links from a given point to all other points, this *local map* view of the hypertext world allowed you to focus on a single (albeit constantly shifting) path: start at A, then proceed to B (which shares some relationship with A), then to C, and so on. As you will see by the end of this book, while concentrating on individual paths causes you to lose sight of the "big picture," it also enables you to get from any given point to any other. (Tellingly, Intermedia itself eventually dropped support for the big-picture "global maps," having learned they were so complicated that no one wanted to use them anyway.)

## XPath, XPointer, and Other XML-Related Specs

It's highly unlikely, if you're at the point of wanting to learn about XPath and XPointer, that you'll be surprised by one ugly reality: everything in XML seems to hinge on everything else. For a brief period of a year or two, you could pick up a couple of general-purpose books on XML and learn everything you needed to know about the subject; that time is long gone.

So let's pretend that XML as a whole is represented graphically by one of Intermedia's global maps. It's a mess, isn't it? There's no way to figure it all out, even if by "it" you just mean that part of it relating to XPath and XPointer—or so it seems. But let's narrow the focus a bit, following the Intermedia Web view's local-map approach.

Let's start with XPath. Successfully getting your mind around XPath currently requires that you have some knowledge of XML itself (including such occasionally overlooked little dark corners as ID-type attributes and whitespace handling). It also requires that you "get" at least the rudiments of XML namespaces.*

XPointer is a bit more complicated. First, it's built principally on an XPath foundation. While it's possible to use XPointer with no knowledge at all of XPath, the range of applications in which you can do so is quite limited.

Second, XPointers themselves are used by the XLink standard for linking from one XML resource to another (in the same or a different document). You can come to understand *how to use* XPointers quite completely without ever actually using them, and hence without any working knowledge of XLink; nonetheless, an elementary grasp of at least basic XLink terminology and syntax is necessary for true understanding.

Third, a couple of XML-related standards—XML Base and the XML Infoset—are referenced by the XPointer spec but don't require that you understand much about them to effectively use XPointer.

---

* Understanding certain XPath features seems to presume familiarity with such non-XML issues as how computers perform floating-point arithmetic and the dozens of ways in which legitimate Uniform Resource Identifiers (URIs) may be formed. I'd argue, though, that you don't need an intimate, profound familiarity with those issues—just some common sense.

Finally, as you will see, an ability to use XPointer depends to a certain extent on a number of non-XML standards (particularly, Internet media types, URIs, and character encodings).

 Don't panic; I'll cover what you need to know of these more-obscure standards when the need arises.

In short, the route to XPath and XPointer mastery might look something like Figure 1-1.

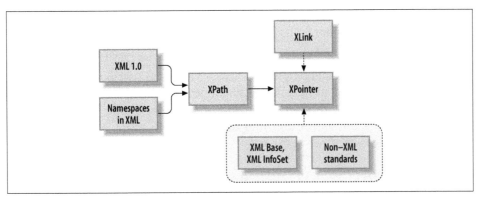

*Figure 1-1. Interdependencies among XML-related standards*

In this diagram, the connections you really have to be concerned with are the ones depicted with solid lines; the connections—and the one box—depicted with dashed lines will be of less critical concern.

---

### Intentional (and Temporary) Oversight

*Not* shown in Figure 1-1 is the 800-pound gorilla of XML standards, XML Schema. The current version of XPath is already being revised to make the collision between it and XML Schema less painful, at least in theory. This issue is discussed at greater length in Chapter 6.

XPointer knows very little of XML Schema, though some of its parts can work with ID values defined in XML Schema. Beyond that, the future is open. The best we can hope at this point is that XML Schema will have some (ideally, some *pleasant*) effect on XPointer.

---

## Specs Dependent on XPath and XPointer

The other side—not what you need to know to use XPath and XPointer, but what you need to know XPath and XPointer *for*—is rich. (One of this book's early reviewers said that she gets "quite excited" by the range. I'm not sure I'd go that far, but I take her point.) Here's a sampling.

First, XPath. As you already know from what I've covered, you can use XPath to leverage yourself into practical use of XSLT, XPointer, and XQuery. XPath syntax is also used in the following standards, which need to refer to portions of XML documents:

- XForms (current version at *http://www.w3.org/TR/xforms/*)
- The Document Object Model (DOM), level 3 (see *http://www.w3.org/TR/DOM-Level-3-XPath/xpath.html*)
- XML Schema (see *http://www.w3.org/TR/xmlschema-1/*, particularly Section 3.11)

XPointer is more of a special-purpose tool than XPath and its range of usefulness is therefore narrower. You already know about its usefulness to XLink. However, XPointer is also at the heart of the XInclude spec for incorporating fragments of one document within another. You can find the current version of XInclude at *http://www.w3.org/TR/xinclude/*.

# XPath and XPointer Versus XQuery

To get one other important question out of the way immediately: XPath and XPointer are *not* XQuery. The latter is a recent addition to the (rather crowded) gallery of the W3C's XML-related standards. Its purpose is to provide to XML-based data stores some (ideally all) of the advantages of Structured Query Language (SQL) in the relational-database world. In SQL, a very simple query might look something like this:

```
SELECT emp_id, emp_name
FROM emp_table
WHERE emp_id = "73519"
```

As you can see, this comprises a straightforward mix of SQL keywords (shown here in uppercase), the names of relational tables and fields, operators (such as the equals sign), and literal values (such as 73519). The result of "running" such a query is a list, in table form (that is, rows and columns), of data values.

The XQuery form of the above SQL query might look as follows (note in particular the relationship between the above WHERE clause and the boldfaced portion of the XQuery query):

```
{for $b in document("emp_table.xml")//employee[emp_id = "73519"]
    return
        <p>{ emp_id }{ emp_name }</p>
}
```

The result of "running" this query is a well-formed XML document or document fragment, such as:

```
<p>
   <emp_id>73519</emp_id>
   <emp_name>DeGaulle,Charles</emp_name>
</p>
```

XQuery is still wending its way through the sometimes-tortuous route prescribed for all W3C specifications; at the time of this writing, it's still a Working Draft, dated April 2002. A number of controversies swirl about it. First is that, while its equivalent of the SQL WHERE clause is based on XPath, it's not *quite* XPath as you will come to understand it. (The XPath-based portion of the above XQuery statement is in boldface.) Second, XQuery's approach to returning an XML result from an XML source conflicts with the approach taken by the XSLT spec for the same purpose. And third is the XQuery syntax itself, which though vaguely resembling XML,[*] is not exactly XML. The "meaning" of an XQuery query is bound up not in elements and attributes but in special element text content delimited by curly braces (the { and } characters).

Now, there are valid reasons for not using pure XML syntax in general-purpose languages, such as XQuery and (as you will see) XPath and XPointer. Chief among these reasons—the reason why these specs' authors almost always drop the use of purely XML-based syntax after first considering it—is that the verbosity is overwhelming. For instance, the W3C has prepared a Working Draft version (dated, as of this writing, June 2001) of something called XQueryX: a purely XML syntax representation of XQuery queries. Section 3 of this document provides examples of XQuery queries and their XQueryX counterparts; a typical XQuery query takes up seven lines, while the equivalent XQueryX form is 57 lines long.

 If you're interested in seeing some of these rather gruesome (in my opinion) examples for yourself, you can find the current version of the XQueryX standard at *http://www.w3.org/TR/xqueryx*.

Another problem with using purely XML syntax for general-purpose applications is namespaces. If queries (or path/pointer language expressions) had to use XML syntax, they'd need to include namespace qualifications to distinguish the queries, paths, and pointers from the surrounding document's content, greatly increasing the complexity of any document that needed to use them. That's why XPath and XPointer expressions are served up in attribute values and why XQuery's counterparts appear in element content.

---

[*] For example, the XQuery snippet here includes a <p> and </p> start tag/end tag pair.

I don't mean to imply here, as you will see, that you can ignore namespace issues in constructing path and pointer expressions. For instance, if you wish to locate an element with a particular name in a document, you must still carry—at least in the back of your head—the question, "Do I mean the name and its namespace prefix, if one, or just the name itself?" My point here relates strictly to the syntax of the general-purpose "querying" language itself. That said, XQuery's use of specially delimited and formatted element content seems to me to fly in the face of XML's classic emphasis on supplying meaning via markup (as opposed to embedding it in text strings outside the markup), in not entirely satisfactory ways.

# CHAPTER 2

# XPath Basics

Chapter 1 provided sketchy information about using XPath. For the remainder of the book, you'll get details aplenty. In particular, this chapter covers the most fundamental building blocks of XPath. These are the "things" XPath syntax (covered in succeeding chapters) enables you to manipulate. Chief among these "things" are XPath *expressions*, the *nodes* and *node-sets* returned by those expressions, the *context* in which an expression is evaluated, and the so-called *string-values* returned by each type of node.

## The Node Tree: An Introduction

You'll learn much more about nodes in this chapter and the rest of the book. But before proceeding into even the most elementary details about *using* XPath, it's essential that you understand what, exactly, an XPath processor deals with.

Consider this fairly simple document:

```
<?xml-stylesheet type="text/xsl" href="battleinfo.xsl"?>
<battleinfo conflict="WW2">
   <name>Guadalcanal</name>
   <!-- Note: Add dates, units, key personnel -->
   <geog general="Pacific Theater">
      <islands>
         <name>Guadalcanal</name>
         <name>Savo Island</name>
         <name>Florida Islands</name>
      </islands>
   </geog>
</battleinfo>
```

As the knowledgeable human eye—or an XML parser—scans this document from start to finish, it encounters signals that what follows is an element, an attribute, a comment, a processing instruction (PI), whatever. These signals are of course the markup in the document, such as the start and end tags delimiting the elements.

XPath functions at a higher level of abstraction than this simple kind of lexical analysis, though. It doesn't know anything about a document's tags and thus can't communicate anything about them to a downstream application. What it knows about, and knows about intimately, are the *nodes* that make up the document: the discrete chunks of information encapsulated within and among the markup. Furthermore, it recognizes that these chunks of information bear a relationship to one another, a relationship imposed on them by their physical arrangement within the document. (such as the successively deeper nesting of elements within one another) Figure 2-1 illustrates this node-tree view of the above document as seen by XPath.

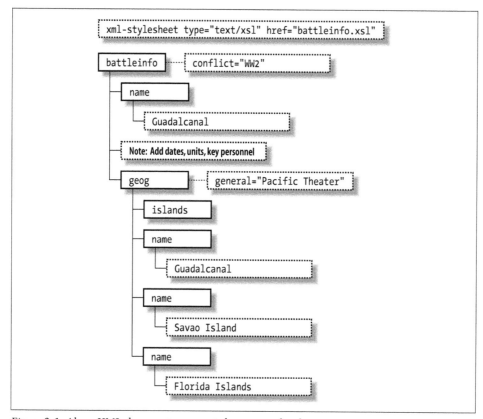

*Figure 2-1. Above XML document represented as a tree of nodes*

There a few things to note about the node tree depicted in Figure 2-1:

- First, there's a hierarchical relationship among the different "things" that make up the tree. Of course, all the nodes are contained by the document itself (represented by the overall figure). Furthermore, many of the nodes have "offshoot" nodes. The battleinfo element sits on top of the outermost name element, the comment, and the geog element (which are all in turn subordinate to battleinfo).

- Some discrete portions of the original document contribute to the hierarchical nature of the tree. The elements (solid boxes) and their offspring—subordinate elements, text strings (dashed boxes), and the comment—are connected by solid lines representing true hierarchical relationships. Attributes, on the other hand, add nothing to the structure of the node tree (although they do have relationships, depicted with dotted-dashed lines, to the elements that define them). And the xml-stylesheet PI at the very top of the document is connected to nothing at all.

- Finally, most subtly yet most importantly, there is not a single scrap of markup in this tree. True enough, the element, attribute, and PI nodes all have names that *correspond to* bits of the original document's markup (such as the elements' start and end tags). But there are no angle brackets here. All that the XPath processor sees is content, stacked inside a tower of invisible boxes. The processor knows what kind of box each thing is, and if applicable it knows the box's name, but it does not see the box itself.

# XPath Expressions

If you've never worked with XPath before, you may be expecting its syntax to be XML-based. That's not the case, though. XPath is *not* an XML vocabulary in its own right. You can't submit "an XPath" to an XML parser—even a simple well-formedness checker—and expect it to pass muster. That's because "an XPath" is meant to be used as an attribute value.

 Chapter 1 discussed why using XML syntax for general-purpose languages, such as XPath and XPointer, is impractical. As mentioned there, the chief reason might be summed up as: such languages are needed in the context of special-purpose languages, such as XSLT and XLink. Expressing the general-purpose language *as* XML would both make them extremely verbose and require the use of namespaces, complicating inordinately what is already complicated enough.

"An XPath"[*] consists of one or more chunks of text, delimited by any of a number of special characters, assembled in any of various formal ways. Each chunk, as well as the assemblage as a whole, is called an XPath *expression*.

Here's a handful of examples, by no means comprehensive. (Don't fret; there are more detailed examples aplenty throughout the rest of the book.)

taxcut
  Locates an element, in some relative context, whose name is "taxcut"

/
  Locates the document root of some XML instance document

---

[*] Not that you'll see any further references to something by that name, in the spec or anywhere else.

`/taxcuts`

Locates the root element of an XML instance document, only if that element's name is "taxcuts"

`/taxcuts/taxcut`

Locates all child elements of the root taxcuts element whose names are "taxcut"

`2001`

The number 2001

`"2001"`

The string "2001"

`/taxcuts/taxcut[attribute::year="2001"]`

Locates all child elements of the root taxcuts element, as long as those child elements are named "taxcut" and have a year attribute whose value is the string "2001"

`/taxcuts/taxcut[@year="2001"]`

Abbreviated form of the preceding

`2001 mod 100`

Calculated remainder after dividing the number 2001 by 100 (that is, the number 1)

`/taxcuts/taxcut[@year="2001"]/amount mod 100`

Calculated remainder after dividing the indicated amount element's value by 100

`substring-before("ill-considered", "-")`

The string "ill"

## Location Steps and Location Paths

Chapter 3 details both of these concepts. To get you started in XPath, here's a broad outline.

Most XPath expressions, by far, locate a document's contents or portions thereof. (Expressions such as the number 2001 and the string "2001" are exceptions; they don't locate anything, you might say, except themselves.) These pieces of content are located by way of one or more *location steps*—discrete units of XPath "meaning"—chained together, usually, into *location paths*.

This XPath expression from the above list:

`/taxcuts/taxcut`

consists of two location steps. The first locates the taxcuts child of the document root (that is, it locates the root element); the second locates all children of the preceding location step whose names are "taxcut." Taken together, these two location steps make up a complete location path.

# Expression Syntax

As you can see from the previous examples, an XPath expression can be said to consist of various components: tokens and delimiters.

## Tokens

A token, in XPath as elsewhere in the XML world, is a simple, discrete string of Unicode characters. Individual characters within a token are not themselves considered tokens. If an XPath expression is analogous to a chemical molecule, the tokens of which it's composed are the atoms. (And the individual characters, I guess, are the sub-atomic particles.)

If quotation marks surround the token, it's assumed to be a string. If no quotation marks adorn the token, an XPath-smart application assumes that the token represents a node *name*.[*] I'll have more to say about nodes and their names in a moment and much more to say about them throughout the rest of the book. For now, though, consider the first example listed above. The bare token taxcut is the name of a node. If I had put it in quotation marks, like "taxcut", the XPath expression wouldn't necessarily refer to anything in a particular document; it would simply refer to a string composed of the letters t, a, x, c, u, and t: almost certainly not what you want at all.

As a special case, a node name can also be represented with an asterisk (*). This serves as a wildcard (all nodes, regardless of their name) character. The expression taxcut/* locates all elements that are children of a taxcut element.

 You cannot, however, use the asterisk in combination with other characters to represent portions of a name. Thus, tax* doesn't locate all elements whose names start with the string "tax"; it's simply illegal as far as XPath is concerned.

## Delimiters

Tokens in an XPath expression are set off from one another using single-character delimiters, or pairs of them. Aside from quotation marks, these delimiters include:

/
    A forward slash separates a location step from the one that follows it. While I introduced location steps briefly above, Chapter 3 will discuss them at length.

[ *and* ]
    Square brackets set off a predicate from the preceding portion of a location step. Again, detailed discussion of predicates is coming in Chapter 3. For now,

---

[*] Depending on the context, such an unquoted token may also be interpreted as a function (covered in Chapter 4), a node test (see Chapter 3), or of course a literal *number* instead of a string.

understand that a predicate tests the expression preceding it for a true or false value. If true, the indicated node in the tree is selected; if false, it isn't.

=, !=, <, >, <=, *and* >=

These Boolean "delimiters" are used in a predicate to establish the true or false value of the test. Note that when used in an XML document, the markup-significant < and > characters must appear in their escaped forms to comply with XML's well-formedness constraints, even when used in attribute values. (For instance, to use the Boolean less-than-or-equal-to test, you must code the XPath expression as &lt;=.) While XPath itself isn't expressed as an XML vocabulary, the documents in which XPath expressions most often appear *are* XML documents; therefore, well-formedness will haunt you in XPath just as elsewhere in the XML world.[*]

::

A double colon separates the name of an axis type from the name of a specific node (or set of nodes). Axes (more in Chapter 3) in XPath, as in plane and solid geometry, indicate some orientation within a space. In an XPath expression, an axis "turns the view" from a given starting point in the document. For instance, the attribute axis (abbreviated @) looks only at attributes of some element or set of elements.

//, @, ., *and* ..

Each of these—the double slash, at sign, period, and double period—is an abbreviated or shortcut form of an axis or location step. Respectively, these symbols represent the concepts of descendant-or-self, attribute, self, and parent (covered fully in Chapter 3).

|

A pipe/vertical bar in an XPath expression functions as a Boolean union operator. This lets you chain together complete multiple expressions into compound location paths. Compound location paths are covered at the end of Chapter 3.

( *and* )

Pairs of parentheses in XPath expressions, as in most other computer-language contexts, serve two purposes. They can be used for grouping subexpressions, particularly in cases where the ungrouped form would introduce ambiguities, and they can be used to set off the name of an XPath function from its argument list. Details on XPath functions appear in Chapter 4.

+, -, *, div, *and* mod

These five "delimiters" actually function as numeric operators: ways of combining numeric values to calculate some other value. Numeric operators are also covered in Chapter 4. Note that the asterisk can be used as either a numeric

---

[*] Be careful on this issue of escaping the < and > characters. XPath is used in numerous contexts (such as Java-Script and other scripting languages) besides "true XML"; in these contexts, use of a literal, unescaped < or > character may actually be mandated.

operator or as a wildcard character, depending on the context in which it appears. The expression tax*income multiplies the values of the tax and income elements and returns the result; it does *not* locate all elements whose names start with the string "tax" and end with the string "income."

whitespace

When not appearing within a string, whitespace can in some instances delimit tokens (and even other delimiters) for legibility, without changing the meaning of an expression. For instance, the two predicates [@year="2001"] and [@year = "2001"] are functionally identical, despite the presence in the second case of blank spaces before and after the =. Because the rules for when you can and can't use whitespace vary depending on context, I'll cover them in various places throughout the book.

## Combining tokens and delimiters into complete expressions

While the rules for valid combinations of tokens and delimiters aren't spelled out explicitly anywhere, they follow the rules of common sense. (Whether the sense is in fact common depends a little on how comfortable you are with the concepts of location steps and location paths.)

For instance, the following is a syntactically illegitimate XPath expression; it also, if you think a little about it, doesn't make *practical* sense:

```
book/
```

See the problem? First, for those of you who simply want to follow the rules without thinking about them, you can simply accept as a given that the / (unless used by itself) must be used as a delimiter between location steps; with no subsequent location step to the right, it's not separating book from anything.

Second, there's a more, well, let's call it a more philosophical problem. What exactly would the above expression be meant to say? "Locate a child of the book element which...." Which what? It's like a sentence fragment.

> Note the difference here between XPath expressions and their counterparts in some other "navigational" languages, such as Unix directory commands and URIs. In these other contexts, a trailing slash might mean "*all* children of the present context" (such as a directory) or "the *default* child of the present context" (such as a web document named *index.html* or *default.html*). In XPath, few of these matters are implicit. If you want to get all children of the current context, follow the slash with something, such as an asterisk wildcard (to get all named children), as in book/*. Chapter 3 describes other approaches, particularly the use of the node( ) node test.

I'll cover these kinds of common-sense rules where appropriate. (See Chapter 3, especially.)

# XPath Data Types

A careful reading of the previous material about XPath expressions should reveal that XPath is capable of processing four data types: string, numeric, Boolean, and nodes (or node-sets).

The first three data types I'll address in this section. Nodes and node-sets are easily the most important single XPath data type, so I've relegated them to a complete section in their own right, following this one.

## Strings

You can find two kinds of strings, explicit and implicit, in nearly any XPath expression. Explicit (or literal) strings, of course, are strings of characters delimited by quotation marks. Now, don't get confused here. As I've said, XPath expressions themselves appear as attribute values in XML documents. Therefore, an expression as a whole will be contained in quotation marks. Within that expression, any literal strings must be contained in *embedded* quotation marks. If the expression as a whole is contained in double quotation marks, ", then a string within it must be enclosed in single quotation marks or apostrophes: '. If you prefer to enclose attribute values in single quotes, the embedded string(s) must appear in double quotes.

 This nesting of literal quotation marks and apostrophes—or vice versa—is unnecessary, strictly speaking. If you prefer, you can *escape* the literals using their entity representations. That is, the expressions "a string" and &quot;a string&quot; are functionally identical. The former is simply more convenient and legible.

For example, in XSLT stylesheets, one of the most common attributes is select, applied to the xsl:value-of element (which is empty) and others. The value of this attribute is an XPath expression. So you might see code such as the following:

```
<xsl:value-of select="fallacy[type='pathetic']"/>
```

If the string "pathetic" were not enclosed in quotation marks, of course, it would be considered a node name rather than a string. (This might make sense in some contexts, but even in those contexts, it would almost certainly produce quite different results from the quoted form.) Note that the kind of quotation marks used in this example alternates between single and double as the quoted matter is nested successively deeper.

Explicitly quoted strings aside, XPath also makes very heavy use of what might be called implicit strings. They might be called that, that is, except there's already an official term for them: string-values. I will have more to say about string-values later in this chapter. For now, a simple example should suffice.

Consider the following fragment of an XML document:

```
<type>logical</type>
<type>pathetic</type>
```

Each element in an XML document has a string-value: the concatenated value of all text contained by that element's start and end tags. Therefore, the first type element here has a string-value of logical; the second, pathetic. An XPath expression in a predicate such as:

```
type='logical'
```

would be evaluated for the two elements, respectively, as:

```
'logical'='logical'
'pathetic'='logical'
```

That is, for the first type element the predicate would return the value true; for the second, false.

## Numeric Values

There's no special magic here. A numeric value in XPath terms is just a number; it can be operated on with arithmetic, and the result of that operation is itself a number. (XPath provides various facilities for converting numeric values to strings and vice versa. Detailed coverage of these facilities can be found in Chapter 4.) Formally, XPath numbers are all assumed to be floating-point numbers even when their explicit representation is as integers.

 While XPath assumes all numbers to be of floating-point type, you cannot represent literal numbers in XPath using scientific notation. For example, many languages allow you to represent the number 1960 as 1.96E3 (that is, 1.96 times 10 to the 3rd power); such a value in XPath is not recognized as a legitimate number.

Although the XPath specification does not define "numeric-values" for nodes analogous to their string-values, XPath-aware applications can treat as numeric any string-value that can be "understood" as numeric. Thus, given this XML code fragment:

```
<page_ref>23</page_ref>
```

you can construct an XPath expression such as:

```
page_ref + 10
```

This would be understood as 23 (the numeric form of the page_ref element's string-value) plus 10, or 33.

The XPath specification also defines a special value, NaN, for simple "Is this value a number?" tests. ("NaN" stands for "not a number.") While the spec repeatedly refers to something called NaN, it doesn't show you how to use it except as a *string* (returned by the XPath string( ) function, as it happens). If you wanted to locate only those year elements which had legitimately numeric values, you could use an XPath expression something like this:

```
string(number(year)) != "NaN"
```

This explicitly attempts to convert the string-value of the year element to a number, then converts the result of that attempt to a string and compares it to the string "NaN."* Only those year elements for which those two values are not equal (that is, only those year elements whose string-values are *not* "not a number") will pass.

 The string( ) function, covered at length in Chapter 4, is extremely important in XPath. That's not because it's used that much in code— in my experience it isn't used much at all—rather, its importance is due to the XPath spec's being rife with phrases such as "...as if converted to a string using the string( ) function." As a practical matter, the string( ) function's use is implicit in many situations. From a certain standpoint, you could almost say that *all* an XML document's text content is understood by an XPath-aware application "as if converted to a string using the string( ) function."

## Boolean Values

As elsewhere, in XPath a Boolean value is one that equals either true or false. You can convert a Boolean value to the string or numeric data types, using XPath functions. The string form of the values true and false are (unsurprisingly) the strings "true" and "false"; their numeric counterparts are 1 and 0, respectively.

Probably the single most useful application of XPath Booleans is in the predicate portion of a location step. As I mentioned earlier, the predicate tests some candidate node to see if it fulfills some condition expressed as a Boolean true or false. Thus:

```
concerto[@key="F"]
```

locates a concerto element only if its key attribute has a value of "F".

Importantly, as you will see in Chapter 3, the predicate's true or false value can also test for the simple *existence* of a particular node. If the node exists, the Boolean value of the predicate is true; if not, false. So:

```
concerto[@key]
```

locates a concerto element only if it has any key attribute at all.

---

* Note the importance here of quoting the string "NaN." If this code fragment had omitted the quotation marks, the XPath processor would not be testing for the special NaN value but for the string-value of an *element* whose name just happens to be NaN.

# Nodes and Node-Sets

The fourth and most important data type handled by XPath is the node-set data type.

Let's look first at nodes themselves. A node is any discrete logical *something* able to be located by an XPath location step. Every element in a document constitutes a node, as does every attribute, PI, and so on.

## Node Properties

Each node in a document has various properties. I've discussed one of these properties briefly already—the string-value—and will provide more information about it at the end of this chapter. The others are its name, its sequence within the document, and its "family relationships" with other nodes.

### Node names

Most (but not all) nodes have *names*. To understand node names, you need to understand three terms:

*qualified name*
This term, almost always contracted to "QName," is taken straight from the W3C "Namespaces in XML" spec, at *http://www.w3.org/TR/REC-xml-names*. The QName of a node, in general, is the identifier for the node as it actually appears in an instance document, including any namespace prefix. For example, an element whose start tag is `<concerto>` has a QName of "concerto"; if the start tag were `<mml:concerto>`, the QName would be "mml:concerto."

*local-name*
The local-name of a node is its QName, *sans* any namespace prefix. If an element's QName is "mml:concerto," its local-name is "concerto." If there's no namespace in effect for a given node, its QName and local-name are identical.

*expanded-name*
If the node is associated with a particular namespace, its expanded-name is a pair, consisting of the URI associated with that namespace and the local-name. Because the expanded-name doesn't consider the namespace prefix at all, two elements, for example, can have the same expanded-name even if their QNames are different, as long as both their associated namespace URIs (possibly null) and their local-names are identical. For more information, see the sidebar, "Expanded but Elusive," later in this chapter.

These three kinds of name conform to common sense in most cases, for most nodes, but can be surprising in others. When covering node types, below, I'll tell you how to determine the name of a node of a given type.

## Document order

Nodes in a document are positioned within the document before or after other nodes. Take a look at this sample document:

```
<?xml-stylesheet type="text/xsl" href="invoice.xsl"?>
<statement acct="112233">
    <history>
        <credits>
            <payment date="2001-09-09" curr="EU">13.99</payment>
            <adjustment date="2001-09-30" curr="USD">12.64</adjustment>
        </credits>
        <debits>
            <fin_chg date="2001-09-09" curr="USD">1.98</fin_chg>
        </debits>
    </history>
    <current>
        <!-- No current charges for this customer? -->
    </current>
</statement>
```

If you were an XML parser reading this document from start to finish, you'd be following normal *document order*. The xml-stylesheet PI comes before any of the elements in the document, the history element precedes the current element, the fin_chg element precedes the comment contained by the current element, and so on. Also note that XPath considers the attributes to a given element to come before that element's children and other descendants.

This all is pretty much common sense. Be careful when dealing with attributes, though: XPath considers an element's attributes to be in no particular document order at all. In the above document, whether the various date attributes are "before" the corresponding curr attributes is entirely XPath application dependent. As a practical matter, most XPath applications will probably be indexing attributes alphabetically, by their names—so each curr will precede its date counterpart. But you cannot absolutely count on this behavior.

As you'll see in Chapter 3, under the discussion of axes, it's also possible to access nodes in *reverse document order*.

## Family relationships

XML's strict enforcement of document structure, even under simple well-formedness constraints, ensures that nodes don't just have a simple document order—even the "nodes" in a comma-separated values (or other plain text) file do that much—but also a set of more complex relationships to one another. Some nodes are parents of others (which are, in turn, children of their parents), and nodes may have siblings, ancestors, and so on.

Because these family relationships are codified in the concept of XPath axes, I'll defer further discussion of them until Chapter 3.

## Node-Sets

XPath doesn't for the most part deal in nodes, but in *node-sets*. A node-set is simply a collection of nodes, related to one another in some arbitrary way by means of an XPath location step (or full location path). In some cases, sure, a node-set might consist of a single node. But in most cases—especially when the location step is unqualified by a predicate—this is almost an accident, an artifact of the XML instance being navigated via XPath.

Here's a simple XML document:

```
<publications>
    <book>...</book>
    <book>...</book>
    <book>...</book>
    <magazine>...</magazine>
</publications>
```

This location path:

```
/publications/book
```

returns a node-set consisting of three book elements. This location path:

```
/publication/magazine
```

returns a single magazine node. Technically, though, there's nothing inherent in this location path that forces only a single node to be located. This document *just happens* to have a single magazine element, and as a result, the location path locates a node-set that *just happens* in this case to consist of a single node.

This concept of node-sets returned by XPath radically departs from the more familiar counterparts in HTML hyperlinking. Under HTML, a hyperlink "gets" an entire document. This is true even if the given HTML link uses a fragment identifier, such as #top or #section1. (The whole document is still retrieved; it's simply positioned within the browser window in a particular way.) Using XPath, though, what you're manipulating is in most cases truly not the entire target document, but one or more discrete portions of it. In this sense, XPath isn't a "pointing-to" tool; it's an *extraction* tool.[*]

Also worth noting at this point is that the term node-*set* carries some implicit baggage of meaning: like a set in mathematical terms, a node-set contains no duplicate nodes (although some may have duplicate string-values) and is intrinsically unordered.

---

[*] XHTML, the "reformulation as XML" of the older HTML standard, is kind of a special case. Because an XHTML document is an XML document, it may use XPath-based XPointers in the value of an href attribute. But you can't assume that a browser, for now, will conform to the expected behavior of a true XPointer-aware application. Browser vendors don't exactly leap out of the starting gate to adopt new standards.

When you use XPath to locate as a node-set all elements in a document, there's no guarantee that you'll get the members of the node-set back in any particular sequence.

## Node Types

The kinds of node(-set)s retrievable by XPath cover, in effect, any kind of content imaginable: not just elements and attributes, but PIs, comments, and anything else you might find in an XML document. Let's take a look at these seven node types.

> Conspicuously missing from the following list of "any kind of content imaginable" are entity references. There's no such thing as an "entity reference node," for example. Why not? Because by the time a document's contents are scanned by an XPath-aware application, they've already been processed by a lower-level application—the XML parser itself. All entity substitutions have already been made. By the same token, XPath can't locate a document's XML or DTDs, can't return to your application any of the contents of an internal DTD subset, and can't access (for example) *tags* instead of *elements*. XPath, in short, can't "read" a document lexically; it can only "read" it logically.
>
> (See the short section, "XPath node types and the XML Infoset" later in this chapter, for a comparison of XPath node types with what the Infoset refers to as "information items.")

### The root node

Every XML document has one and only one root node. This is the logical something that contains the entire document—not only the root element and all its contents, but also any whitespace, comments, or PIs that precede and follow the root element's start and end tags. This "something" is analogous to a physical file, but there may be no precise physical file to which the root node refers (especially in the case of XML documents generated or assembled on the fly and not saved in some persistent form).

In a location path, the root node is represented by a leading / (forward slash) character. Any location path that starts with / is an absolute location path, instructing the XPath-aware application, in effect, to start at the very top of the document before considering the location steps (if any) that follow. The root node does not have an expanded-name. Its local-name is an empty string.

### Element nodes

Each element node in the document is composed of the element's start and end tags and everything in between. (Thus, when you retrieve a document's root element, you're retrieving everything in the document except any comments and PIs that precede or follow it.) Consider a simple code fragment:

```
<year>
   <month monthnum="4">April</month>
   <month monthnum="8">August</month>
```

```
<month monthnum="12">December</month>
<month monthnum="2">February</month>
<month monthnum="1">January</month>
<month monthnum="3">March</month>
<month monthnum="5">May</month>
<month monthnum="6">June</month>
<month monthnum="7">July</month>
<month monthnum="11">November</month>
<month monthnum="10">October</month>
<month monthnum="9">September</month>
</year>
```

This location path (which says, "Locate all month children of the root year element whose monthnum attributes have the value 3"):

```
/year/month[@monthnum="3"]
```

selects the sixth month element in the fragment—that is, the element whose contents (the string "March") are bounded by the <month monthnum="3"> start tag and the corresponding </month> end tag. To emphasize, and to repeat a point made early in this chapter: while the physical representation of the element is *bounded by* its start and end tags, XPath doesn't have any understanding at all of tags or any other markup. It just gets a particular invisible box corresponding to this physical representation and holding its contents. Importantly, though, it selects the element as a single node with various properties and subordinate objects (a name, a string-value, an attribute with its value).

 Note especially that this example does *not* locate the third month element. It selects all month elements with the indicated monthnum attribute value.

You sometimes must take care, when selecting element nodes, not to be confused by the presence of "invisible whitespace" in their string-values.

Yes, true: all whitespace is invisible. (That's why it's called whitespace, right?) But the physical appearance of XML documents can trick you into thinking that some whitespace "doesn't count," even though that's not necessarily true. For instance, consider Figure 2-2, depicting a greatly simplified version of a document in the same vocabulary we've been using in this section.

```
<year><month monthnum="4">April</month></year>
```

*Figure 2-2. An XML document with no whitespace*

In this figure, as you can see, there's no whitespace in any of the document's content, only within element start tags (and not always there). While many real-world XML documents (especially those that are machine generated) appear this way, it's just as likely that the documents you'll be excavating with XPath will look like Figure 2-3.

```
<year>
    <month monthnum="4">April</month>
</year>
```

*Figure 2-3. The same XML document with whitespace*

The human eye tends to ignore the whitespace-only blocks of text (represented with gray blocks in the figure) in a document like this one, discarding them as insignificant to the document's meaning. But XML parsers, bound by the XML spec's "all text counts" constraint, are not free to ignore these scraps of whitespace. (Some parsers may flag the whitespace as potentially "insignificant," leaving to some higher-order application the task of ignoring it or not.) So consider now the effect of an XPath expression such as the following, when applied to the document in Figure 2-3:

```
/year
```

This location path doesn't return just the year element node, the month element node and its attribute. It also returns:

- Some blank spaces, a newline, and some more blank spaces preceding the month element

- A newline following the month element

Whether this will present you with a problem depends on your specific need. If it is a problem, there's an XPath function, `normalize-space()` (covered in Chapter 4), that trims all leading and trailing whitespace from a given element's content.

 In XPath, as in many other XML-related areas, dealing with whitespace can induce either euphoria or migraines. In addition to the `normalize-space()` XPath function covered in Chapter 4, you should consider the (default or explicit) behavior of XML's own built-in `xml:space` attribute, and—depending on your application's needs—the effects of the XSLT `xsl:strip-space` and `xsl:preserve-space` elements, as well as the `preserveWhiteSpace` property of the MSXML Document object (if you're working in a Microsoft scripting environment).

The local-name of an element node is the name of the element type (that is, its generic identifier (GI), as it appears in the element's start and optional end tags). Thus, its expanded-name equals either its local-name (if there isn't a namespace in effect for that element) or its associated namespace URI paired with the local-name. Consider this code fragment:

```
<xsl:stylesheet version="1.0"
    xmlns:xsl="http://www.w3.org/1999/XSL/Transform">
    <xsl:template match="/">
        <html>
            ...
        </html>
    </xsl:template>
</xsl:stylesheet>
```

All elements in this document whose names carry the xsl: prefix are in the namespace associated with the URI "http://www.w3.org/1999/XSL/Transform." Thus, the expanded-name of the xsl:stylesheet element consists of that URI paired with the local-name, "stylesheet."

---

## Expanded but Elusive

The XPath spec is vague on how exactly the thing called an "expanded-name" should be represented. Those of you obsessed with such matters might wonder, for example, if it's represented in the form of a simple string concatenation such as "http://www.w3.org/1999/XSL/Transform:stylesheet" or as a tuple, such as {"http://www.w3.org/1999/XSL/Transform", "stylesheet"}, or whatever. As discussed in Chapter 3, there are XPath functions for returning a node's QName, its local-name, and its namespace URI; tellingly, though, there's none for returning its expanded-name.

In a note to the *XML-DEV* mailing list in 1998, the editor of the XPath specification, James Clark, provided a sample Java function for generating an expanded-name. (A copy of the note appears on Robin Cover's "XML Cover Pages," at *http://xml.coverpages.org/clarkNS-980804.html*.) According to this code, the expanded-name of a node associated with a namespace consists of the namespace URI, a "+" character, and the local-name. Thus, the expanded-name of the xsl:stylesheet element in the above example will be:

```
http://www.w3.org/1999/XSL/Transform+stylesheet
```

As it happens, few XPath-aware processors use Clark's algorithm. Instead, they seem universally to represent the expanded-name as the namespace URI enclosed in curly braces (the { and } characters), immediately followed by the local-name. Therefore, you're more likely to encounter:

```
{http://www.w3.org/1999/XSL/Transform}stylesheet
```

Whether you can actually count on either result in your own application depends on whether Clark's algorithm or the latter *de facto* "standard"—or something altogether different—is in use by the processor. This shouldn't affect your XPath processing directly but may be something to watch for if you dig into implementation internals.

---

### Attribute nodes

Attributes, in a certain sense, "belong to" the elements in which they appear, and in the same sense, they might be thought to adopt the namespace-related properties of those elements. For instance:

```
<xsl:template match="/" />
```

Logically, you might conclude that the match attribute is "in" the same namespace as the xsl:template element—it does, after all, belong to the same XML vocabulary—and that it, therefore, has something like an implied namespace prefix.

This isn't the case, though. An attribute's QName, local-name, namespace URI, and hence, expanded-name are all determined solely on the basis of the way the attribute is represented in the XML source document. Attributes such as match in the above example—with no explicit prefix—have a null namespace URI. That is, unprefixed attributes are in *no* namespace, including the default one; thus, their QName and local-name are identical.

Note that namespace declarations, which look like attributes (and indeed are attributes, according to the XML 1.0 and "Namespaces in XML" Recommendations), are not considered the same as other attributes when you're using XPath. As one example, the start tag of a typical xsl:stylesheet root element in a typical XSLT stylesheet might look something like this:

```
<xsl:stylesheet version="1.0"
   xmlns:xsl="http://www.w3.org/1999/XSL/Transform"
   xmlns="http://www.w3.org/1999/xhtml">
```

A location path intended to locate all this element's attributes might be:

```
/xsl:stylesheet/@*
```

(As a reminder, the wildcard asterisk here retrieves all attribute nodes, regardless of their names.) In fact, this location path locates only the version attribute. The xmlns:xsl and xmlns attributes, being namespace declarations instead of "normal" attributes, are *not* locatable as attribute nodes.

 If the document referred to by the XPath expression is validated against a DTD, it may contain more attributes than are present explicitly—visibly—in the document itself. That's because the DTD may declare some attributes with default values in the event the document author has not supplied those attributes explicitly. Always remember that the "document" to which you're referring with XPath is the source document *as parsed*, which may be only more or less the source document that you "see" when reading it by eye.

### PI nodes

Processing instructions, by definition, stand outside the vocabulary of an XML document in which they appear. Nonetheless, they do have names in an XPath sense: the name of a PI is its target (the identifier following the opening <? delimiter). For this PI:

```
<?xml-stylesheet type="text/css" href="mystyle.css"?>
```

the QName and local-name are both xml-stylesheet. However, because a PI isn't subject to namespace declarations anywhere in a document—PIs, like unprefixed attributes, are always in *no* namespace—its namespace URI is null.

The other thing to bear in mind when dealing with PI nodes is that their pseudo-attributes look like, but are *not*, real attributes (hence, the "pseudo-" prefix). From an XPath processor's point of view, everything between the PI target and the closing

?> delimiter is a single string of characters. In the case of the PI above, there's no node type capable of locating the type pseudoattribute separate from the href pseudoattribute, for example. (You can, however, use some of the string-manipulation functions covered in Chapter 4 to tease out the discrete pseudoattributes.)

### Comment nodes

Each comment in an XML source document may be located independently of the surrounding content. A comment has no expanded-name at all, and thus has neither a QName, a local-name, nor a namespace URI.

### Text nodes

Any contiguous block of text—an element's #PCDATA content—constitutes a text node. By "contiguous" here I mean that the text is unbroken by any element, PI, or comment nodes. Consider a fragment of XHTML:

```
<p>A line of text.<br/>Another line.</p>
```

The p element here contains not just one but two text nodes, "A line of text." and "Another line." The intervening br element breaks them up into two. The presence or absence of whitespace in the #PCDATA content is immaterial. So in the following case:

```
<p>A line of text.
Another line.</p>
```

there's still a single text node, which, like a comment, has no expanded-name at all.

### Namespace nodes

Namespace nodes are the chimeras and Loch Ness monsters of XPath. They have characteristics of several other node types but at the same time are not "real," but rather fanciful creatures whose comings and goings are marked with footprints here and there rather than actual sightings.

The XPath spec says every element in a given document has a namespace node corresponding to each namespace declaration in scope for that element:

- One for every explicit declaration of a namespace prefix in the start tag of the element itself
- One for every explicit declaration of a namespace prefix in the start tag of any *containing* element
- One for the explicit xmlns= declaration, if any, of a namespace for *un*prefixed element/attribute nodes, whether this declaration appears in the element's own start tag or in that of a containing element

Here's a simple fragment of an XSLT stylesheet:

```
<xsl:stylesheet version="1.0"
    xmlns:xsl="http://www.w3.org/1999/XSL/Transform"
    xmlns="http://www.w3.org/1999/xhtml">
```

```
<xsl:template match="/">
  <html xmlns:xlink="http://www.w3.org/1999/xlink/namespace">
  ...
  </html>
</xsl:template>

</xsl:stylesheet>
```

Three explicit namespace declarations are made in this fragment:

- The xsl: namespace prefix is associated (in the xsl:stylesheet element's start tag) with the XSLT namespace URI, "http://www.w3.org/1999/XSL/Transform."

- The default namespace—that is, for any unprefixed element names appearing within the xsl:stylesheet element—is associated with the XHTML namespace, "http://www.w3.org/1999/xhtml."

- The xlink: namespace prefix is associated (in the html element's start tag) with the namespace URI set aside by the W3C for XLink elements and attributes, "http://www.w3.org/1999/xlink/namespace."

 There's also one other namespace implicitly in effect for all elements in this, and indeed any, XML document. That is the XML namespace itself, associated with the reserved xml: prefix. The corresponding namespace URI for this implied namespace declaration is "http://www.w3.org/XML/1998/namespace."

The namespace declarations for the xsl: and default namespace prefixes both appear in the root xsl:stylesheet element's start tag; therefore, they create implicit namespace nodes on every element in the document—including those for which those declarations might not seem to make much sense. The html element, for instance, will probably not be able to make much use of the namespace node associated with the xsl: prefix. Nonetheless, in formal XPath terms that namespace node is indeed in force for the html element.

The namespace declaration for the xlink: prefix, on the other hand, is made by a lower-level element (html, here). Thus, there is no namespace node corresponding to that prefix for the higher-level xsl:template and xsl:stylesheet elements.

Each namespace node also has a local-name: the associated namespace prefix. So the local-name of the namespace node representing the XSLT namespace in the above document is "xsl." When associated with the default namespace, the namespace node's local-name is empty. The namespace URI of a namespace node, somewhat bizarrely, is always null.

In XPath, as in most—maybe all—XML-related subjects, namespaces sometimes seem like more trouble than they're worth. The basic purpose of namespaces is simple: to disambiguate the names of elements, and perhaps attributes, from more than one XML vocabulary when they appear in a single document instance. Yet the *practice* of using namespaces leads one down many hall-of-mirrors paths, with concepts and syntax nested inside other concepts and syntaxes and folding back on themselves.

As a practical matter, you will typically have almost no use for identifying or manipulating namespace nodes at all; your documents will consist entirely of elements and attributes from a single namespace.

### XPath node types and the XML Infoset

The XML Information Set (commonly referred to simply as "the Infoset") is a W3C Recommendation published in October 2001 (*http://www.w3.org/TR/xml-infoset/*). Its purpose, as stated in the spec's Abstract, is to provide "a set of definitions for use in other specifications that need to refer to the information in an XML document."

The definitions the Infoset provides are principally in terms of 11 *information items*: document, element, attribute, processing-instruction, unexpanded entity reference, character, comment, document type declaration, unparsed entity, notation, and namespace. As you can see, there's a certain amount of overlap between this list and the node types available under XPath—and also a certain number of loose ends not provided at all by one or the other of the two Recommendations.

XPath 2.0 will resolve the conflicts in definitions of Infoset information items and XPath node types; at the same time, XPath will continue to need things the Infoset does not cover. For instance, XPath does not generally need to refer to atomic-level individual character information items. Instead, it needs to refer to the more "molecular" text nodes. For these "needed by XPath but not defined under the Infoset" information items, XPath 2.0 will continue to provide its own definitions.

For more information about XPath 2.0 and the Infoset, refer to Chapter 5.

# Node-Set Context

It's hard to imagine a node in an XML document that exists in isolation, devoid of any context. First, as I've already mentioned, nodes have relationships with other nodes in the document—both document-order and "family" relationships. Maybe more importantly, but also more subtly, nodes in the node-set returned by a location path also have properties relative to the other nodes in that node-set—even when document order is irrelevant and family relationships, nonexistent. These are the properties of *context size*, *context position*, and *namespace bindings*.

Consider the following XML document:

```
<ChangeInMyPocket>
    <Quarters quantity="1"/>
    <Dimes quantity="1"/>
    <Nickels quantity="1"/>
    <Pennies quantity="3"/>
    <!-- No vending-machine purchase in my immediate future -->
</ChangeInMyPocket>
```

It's possible, in a single location path, to locate only the four quantity attributes (or any three, two, or one of them) and the comment; or just the root node and the comment; or just the Quarters element, the Pennies element, and the quantity attribute of the Nickels element. The nodes in the resulting node-set need not share any significant formal relationship in the context of the document itself. But in all cases, these nodes suddenly acquire relationships to others in a given node-set, simply by virtue of their membership in that node-set.

The *context size* is simply the number of nodes in the node-set, irrespective of the type of nodes. A location path that returned a node-set of all element nodes in the above document would have a context size of 5 (one for each of the ChangeInMyPocket, Quarters, Nickels, Dimes, and Pennies elements). A location path returning all the quantity attributes and the comment would also have a context size of 5.

The *context position* is different for every member of the node-set: it's the integer representing the ordinal position that a given node holds in the node-set, relative to all other nodes in it, in document order. If a node-set consists of all child elements of the ChangeInMyPocket element, the Quarters element will have a context position of 1, the Dimes element, 2, and so on. In a different node-set, the Quarters element might be node 2 and Dimes, 1, and so on.

> I've alluded to this before but just as a reminder: when determining context position, particularly of elements, be aware of "invisible whitespace" separating one element's end tag from the succeeding one's start tag. In the above document, a location path that retrieves *all* children of the ChangeInMyPocket element, not just the child *elements*, will also locate all the newline and space characters used for "pretty-printing"; each block of these characters constitutes a text-node child of ChangeInMyPocket. Thus, the Quarters element will have a context position of 2, the Dimes, 4, and so on.

Chapters 3 and 4 go into more detail about dealing with context position and context size. Note especially, in Chapter 3, the material about reverse document order in certain XPath axes, because this inverts the normal sequence of context positions.

The term *namespace bindings* refers to any namespace declarations in effect at the time an XPath expression is evaluated. In the previous document, which has no explicit namespace declarations, the only namespace binding in any expression's evaluation context will be the "built-in" namespace for elements and attributes whose names are prefixed xml:. Note that any namespace binding is not tied to a particular prefix, however; what's important is the *URI* to which the prefix is bound. Consider the following fragment:

```
<myvocab:root
    xmlns:myvocab="http://myvocab.com/namespace"
    xmlns:yourvocab="http://myvocab.com/namespace">
    <yourvocab:subelem>
        [etc.]
    </yourvocab>
</myvocab>
```

A superficial consideration of the namespace bindings in effect for the above yourvocab:subelem document might suggest that there are two, one for the myvocab: prefix and one for yourvocab:. Not true. There's only one namespace URI in play at that point (although it's aliased, after a fashion, by the two prefixes), and hence, there's only one namespace binding in that element node's context.

# String-Values

By definition, a well-formed XML document is a text document, incapable of containing such "binary" content as multimedia files and images. Thus, it stands to reason that in navigating XML documents via XPath the strings of text that make up the bulk of the document (aside from the element names themselves) would be of supreme importance. This notion is codified in the concept of *string-values*. And the importance of string-values lies in the fact that most of the time, when you locate a node in a document via XPath, what you're after is not the node per se but rather its string-value.

Each node returned by a location path has its own string-value. The string-value of a node depends on the node type, as summarized in Table 2-1. Note that the word "normalized" used to describe the string-value for the attribute node type is the same as elsewhere in the markup world: it means stripped of extraneous whitespace, by trimming leading and trailing whitespace and collapsing multiple consecutive occurrences of whitespace into a single space. For example, given an attribute such as region=" NW    SE" (note leading blank spaces and multiple spaces between the "NW" and "SE"), its normalized value would be "NW SE". Also note, though, that this normalization depends on the attribute's type, as declared in a DTD or schema. If the attribute type is CDATA, those interior blank spaces would be assumed to be significant and not normalized. Therefore, if the region attribute is (say) of type NMTO-KENS, the interior whitespace is collapsed; if it's CDATA, the whitespace remains.

*Table 2-1. String-values, by node type*

| Node type | String-value |
|---|---|
| Root | Concatenated value of all text nodes in the document |
| Element | Concatenated value of all text nodes within the scope of the element's start and end tags, including the text nodes contained by any descendant elements |
| Attribute | Normalized value of the attribute |
| PI | Everything in the PI between its target (and whitespace following the target) and the closing ?> delimiter |
| Comment | The comment's content—the text between the opening and closing <!-- and --> delimiters |
| Text | The character data in the node (note that every text node consists of at least one character) |
| Namespace | The namespace URI associated with the corresponding namespace prefix |

If you're using DOM, note that Table 2-1 establishes a loose correspondence between XPath string-values and the values returned by the DOM nodeValue method. The exceptions—and they're important ones—are that nodeValue, when applied to the document root and element nodes, returns not a concatenated string but a null value. The only way to get at these node types' text content through the DOM is to apply nodeValue to their descendant text nodes.

Consider an XML document such as the following:

```
<?xml-stylesheet type="text/xsl" href="4or5guys.xsl"?>
<quotation xmlns:xlink="http://www.w3.org/1999/xlink">
    <source>
        <author>Firesign Theatre</author>
        <work year="1970">Don't Crush that Dwarf, Hand Me The Pliers</work>
    </source>
    <text>And there's hamburger all over the highway in Mystic, Connecticut.</text>
    <!-- Following link last verified 2001-09-15 -->
    <allusion xlink:href="http://www.dern.com/ng_burgr.html"/>
</quotation>
```

All seven XPath node types are present in this document. String-values for some of them are as follows:

*root node*

Concatenated values of all text nodes in the document, that is:

```
Firesign Theatre
Don't Crush that Dwarf, Hand Me The Pliers
```

```
And there's hamburger all over the Highway in Mystic, Connecticut.
```

(Note how the whitespace-only text nodes, included for legibility in the original document, are carried over into the string-value.)

source *element node*
> Concatenated value of all text nodes within the element's scope (including whitespace-only text nodes):
> ```
> Firesign Theatre
> Don't Crush that Dwarf, Hand Me The Pliers
> ```

year *attribute*
> ```
> 1970
> ```

xml-stylesheet *PI*
> ```
> type="text/xsl" href="4or5guys.xsl"
> ```

*comment*
> ```
> Following link last verified 2001-09-15
> ```

*first text node (not counting whitespace-only text nodes)*
> ```
> Firesign Theatre
> ```

*namespace node on all elements*
> The namespace for the xlink: prefix, declared in the root quotation element, does not apply to any elements, because none of their names use that prefix. All of these elements have empty strings because they are not in a namespace.

## String-Value of a Node-Set

Not only does each node in a node-set have a string-value, as described above; the node-set as a whole has one.

If you followed the logic behind each of the previous examples, especially the concatenation of text nodes that makes up the string-value of a root or element node, you might think the string-value of a node-set containing (say) two or more element nodes is the concatenation of all their string-values. Not so. The string-value of a multinode node-set is the *string-value of the first node* in that node-set.

(Actually, the apparent inconsistency goes away if you just remember that last sentence, eliminating the word "multinode." Thus, the value of any single node is just a special case of the general rule; the node-set in this case just happens to be composed of a single node—which is, of course, the first in the node-set.)

In the previous example, the source element has two child element nodes, author and work. This location path:

```
/quotation/source/*
```

thus returns a node-set of two nodes. The node-set's string-value is the string-value of the first node in the node-set, that is, the author element: "Firesign Theatre."

# CHAPTER 3

# Location Steps and Paths

In Chapter 2, I covered the kinds of content XPath is capable of locating: essentially, any content at all in an XML document. Now it's time to take a look at how exactly you locate it—a look, in short, at XPath syntax.

## XPath Expressions

As earlier chapters (notably Chapter 1) have explained, knowing XML's own syntax does not prepare you for knowing XPath syntax. Unlike the languages that make use of XPath, XPath itself is not an XML vocabulary. A given "XPath" doesn't contain all the characteristic left and right angle brackets, ampersands, and other hallmarks of XML syntax dear (or not) to your heart from your other XML work.

Instead, units of XPath meaning, called *expressions*, are typically used in attribute values. Thus you'll be creating and using XML code that uses these expressions in ways such as:

```
<xsl:value-of select="expression"/>
```

and:

```
<a xlink:href="xpointer(expression)">Table of Contents</a>
```

Sometimes, when you see the term *XPath expression*, what's being referred to is simply a speck of meaning—a subatomic particle, as it were, that has a sort of abstract academic interest but little practical value by itself. This sort of expression is a string or numeric value. For instance, both of the following are valid XPath expressions in this limited sense:

```
"I should have been a pair of ragged claws"
119.725
```

In the real world of XPath, though, such literal expressions are pretty pointless. If you locate the literal string "I should have been a pair of ragged claws," you simply locate that string—outside the context of an XML document or, for that matter, devoid of any context at all. XPath expressions are meant primarily to locate content *in context*. The most familiar real-world analogy for the syntax to accomplish this is a computer's filesystem or a web server's directory structure.

 Although I probably sounded scornful just now of literal-valued XPath expressions, don't write them off. The ability to "find" a literal value (instead of a chunk of content in the source document) is actually quite useful. You'll see many examples later in this chapter, particularly in the section on the predicate portion of an XPath expression. There, you'll learn how to locate a particular node (represented by a location path) when its value equals, say, some particular literal value. There's no way to represent the righthand side of this equation other than with a literal XPath expression. The point is merely that locating the literal value itself is absurd.

## The Filesystem Analogy

In Chapter 2, Figure 2-1 depicted the structure of a well-formed XML document. Although I didn't make the comparison explicit, you may have observed that Figure 2-1 could also represent a directory tree: there's a root directory, beneath which you find one or more subdirectories, and so on. Within any directory along the way you might find one or more files.

The analogy between locating files and other resources on the one hand and XML-based content in a document on the other is not just abstract but explicit, codified in the syntax. An expression such as the following might be a perfectly legitimate XPath expression as well as a path to one or more files in a computer filesystem:

```
/root/dir1/dir1_1/file
```

If you're dealing with a computer operating system or a web URI, this entire syntactic construct is called (among other things) a directory path; in XPath, it's known as a *location path*.

## Points of Similarity, Points of Difference

Before getting into the nuances of location paths in their own right, I want to make plain some of the ways in which they are both similar to and different from directory paths. First, the similarities:

- Most obviously, the syntax is very similar. Each incremental move through the tree of directories or nodes is separated from others by a slash, /.

- The most common way to move through the directory or node tree is down: start at the root, select one of its children, then one of that child's children, and so on, until finding the resource at the very end of the path.

- Both a directory path and a location path can begin with a slash, in which case they're referred to as absolute paths. They can also dive right in with the name of some subordinate resource, with no leading slash, and in this case, they're called relative paths. What they're relative to is "wherever you are" in the filesystem or document in question.

- A syntactically correct path is no guarantee that you'll find anything there. When navigating—or attempting to navigate—a directory path to a resource that doesn't exist, you get a "File does not exist" error message from the operating system, or an HTTP 404 message from the web server; an XPath expression that "locates" a nonexistent resource fails less egregiously, but fails nonetheless: it returns an empty node-set.

And now the chief differences, neither of them obvious from the simple example already presented:

- Within a filesystem, you can easily "move up" or "move down" the directory tree to related resources (directories or files) in the same branch of the directory tree. "Moving sideways" isn't so easily accomplished, though, especially if you need to "move sideways" to different branches of the tree and/or to other resources whose names share nothing in common. XPath, as you will see, is amazingly flexible in terms of its knowledge of a document's tree of nodes and the multiple relationships a given node has with others.

- While you can use wildcard characters such as * and ? to locate files that share some common naming characteristics, you cannot locate files that share the same *type* if their names share nothing in common. For instance, it's become common to name text files with a filename extension of *.txt*. Using this ad-hoc and totally unofficial "standard," however, both fails to locate text files with some other extension and possibly locates some *non*–text files as well. That is, the name is no absolute guarantee of the type. XPath, in contrast, can easily locate types of content in a given document, as well as content with specific names.

# Location Paths

"Understanding" a location path and how to code it requires no great intellectual leap. If you know how to walk a filesystem directory tree, separating each level in the navigation from the others with slashes, you already grasp the rudiments of location paths. Still, you need to keep a few points in mind.

## The Importance of Context

Chapter 2 discussed context, particularly the notion that each node in a given node-set shares with all the others a context size, and has its own context position within that size—the "Node X of Y" notion.

More subtly, using a multilevel location path imposes a successively finer sieve of context on each level in the path. Consider:

```
/customers/customer/invoice/item/quantity
```

As you move to the right in this location path, you're not only "walking down" into the document's nether regions, you're also almost certainly excluding from consideration various portions of the document not of interest at the moment. That is, each level in the location path *implicitly changes the context node* in terms of which levels to the right will be evaluated. Figure 3-1 illustrates this process.

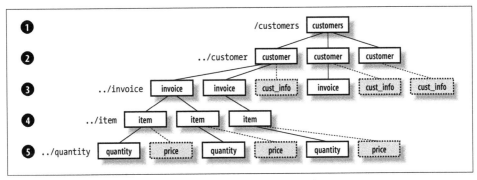

*Figure 3-1. Filtering content via successive steps in a location path*

The full location path can be decomposed into five *location steps*, each separated from the others by slashes; each step narrows the view already established by those that preceded it. Step 1 limits the selection to the root customers element, and step 2, to the customer elements that are children of that root element.

So far, there's been no filtering at all occurring; every element down to this level in this sample document is still visible. In step 3, though, something interesting happens: the location path selects the invoice children of each customer element. The first and second customer elements have two and one such children, respectively; the third customer element has no invoice children, and as a result this customer effectively drops out of consideration as a match for further location steps. For purposes of content retrieved by this location path, in other words, customer #3 might as well not exist at all.

The filtering continues in steps 4 and 5. For some reason—perhaps data entry in this document is not complete—the invoice child of customer #2 has no item children and thus disappears from view in step 4. In the fifth and final step, the location path says that ultimately, only the quantity children of each item element are of interest, eliminating the price children and selecting, in the end, only those quantity elements descended from ("belonging to") the first customer.

What does this have to do with context? The point is that each succeeding location step does not stand in isolation: the full location path doesn't select *all* customer elements, *all* invoice elements, and so on. In fact, it selects only those nodes (elements, in this case) at the very end of the location path, and of those, only the nodes that have met all preceding conditions in the path.

## Absolute Versus Relative Location Paths

As I've already mentioned, location paths—just like directory paths—can be either absolute or relative. An absolute location path begins with a slash, which effectively denotes the root node of the document. If the path starts with *no* leading slash, it's a relative path.

Practically speaking, when you're using XPath in an XPointer context, you'll always use an absolute path except when locating content within the same document containing the XPointer.

In an XSLT stylesheet, the situation's a little more complicated. A typical stylesheet consists of numerous so-called template rules (one xsl:template element apiece), each of which matches (via a location path) some portion(s) of the source document.[*] Within the template rule may be any number of XPath-based references to other portion(s) of the document, and these latter references are most commonly relative location paths—that is, relative to the context established by the containing template rule. For instance, a template rule might look something like this:

```
<xsl:template match="/books">
   <xsl:for-each select="book/title">
      <xsl:value-of select="."/>
   </xsl:for-each>
</xsl:template>
```

The location path bound to the template rule's match attribute is absolute, matching the root books element. Within the template rule, however, the location path bound to the xsl:for-each element's select attribute is relative—as is the one bound to the xsl:value-of element's select attribute. The former select attribute locates each title element of each given book child of books. The latter simply re-selects (for a different purpose) the node already established by the containing xsl:for-each. (By the way, note in this example the period, also called the "full stop," which may be familiar to you from its occasional use in directory paths.)

---

[*] Actually, to say the template rule "matches content via a location path" isn't quite accurate. The value of an xsl:template element's match attribute is not, strictly speaking, a location path, but rather something called a "location path pattern" or "match pattern"—whose syntax is dictated not by XPath, but by the XSLT spec. There's also a practical difference, in that a match pattern doesn't really select something in the source document; it simply (as the term indicates) *matches* that something, for purposes of specifying how the template will behave when a match is found.

In XSLT, template rules may invoke other template rules, using the xsl:apply-templates element. The select attribute of this element directs the XSLT processor to next process any template rule that matches the indicated relative location path. Thus, the example template rule I just provided could also be coded in the form of two separate template rules, like this:

```
<xsl:template match="/books">
    <xsl:apply-templates select="book/title">
</xsl:template>

<xsl:template match="book/title">
    <xsl:value-of select="."/>
</xsl:template>
```

The practical effect of a stylesheet structured in this way is that only one template rule's match pattern may be an absolute location path; all others will "trickle down" to successively lower-level template rules, chained together by linking the select attributes of xsl:apply-templates elements to the corresponding template rules (even when the latter's match attributes specify absolute rather than relative paths).

## Compound Location Paths

It's frequently desirable to select not just the nodes found by way of a single location path, but all the nodes found by way of two or more paths. This is accomplished using the union operator, a "pipe" or vertical-bar character, (|), to delimit the constituent paths. (Whitespace on either side of the pipe is not significant.)

Referring back to the sample document depicted in Figure 3-1, you could select all the invoice elements *and* all the cust_info elements with a single compound location path:

```
/customers/customer/invoice | /customers/customer/cust_info
```

Here, the selected nodes just happen to be elements at the same level of the node tree. As you will soon see, however, there's no particular requirement that this be the case; you can just as easily select a node-set consisting of elements at different levels of the hierarchy and/or nodes of any types at all, elements or otherwise.

# Location Steps

Location paths are interesting on a grand, macroscopic level. But (at least to my way of thinking) they're essentially unsophisticated, blunt instruments for extracting content from an XML document. All the real action in XPath is found between the slashes in a full location path—in the *location steps*.

The location steps you've seen so far in this chapter have been extremely simple. They've walked you down into the given XML source document by way of the tree of element nodes, and element nodes only, and only those element nodes with specific names. Easy enough to understand, perhaps (not to deny the value of understandability!), and also arguably the most common sort of location step, but not particularly eye opening. In fact, these elementary location steps have simply taken advantage of various default values and shortcuts for parts of the full location step syntax: the axis, the node test, and the predicate. This syntax is:

```
axis::nodetest[predicate]
```

 As you will see later in this chapter, it's possible for a location step to include multiple predicates—one after the other or even nested.

Of the three components that a location step may contain, only the node test is required. If you omit the axis, you also omit the double colon (::) that delimits it from the node test. If you omit the predicate, you also omit the square brackets ([ and ]) that enclose it.

Before getting into the details of these three pieces of a location step, let's take a look at their general purposes.

## The Big Picture

A common misconception about microscopes, magnifying glasses, telescopes, and binoculars is that they enlarge the image presented to our eyes from some object or other in the real world. Actually, they narrow the field of vision (assuming you're looking into them the right way); the image presented to our eyes always stays the same size. Armed with this information, take a look at Figure 3-2.

Here, you're standing on the rock at the end of a jetty projecting out into a bay, binoculars held to your eyes. Everything outside the field of vision doesn't "exist" for you as long as you're looking through the lenses: the boats on the water behind you and to either side, the colony of seals on the rocks. You have, in effect, no peripheral vision.

But these are special binoculars. Not only can you use the typical thumbwheel to bring perceived objects into and out of focus, or perhaps to zoom in (that is, narrow the field even further) or out. You can also click a button or push a slider along their top edge, which lets you see (in the chosen direction) only boats, or everything but boats, or boats and buoys only, or just those objects whose names begin with the letter "b." (The lighthouse is within the field of vision, for example, but it doesn't fit any of those types of "target.") And you can do even finer tuning: light up just those boats that have sails, or black sails only, or those flying pirate flags, or only flying pirate flags with no cannons visible.

*Figure 3-2. Narrowing the field of vision: "seeing" just boats with sails in a particular direction*

There's your XPath location step: the axis selects the direction you're looking; the node test selects particular generic kinds of objects to see; and the predicate highlights only those objects of the right generic kinds that have other specific characteristics.

Let's start by examining the one required portion of a location step: the node test.

## The Node Test

The node test singles out in a document the sort of nodes in which you're interested. You have two approaches here: identify the names you're interested in or identify the types. Table 3-1 summarizes the available options.

*Table 3-1. Location step node tests*

| To select... | Use... |
| --- | --- |
| elements with a particular name | the element name in which you're interested (e.g., /books/book selects all elements named book that are children of the root element named books) |
| elements with any name | an asterisk (*) wildcard character in place of the element name (e.g., /books/* selects *all* child elements of the root books element, regardless of those child elements' names) |
| text nodes | The text( ) node test (e.g., paragraph/text( ) selects all text nodes that are immediate children of the paragraph elements that are children of the context node) |

Table 3-1. Location step node tests (continued)

| To select... | Use... |
|---|---|
| comment nodes | The comment( ) node test (e.g., simply using comment( ) locates all comments that are children of the context node) |
| processing instructions with a particular target | The processing-instruction(target) node test (e.g., /processing-instruction('xml-stylesheet') selects all xml-stylesheet PIs which are children of the root node) |
| processing instructions regardless of the target | The processing-instruction( ) node test (e.g., /processing-instruction( ) selects *all* PIs that are children of the root node) |
| all nodes, regardless of their type or name | The node( ) node test (e.g., in an XHTML source document, /html/node( ) locates not only the meta, head, and body elements, but also any comments and/or PIs that are children of the root html element) |

Neither attributes nor namespace nodes can be located using the node test alone. You must use an axis in a location step to locate these two node types. See the information about the attribute:: and namespace:: axes later in this chapter for more information.

One other point: Note that the text( ), comment( ), processing-instruction( ), and node( ) node tests—technically called node *type* tests—are not functions, and all require the use of parentheses even though the parentheses are empty. This distinguishes these node tests from those simply seeking elements whose *names* just happen to be, for example, comment and text.

## The Axis

Having determined that you want a location step (via the node test) to "see" only nodes of a certain kind, you can specify the direction—the line of sight, if you will—in which you want to see them. (The direction is always relative to the context node at the point of the location step.) This is accomplished using an axis.

The XPath spec defines 13 different axes, many of which are modeled on a "family" view of the source document's nodes. That is, in a genealogical family tree, each person represents a node; each node (except the one at the very top) has a parent and ancestors, many have children and other descendants, siblings, and so on. So it is in an XML source document, which—thanks to the rules of well-formedness—always contains at least two strictly structured nodes (the root node and the root element).

Let's take a look at a summary of the 13 axes first, presented as Table 3-2. (I use the word "visible" in this table advisedly. I mean, of course, whether nodes of a given type are visible to an XPath-aware processor—not whether they're visible to a human reader of the document. By the latter standard, whitespace-only text nodes might be considered "invisible," even though they're just as substantial to a processor as any other nodes in the tree.)

*Table 3-2. Location step axes*

| Axis | Description | Direction | Visible node types |
|------|-------------|-----------|--------------------|
| child:: | Locates node(s) immediately descended from the context node | Forward | Elements, comments, PIs, text nodes |
| parent:: | Locates the one node immediately above the context node in the node tree | Reverse | Root node, elements |
| descendant:: | Extends the child:: axis all the way down the node tree, locating children, children of children, and so on | Forward | Elements, comments, PIs, text nodes |
| ancestor:: | Extends the parent:: axis all the way up the node tree, locating parents, parents of parents, and so on | Reverse | Root node, elements |
| descendant-or-self:: | Like the descendant:: axis, but locates the context node itself as well as all descendants | Forward | Any but attributes or namespaces |
| ancestor-or-self:: | Like the ancestor:: axis, but locates the context node itself as well as all ancestors | Reverse | Root node, elements |
| following:: | Locates all visible nodes that follow the context node (excludes descendants) | Forward | Any but root node, attributes, or namespaces |
| preceding:: | Locates all visible nodes that precede the context node (excludes ancestors) | Reverse | Any but root node, attributes, or namespaces |
| following-sibling:: | Locates all visible nodes that both follow the context node and share the same parent | Forward | Any but root node, attributes, or namespaces |
| preceding-sibling:: | Locates all visible nodes that both precede the context node and share the same parent | Reverse | Any but root node, attributes, or namespaces |
| attribute:: | Locates attributes of the context node | Forward | Attributes only |
| namespace:: | Locates namespace nodes | Forward | Namespaces only |
| self:: | Locates the context node itself | (N/A) | Any |

In this table, note that each axis is designated as a forward or reverse axis. These terms refer to the direction, relative to the context node, in which nodes are visible—in document order or reverse document order, respectively.

Now let's look at some nuances of using axes in your own XPath location steps.

### Defaults and shortcuts

First, there's a default axis, child::. Therefore, the following two location steps are functionally identical:

```
child::circle
circle
```

Both locate all circle elements that are children of the context node.

Steps that access the parent node via the parent:: axis in XPath, as in common file-system directory path syntaxes, can be abbreviated using a double period. These two location steps are thus equivalent:

```
parent::node( )
..
```

Similarly, the self:: axis can be abbreviated with a single period. (As with the parent:: axis, this is technically an abbreviation for the axis in combination with the node( ) node test.)

When using the parent:: and self:: axes, you almost never have to specify the name of the node in question; no node in an XML document ever has more than one parent or "self," and the name of that parent/self node is thus almost always immaterial. The exception is when a given element type may appear at any of several levels of a document conforming to a given vocabulary, and you want to select only those with a particular parent element type.

Note that the self:: axis is useful for testing the name of the context node in the predicate portion of a location step. (Predicates are covered in the next section of this chapter.) The name( ) XPath function, covered in Chapter 4, can also be used for this purpose. However, the self:: axis is "namespace aware" and works specifically with the namespace prefix supplied as the tested value; the name( ) function permits the processor to substitute any prefix it wants, as long as the namespace URI is correctly mapped. Consider these two examples:

```
self::someprefix:somename
name( )="someprefix:somename"
```

The first example is true only if the context node's name is "somename" *and* its namespace prefix is "someprefix"; the second is true if the context node's name is "somename" *and* its namespace prefix, whatever it is, maps to the same namespace URI as does "someprefix."

When seeking content along the attribute:: axis, you can replace that axis with a simple at sign (@). Both of the following location steps locate the copyright attribute of the context node:

```
attribute::copyright
@copyright
```

Finally, while not strictly a shortcut for an axis, the location step (plus separators) /descendant-or-self::node( )/ can be abbreviated with a simple double slash, //. Here's a sample document, a peek into a particularly unruly kitchen pantry (entirely fictional, of course):

```
<pantry>
  <shelf>
    <supplies>
      <paper_goods>
        <paper_good>paper towels</paper_good>
```

```
            <paper_good>paper plates</paper_good>
        </paper_goods>
    </supplies>
    <snack_foods>
        <snack_food>popcorn</snack_food>
        <snack_food>chips</snack_food>
    </snack_foods>
</shelf>
<shelf>
    <supplies>
        <paper_goods>
            <paper_good>napkins</paper_good>
        </paper_goods>
    </supplies>
    <snack_foods>
        <snack_food>dried tofu</snack_food>
    </snack_foods>
</shelf>
</pantry>
```

To locate all snack_food elements descended from this document's root pantry element, no matter where they are in its tree of descendants, either of the following will suffice:

```
/pantry/descendant-or-self::node( )/snack_food
/pantry//snack_food
```

If locating all nodes of a particular name or type, the double slash can begin the location path alone—there is no need to precede them with yet another slash representing the root node. For instance, to locate all elements in a document, use:

```
//*
```

and *not*:

```
///*
```

The double-slash shortcut is so useful that you will probably find yourself using it as a shortcut for the descendant::node( ) location step as well—failing to recognize a potential pitfall in doing so: the double slash is *not* associated with just the descendant::node( ) location step, but with the descendant-**or-self**::node( ) location step. In many cases, the results of using either are identical. For instance:

```
/pantry//snack_food
```

works because selecting "all descendants of the pantry element, as well as the pantry element itself, as long as the given node is a snack_food element" obviously eliminates the pantry element itself, leaving only the snack_food descendants.

But if you use the wildcard asterisk or the node( ) node test together with the double slash, you may get a surprise. The following two location paths each select the pantry element in addition to all the desired descendants:

```
/pantry//*
/pantry//node( )
```

## Restrictions by context node type

The last column in Table 3-2 shows which node types are visible, looking from the context node along the indicated axis. However, it's also important to note that the axes available at a given moment vary depending on the type of the context node. An XPath processor will not reject outright invalid axis/context node type combinations; it will simply return an empty node-set for that location step. Table 3-3 summarizes these restrictions.

*Table 3-3. Valid axis/context node combinations*

| Axis | Use when context node type is |
| --- | --- |
| child:: | Root or element |
| parent:: | Any but the root node (which has no parent) |
| descendant:: | Root or element |
| ancestor:: | Any but the root node (which has no ancestors) |
| descendant-or-self:: | Root or element |
| ancestor-or-self:: | Any |
| following:: | Any but root, attribute, or namespace |
| preceding:: | Any but root, attribute, or namespace |
| following-sibling:: | Any but root, attribute, or namespace |
| preceding-sibling:: | Any but root, attribute, or namespace |
| attribute:: | Element |
| namespace:: | Element |
| self:: | Any |

A curious side effect of the information in Tables 3-2 and 3-3, taken together, is that although attribute and namespace nodes "belong to" their declaring elements—in the sense that such an element acts as an attribute/namespace node's parent and is therefore visible along the parent:: axis—the reverse is not true: you can't see attribute or namespace nodes along an element's child:: axis.

## Axes and efficiency

Something to remember when selecting axes to navigate around your XML documents is while the end result achieved by using one axis may be identical to that achieved by using another, one *means* to the end may be significantly more efficient than another. The following XML document illustrates this:

```
<dictionary>
  <letter>
    <forms>
      <form type="upper">A</form>
      <form type="lower">a</form>
    </forms>
```

```
<word>
    <spelling>aardvark</spelling>
    <part_of_speech>noun</part_of_speech>
    <definition>a nocturnal mammal of southern Africa with a tubular
    snout and a long tongue</definition>
  </word>
  </letter>
</dictionary>
```

Both of the following location paths locate the `definition` element:

```
//definition
/dictionary/letter/word/definition
```

The second, however, is a much more direct route to the desired result. It leads the processor down the tree with no side trips, right to the `definition` element. The first, in contrast, takes a leisurely stroll through all descendants of the root node, picking up each one in turn and mulling it over ("Hmm, is this descendant a `dictionary` element...?") before proceeding further through the tree. This includes irrelevant detours into the `forms` branch of the tree and to the `spelling` and `part_of_speech` siblings of the `dictionary` node.

Of course, for this extremely simple example document, the difference in processing time is negligible. Turn this document into an entire dictionary, though, and the difference is considerable. (Of course, explicitly coding the full path to a desired descendant can be more tedious—especially for large, deep node trees. It's hard to argue with performance results, though.)

## The Predicate

Those of you who may have suffered under the yoke of English grammar lessons may be familiar with the term "predicate" as it's commonly used there: the predicate of the sentence is the verb—the word or phrase that drives the sentence's action. So it is with the optional predicate portion of a location step, which drives the filtering performed by the rest of the step to its finest level of granularity.

A more useful way to understand the term as it's used in XPath, though, is to think of its form in such constructions as "Whether Result X will be true is *predicated* upon the truth of Condition Y." That's because a location step's predicate sets forth a Boolean test: if the Boolean test returns true (for a given node selected by the preceding portion of the step), then this node will be selected for inclusion in the resulting node-set. In all other cases, the node is disregarded.

As with Boolean tests in other languages, XPath's predicates are usually coded (within the enclosing square brackets) as Boolean statements of the general form:

```
value1 operator value2
```

where:

- *value1* and *value2* are XPath expressions.
- The whitespace to either side of *operator* is not significant—there can be whitespace there for legibility, or not; and
- *operator* is one of the Boolean operators listed in Table 3-4.

*Table 3-4. Boolean operators in XPath predicates*

| Operator | Meaning |
| --- | --- |
| = | Equal to |
| != | Not equal to |
| > | Greater than |
| >= | Greater than or equal to |
| < | Less than |
| <= | Less than or equal to |

 If (as is likely) you're using XPath expressions within XML documents (as opposed to scripting languages), you must escape any operators that might cause your documents to fail well-formedness constraints. For instance, the < character will need to be escaped as &lt;, and the > may need to be escaped using &gt;. (When used in an attribute value, the greater-than operator (>) never needs to be escaped.)

As I mentioned, the two values being compared by the operator can be either location paths in their own right or literal values. Importantly, any relative location paths appearing in the predicate are considered relative to the context node established by the portions of the location step that precede the predicate, *not* relative to the context node in effect for the location step as a whole. Consider the following simple XML document:

```
<person name="John">
   <child name="John"/>
   <child name="Connie"/>
   <child name="Cindy"/>
   <child name="Mike"/>
</person>
```

Given this document, consider this location path, paying special attention to the predicate:

```
/person/child[@name='John']
```

The context node for the final location step as a whole is the person element. The predicate does *not* look at the name attribute of the person element, however, but rather at the name attribute of each child element. Thus, this predicate results in the selection of only the first child element.

Note that the Boolean condition established by the predicate is an *"any* node that..."
rather than an *"all* nodes that..." condition. For instance, given the above document,
the following location path selects the root person element as long as *any* of its child
children has the indicated name attribute value; the selection doesn't require that *all*
its child children meet the test.

```
/person[child/@name='Cindy']
```

There's no restriction on the number of location steps that might employ predicates,
although the simple examples above show predicates only on the last step. In navigating around an XHTML document with XPath, you might use a location path such
as this:

```
/html/body/p[@align="center"]/img[@border &gt; 0]
```

This selects each img element with a border attribute greater than 0, as long as the img
element's parent is a center-aligned p element that is a child of the body element
(which in turn is a child of the html element).

### Nesting predicates

You may not use or encounter this too much in your own XPath location steps, but
it's entirely legal for an expression being tested by the predicate to include a predicate of its own. (After all, the expressions on either side of the operator, being
expressions, can be and often are location steps in their own right.) Thus, you might
see something like this:

```
//roofing_material[descendant::type[preceding-sibling::manufacturer='Smith']]
```

This selects all roofing_material elements that have a type descendant for which, in
turn, there exists a manufacturer on the preceding-sibling:: axis whose name is
"Smith."

### Compound predicates

You can test for multiple conditions in a single predicate by delimiting the multiple
conditions with logical and/or operators. For instance:

```
camera[brand/@name = 'Minolta' and brand/@list &lt; 300]
```

selects a camera child of the context node only if:

- The camera element has a brand child with a name attribute whose value is
  Minolta.
- The camera element has a brand child, which also has a list attribute whose
  value is less than 300.

As in other computer languages, using multiple ands and ors can become quickly
indecipherable to the human eye and mind, so XPath allows you to group conditions together, using parentheses to eliminate ambiguity. You can nest these grouped
conditions to any arbitrary depth.

Note, in the various example predicates here (and anywhere else in the book), the escaping of markup-significant characters (such as &lt; for the < character). The escaping is required *not* by XPath itself, but by the constraints imposed on XML documents by the XML spec itself; such documents—for example, XSLT stylesheets—are common (perhaps the most common) venues to find XPath expressions. (That's why I'm escaping them.) But when using XPath outside of an XML or other markup context, there's no particular need to escape the special characters. For example, in a non-markup application, the preceding location step could be coded:

```
camera[brand/@name = 'Minolta' and brand/@list < 300]
```

Consider this document:

```
<weather>
    <day date="2001-12-12">
        <readings>
            <reading time="0600">
                <temp>23</temp>
                <wind_spd>5</wind_spd>
                <wind_dir>ESE</wind_dir>
            </reading>
            <reading time="1200">
                <temp>30</temp>
                <wind_spd>2</wind_spd>
                <wind_dir>SE</wind_dir>
            </reading>
            <reading time="1800">
                <temp>34</temp>
                <wind_spd>10</wind_spd>
                <wind_dir>S</wind_dir>
            </reading>
            <reading time="2400">
                <temp>29</temp>
                <wind_spd>15</wind_spd>
                <wind_dir>S</wind_dir>
            </reading>
        </readings>
    </day>
    ...etc....
</weather>
```

As a hypothetical case, you might be interested only in those readings meeting the following conditions:

- The time at which the reading was taken was either noon or 6 p.m.
- The wind speed was less than 15 knots, as long as the wind direction was from the south.
- The temperature was less than 25 degrees.

As a location path, these conditions could be expressed as follows:

```
//reading[(@time="1200" or @time="1800") or (wind_spd &lt; 15 and wind_dir="S")
    or (temp &lt; 25)]
```

If the connecting operators were all either and or or, you wouldn't need to use any grouping at all. The presence of that lone and, though, changes the situation considerably: omit the parentheses, or group (say) the test for wind_dir with the one for temp, and you've suddenly got a subtly (or radically) different test, returning a subtly (or radically) different node-set.

Operator precedence in XPath, in order of *ascending* importance, is as follows: or, and, =, !=, <=, <, >=, and >, so in:

```
a = b or c = d and x = y
```

the and test takes precedence over the or, being evaluated as though they were coded:

```
x = y and (a = b or c = d)
```

When parentheses are used for grouping, conditions are evaluated at their innermost levels first, "boiling up" the respective true or false values to a common level where they can *then* be compared using operator precedence and left-to-right rules.

### Predicates with a single value and no operator

Often, you don't need to determine that a node along some axis has some particular value. You need merely to check for the *existence* of such a node. The way to use an XPath predicate for this purpose is to take advantage of a special form of the predicate, which simply uses a location path with no *operator* or *value2* within the square brackets.

You could select only book elements that contain at least one table, for example:

```
//book[descendant::table]
```

This works because XPath treats an empty node-set as a Boolean false and a *non-empty* node-set as a Boolean true.

Note that this does not disregard a book element that contains an empty table element; it tests for the presence of *any* table element, empty or otherwise. If you want to be sure you're selecting only those book elements with non-empty table descendants, you use an explicit test in the predicate:

```
//book[descendant::table!=""]
```

An earlier note back discussed the general silliness of selecting a node with a particular name on the parent:: axis, because that axis will always locate at most a single node (irrespective of its name). (The root node has no parent, but all other nodes in a document have exactly one parent.) In some XML vocabularies, though, a particular element type may be allowed as a child of *different* element types. A classic case is the XHTML div element, which can appear as a container almost anywhere within the body of an XHTML document. Thus, you can productively use the parent:: axis in a case like this, within a single-valued predicate, to isolate (say) only those div elements that are children of a p element:

```
//div[parent::p]
```

On the other hand, there are often a number of other approaches to the same problem, including the (to my mind) much simpler and easier to digest:

```
//p/div
```

The point here is not to argue the merits of one approach or another in general; it's simply to remind you that as a rule, XPath offers multiple routes to the same solution. If you find yourself trapped by a particular technique that "solves" one problem but creates another, don't forget to investigate an alternative before consigning XPath to the (ever more crowded) dustbin of technologies long on the theoretical dimension but short on the practical.

### Special case: numeric-valued predicates

A very important second exception to the general form of the predicate is when the predicate's value is (or evaluates to) a number. This form is used to select a node that has a particular context position within the node-set selected by the preceding portion of the location step.

Look back at the weather-readings example. If you wanted to select the third reading child of all elements in the document, regardless of its contents, you could do so using:

```
//reading[3]
```

This numeric form of the predicate is actually an abbreviated form of the usual *value1-operator-value2* general syntax. The full form uses the XPath position() function (covered in Chapter 4) in the following fashion:

```
//reading[position() = 3]
```

Note that to test a node's position and some other condition in a compound predicate, you may *not* use the short, numeric form of the position test. Thus, the following:

```
//reading[3 or temp &lt; 25]
```

is *not* correct, and must be coded as:

```
//reading[position() = 3 or temp &lt; 25]
```

### "Stacked" predicates

The XPath spec doesn't use this term, but I think the word "stacked" pretty well describes what's going on. ("Chained" might work equally well. But in a chain, the order of the particular objects usually doesn't make much difference; switch a couple of links and it's still functionally the same chain. In a stack, the sequence can make all the difference in the world.) A location step can have multiple predicates, one following the other, in this fashion:

```
axis::nodetest[predicate1]...[predicateN]
```

where the ellipsis (...) and [predicateN] indicate that you can have as many predicates as you need.

In many cases, this works exactly as though you'd put the stacked predicates together in a single predicate and connected them with and operators. For instance, the following two location steps are functionally identical:

```
day[@date &gt; "2001-12-01"][reading]
day[@date &gt; "2001-12-01" and reading]
```

Both select a day element only if it has a date attribute whose value is greater than 2001-12-01 *and* if it has at least one reading child.

But the operation of these stacked predicates is slightly different from the merely anded-together alternative. In effect, each succeeding stacked predicate is evaluated in terms of the narrowed context provided by the preceding one(s), *not* just in terms of the general context in which a single (perhaps compound) predicate is evaluated. This is especially noticeable when one of the predicates on the stack is numeric, testing for a node's position.

Consider a document that represents tosses of a coin:

```
<tosses>
    <toss result="heads"/>
    <toss result="heads"/>
    <toss result="tails"/>
    <toss result="heads"/>
    ...etc....
</tosses>
```

Now carefully consider the following two location paths into this document, each using a stacked predicate:

```
(//toss)[@result="heads"][3]
(//toss)[3][@result="heads"]
```

See the difference? The first path locates (a) all toss elements whose result attribute equals "heads," and then (b) the third one of those toss elements. Therefore, in the above document, it selects the fourth toss element in the document.

The second path, though, starts out by selecting the third toss element; the stacked predicate applies a further screen, selecting the third toss element only if its result attribute has a value of heads. Because the third toss element's result attribute is tails, therefore, this location path returns an empty node-set.

Also note in these two examples the use of parentheses to isolate a portion of a location path from a predicate. This enables the XPath to apply the predicate(s) to the parenthetical portion as a whole, rather than just to the last location step in the path.

# Compound Location Paths Revisited

Early in this chapter, I mentioned that you could join together multiple location paths into a single one, using the "pipe" character, |. In that section, you saw this example:

```
/customers/customer/invoice | /customers/customer/cust_info
```

For any given location path, you could say that any given location *step* shifts the context in which succeeding location steps are evaluated. Thus, for the first location path in this compound location path, the context is narrowed first to the root customers element (thereby excluding from consideration any content in the document that precedes or follows the root element), then to customer children of the root element, and finally to invoice children of those customer children.

What, you might reasonably wonder, happens to the context in succeeding location paths of a compound location path? Every constituent location path is considered independently—just as if it were the *only* location path. Obviously, if the location path is absolute (as in the example from early in the chapter just repeated here), its context node is immaterial. If the location path is relative, it is evaluated relative to whatever the context node is at that point, *disregarding* any shifts in context effected by preceding portions of the compound location path. Consider this example:

```
invoice | cust_info
```

The first location path selects all invoice children of the context node for the compound location path as a whole. Likewise, the second selects all cust_info children of the context node for the compound location path as a whole—*not* all cust_info children of the invoice elements selected by the first location path. The results of the two selections are simply unioned together into a single node-set.

Along these lines, also note that each constituent location path may employ "stacked" predicates (as discussed earlier in the chapter), compound predicates, or any other location path variations. Predicates used in location path A have no effect on those in location path B and vice versa.

# CHAPTER 4

# XPath Functions and Numeric Operators

The XPath 1.0 Recommendation specifies a number of *functions* and *numeric operations* that can be used to refine the results returned by an XPath expression.

Before getting into the details of these features' uses, let's take a look at a fundamental question: what are functions in the first place? (If you're already familiar with the use of functions in programming languages, such as Java, C++, and Visual Basic, feel free to skip this section.)

## Introduction to Functions

When I was a kid, I loved watching my father work on cars. He'd been a mechanic all his life, and the automotive toolkit he'd acquired over the course of the years was exotic (to my eyes, anyhow).

One of the smaller items in Dad's toolkit was something he called a "spark-plug gapper." It was something like a Swiss-Army knife, with a half-dozen or so stiff steel prongs that you could swivel out from the tool's main body. Each L-shaped prong was of a slightly different thickness; depending on the model of car you were working on and the specific spark plug's specifications, you'd tap the end of the spark plug on the pavement and, using the gapper, ensure that the distance across which the spark was to jump was just right. There was also a small, stiff plane of sheet metal attached to the gapper, which you could use to spread the gap if you'd already closed it up too much. The objective was the get the gap just right, to ensure that the spark plug fired in just exactly the right way.

A function in computer-language terms is like a spark-plug gapper. It's a tool provided by a software developer. You use the tool in the same general way for a given task, whenever you need to obtain some result you can't obtain (or obtain easily) without the tool.

Almost without exception, regardless of the computer language in question, functions are represented syntactically the same way:

```
function_name(arg1, ...)
```

Each function (like each tool in a mechanic's toolbox) has a distinct name. Depending on the function, you may pass one or more arguments to it, which change its behavior in various ways. The arguments are enclosed in parentheses. Thus, the spark-plug gapper might be represented like this:

```
gapper(prong)
```

where gapper is the function name and prong, a single argument provided (or "passed") to the function. Under many circumstances, you wouldn't pass a function like this the literal token p, r, o, n, g; rather, this is just a placeholder, a reminder to you of what you do pass to it. In this form, the function syntax is called a *prototype*. When you actually use (or "call" or "invoke") a function, you typically substitute a literal value for each argument. So an actual call to our hypothetical gapper( ) function might look like this:

```
gapper(1)
```

Now, many functions are fussy about both the number of arguments and the type. Depending on how the gapper( ) function is written, for example, the following might be illegal calls to it:

```
gapper(3, 6)
gapper("1")
```

In the first example, there's more than one argument passed; in the second, the argument being passed is a literal string rather than a literal number. If in fact a legal call to gapper( ) passes only a single numeric argument, either of these two calls will fail—probably resulting in an error message of some kind.

## What Functions Do

The interesting thing about functions is that a call to one of them takes the place of some literal value in a "sentence" in the programming language in question. That is, a function *returns a value*.

So Dad, in my case, might say to me something like, "Here. Set the gap on this plug to fifteen-thousandths of an inch." This would require me to know how to determine which prong on the gapper produced exactly that effect. More likely, especially if this was my first time handling the tool, he'd say, "Set the gap on this plug with prong number one" (or whatever). In a hypothetical computer language to achieve this purpose, this English-language instruction might be rendered:

```
setgap gapper(1)
```

This would achieve the same effect as:

```
setgap .015
```

That is, in formal terms, the gapper( ) function, when passed a numeric value of 1, returns the numeric value .015.

## Functions Within Functions

Given, then, that a function returns a value and that the arguments passed to functions are themselves values, it's entirely legal—even desirable, in many circumstances—to pass one function as an argument to another.

Returning to the spark plug–gapping tool, as you can see from the preceding example, the gapper( ) function returns a value in the form of a fraction of an inch, based on the "prong number" selected. This was eminently reasonable back in Dad's day. Now, though, most spark-plug gaps are expressed in terms of millimeters. So now we'd need a separate method for gapping a plug in metric units instead. The hypothetical computer-language expression of this might look something like:

```
setgap_mm inches_to_mm(gapper(1))
```

which is equivalent to:

```
setgap_mm inches_to_mm(.015)
```

which in turn is equivalent to:

```
setgap_mm .38
```

The gapper( ) function here still returns .015—the value in inches of feeler #1's thickness. This value in turn is passed to a hypothetical conversion function, inches_to_mm( ), which takes a single argument—a number of inches—and converts it to millimeters.

# XPath Function Types

The functions available for use in XPath expressions are categorized by the type of value they return and/or by the type of values they operate on as arguments. These categories are node-set, string, Boolean, and numeric functions.

In each of the function prototypes in this section, I'll use the following scheme to denote the kind of arguments passed:

string
> Argument is a string value, to be enclosed in quotation marks in the function call. If a function call takes more than one string argument, I'll append a number to each, as in string1, string2, and so on.

nodeset
> Argument is a node-set, represented by an XPath location path. Note that if you're using XPath in an XSLT stylesheet, this location path will (if it's a relative path) be sensitive to the context established by the stylesheet at that point. Whether you're using XPath in XSLT or an XPointer, earlier portions of a complete location path can of course establish a context for node-set references in later portions.

boolean

    Argument has a Boolean value of true or false.

number

    Argument has a numeric value. If a function call takes more than one numeric argument, I'll append a number to each, as in number1, number2, and so on.

anytype

    Argument can be any of several types. For instance, you can pass certain functions a string or a numeric argument, and the function will handle any necessary data-type conversion.

?

    A question mark appended to one of the above data types means the argument is optional. For instance, a call to a hypothetical my_func( ) function might come with a prototype such as my_func(string?). This would mean that when you call my_func( ), you may supply a string argument or no argument at all. In such a case, the function will usually assume some default value for the argument, perhaps derived from the context node at the point of the function call.

Note that the type of data returned by each function is documented in a table at the start of the section dealing with the appropriate function type. Unlike functions in some traditional programming languages, XPath functions *always* return a value.

 XSLT and EXSLT both provide functions that go beyond XPath itself. If you need something beyond what this chapter describes, see Appendix A.

## Node-Set Functions

A node-set function, as the name implies, operates on a node-set; one of these functions also *returns* a node-set. Table 4-1 summarizes the functions in this category. Each function is discussed in detail in a separate subsection following the table. These discussions assume that the source document being referenced by XPath expressions is the following fragment of an XML document:

```
<!DOCTYPE book:book
<!ATTLIST book:section id ID #IMPLIED>
]>
<book:book
    xmlns:book="http://mynamespace/uri"
    xmlns:xlink="http://www.w3.org/1999/xlink/ "
    xmlns="http://www.w3.org/2000/svg">

    <book:chapter>
        <book:section id="sect_01">
            <book:para id="para_01">Some text...
                For more information, see:
                <book:ref xlink:href="crossref_01.xml">crossref_01.xml</book:ref>
            </book:para>
```

```
<svg>
    <circle style="fill:yellow"
        cx="100" cy="100" r="50"/>
</svg>
    </book:section>
</book:chapter>

[...remainder of book...]

</book:book>
```

 Note the ATTLIST declaration in this document's prolog. As you'll see, your documents may need such a declaration (in either the internal DTD subset, as here, or an external one) to determine that an attribute is of the ID type. However, if you're using the MSXML XSLT processor, be aware that the ATTLIST declaration alone will not suffice to make the processor recognize the (in this case) id attribute; the processor also requires that the attribute's parent *element* (book:section, here) be declared.

*Table 4-1. Node-set functions*

| Function prototype | Returns | Description |
| --- | --- | --- |
| last() | Number | Returns the number of nodes in the context node-set |
| position() | Number | Returns the ordinal position of the context node within the context node-set |
| count(nodeset) | Number | Returns the number of nodes in nodeset |
| id(string) | Node-set | Returns the element node with an ID-type attribute equal to the value of the passed argument |
| local-name(nodeset?) | String | Returns the local name (that is, the QName without a namespace prefix) of the first node in nodeset |
| namespace-uri(nodeset?) | String | Returns the URI associated with the namespace prefix of the first node in nodeset |
| name(nodeset?) | String | Returns the QName of the first node in nodeset |

## last()

If the context node-set, at the point of the call to last(), contains 12 nodes, last() returns 12.

Assume the context for the call to last() is established by a location path such as the following, referencing the sample XML document above:

```
//book:section/*
```

This locates a node-set consisting of two element nodes, book:para and svg. Therefore, a call to last() at this point returns the value 2.

Probably the most common use of last( ) is in a location step's predicate, as in:

```
/book:book/book:chapter[last( )]
```

which selects the last chapter in the book.

### position( )

This commonly used function returns the integer representing the context node's ordinal position within the context node-set. These positions begin at 1 (for the first node in the node-set) and increment up to the value of the last( ) function.

The sample XML document's root element, book:book, has six element nodes visible along its descendant:: axis (book:chapter, book:section, book:para, book:ref, svg, and circle). Therefore, this location path:

```
/book:book/descendant::*
```

locates a node-set consisting of those six element nodes. You could locate just the svg node by adding a predicate, as here:

```
/book:book/descendant::*[position( )=5]
```

That is, "locate the fifth node in the node-set."

Note that the value returned by the position( ) function is sensitive to the forward or reverse direction of the axis in effect. For forward-type axes, such as descendant:: in the preceding example, nodes are accessed in their natural document order; for reverse-type axes, nodes are accessed in reverse document order. So we could build a location path beginning, say, at the svg element node and locating the ancestor book: chapter element with a location path such as:

```
//svg/ancestor::*[position( )=2]
```

Here, the book:section element is ancestor #1 in reverse document order, and book: chapter is ancestor #2.

The position( ) function is important, as I've said, for two reasons:

- It can be represented in a location step's predicate simply by the value of the position for which you want to test. That is:

```
//svg/ancestor::*[position( )=2]
```

and:

```
//svg/ancestor::*[2]
```

are functionally identical.

- Many XSLT operations must be performed for every *n*th occurrence of some kind of node in the source tree being transformed. For a simple example, perhaps you want to shade every odd row of a table, leaving the even rows unshaded: in other words, to shade every second row. This kind of processing can be achieved easily using position( ) together with the mod numeric operator. I'll describe mod later in this chapter and give an example of its use with position( ).

## count(nodeset)

In every respect but one, the count() function operates identically to the last() function covered earlier. What makes it different is that count() takes one argument; last(), none. Thus, count() can be used to return the number of nodes in some arbitrary node-set other than the current one.

The following XSLT template displays the number of the current section in the chapter within which it appears, then displays (using count()) the total number of book: section nodes in the document as a whole. Note the nested xsl:for-each elements, which cause processing in the template rule to "loop" through some set of operations for every node in a select node-set. Here, the outermost xsl:for-each element loops through every book:chapter element; the innermost xsl:for-each element loops through each book:section child of the selected book:chapter.

```
<xsl:template match="/">
    <xsl:for-each select="book:book/book:chapter">
        Chapter <xsl:value-of select="position()"/>:
            <xsl:for-each select="book:section">
                This is section #<xsl:value-of select="position()"/> of
                <xsl:value-of select="last()"/> within its chapter.
            </xsl:for-each>
    </xsl:for-each>
    The total number of sections in the book is: <xsl:value-of
        select="count(//book:section)"/>
</xsl:template>
```

When you apply this template to a sample document consisting of three book: chapter elements—the first with one book:section child elements, the second with three, and the third with two—the result is:

```
Chapter 1:

        This is section #1 of
        1 within its chapter.

Chapter 2:

        This is section #1 of
        3 within its chapter.

        This is section #2 of
        3 within its chapter.

        This is section #3 of
        3 within its chapter.

Chapter 3:

        This is section #1 of
        2 within its chapter.
```

```
This is section #2 of
2 within its chapter.
```

```
The total number of sections in the whole book is: 6
```

### id(anytype)

Unlike the other functions in the node-set category, the id( ) function actually returns a node-set, given its argument. (The argument is usually, but not always, a string; see the subsection titled "id( ) and node-set arguments," for more information.) The value of the argument locates the set of all element nodes with the indicated ID-type attribute; because the value of an ID-type attribute, by definition, must be unique within a given document, the resulting node-set thus will contain a single element node (or be empty, if no elements have an ID-type attribute with this value). You can also use a whitespace-delimited *list* of values to return all element nodes with any matching ID-type attributes. For instance:

```
id("sect_01 sect_05 sect_88")
```

returns a node-set consisting of up to three element nodes. If no element nodes match a particular value, no error condition exists. In this example, if no element node has an ID-type attribute whose value is sect_05 but there *are* matches for the other two values, the resulting node-set would contain two elements.

It's important that you heed the phrase "ID-type attribute" here. The id( ) function ignores any attributes whose *names* are "id," unless they are declared in the document's DTD as being of the ID type. Thus:

```
id("sect_01")
```

successfully returns the book:section element with that id attribute value, while:

```
id("para_01")
```

returns an empty node-set: the former id attribute is expressly declared to be an ID-type attribute in the document's DTD, while the latter is not. Perhaps more importantly, if there is no DTD at all—if the document is simply well formed—it doesn't make any difference what value you pass to the id( ) function; it will always in this case return an empty node-set. If you're uncertain whether an attribute named id is of the ID type—or know for sure that it isn't—test the attribute value in a location step's predicate, as in:

```
[@id="para_01"]
```

or, if the context node is already the id attribute:

```
[.="para_01"]
```

Such an approach, while perhaps more prosaic, is also closer to failure-proof. (XSLT users can also take advantage of keys to ensure unique identifiers.)

### id( ) and node-set arguments

The id( ) function is unique among functions in the XPath spec in one regard. As with the other functions, if you pass it a value that is *not* a string, the value is treated as if it had been converted to a string by the string( ) function (covered later in this chapter). Typically, when you pass string( ) a node-set, it returns the string-value of only the *first* node in the node-set. However, when you pass id( ) a node-set, the function returns not only a single node (whose ID-type attribute's value would presumably match the string-value of the first node), but rather a node-set containing all element nodes whose ID-type attributes match any of the string-values of nodes in the passed node-set.

### local-name(nodeset?)

The local-name( ) function returns the name of a node, shorn of any namespace prefix. (You might call this the un-QName.) If the optional argument is not supplied, the function operates as if you had passed it a node-set consisting only of the context node. If the node-set contains more than one node, the function returns the local-name of only the first node (in document order) in the node-set:

    local-name(//book:chapter)

returns the string chapter and:

    local-name(//svg)

returns the string svg. On the other hand:

    local-name(//book:section | //svg)

(note the compound location path) returns the string section—that is, the local-name of only the first node in the node-set.

### namespace-uri(nodeset?)

When you need to know the URI associated with a given element or attribute's namespace in an instance document, call the namespace-uri( ) function. If you omit the optional argument, its default value is a node-set consisting of just the context node. If the node-set passed as the argument consists of more than one node, the function returns the URI associated with only the first node in the node-set. If the specified element or attribute has no associated URI, the function returns an empty string.

In the sample XML document, each element node is associated with a namespace URI. The elements with explicit book: prefixes are associated with the URIs tied to those prefixes via the namespace declarations for that prefix. For instance:

    namespace-uri(/book:book)

returns the string "http://mynamespace/uri."

Note that when an attribute node's name is unprefixed—even when there's an explicit *default* namespace declaration (xmlns attribute) in effect for the node—the namespace-uri( ) function returns a null value. This expression:

```
namespace-uri(//circle@style)
```

returns a null string.

An attribute also does not acquire the namespace URI associated with the corresponding element automatically. For attributes in the sample document such as id, style, and cx, an empty string is returned as the namespace URI. However, this expression:

```
namespace-uri(//book:ref/@xlink:href)
```

returns the string "http://www.w3.org/1999/xlink/"—the URI associated (via the xmlns:xlink declaration) with the attribute's xlink: namespace prefix.

By the way, as always when dealing with namespaces, remember that the exact namespace prefix is seldom relevant: what counts is the URI to which the namespace prefix is bound. For instance, at the time the XPath expression is evaluated—say, in an XSLT stylesheet or an XPointer—the namespace URI "http://mynamespace/uri" might be associated with the prefix mybook:. In such a context, the following two function calls return exactly the same results as long as the document containing the XPath expression binds both prefixes to the same URI:

```
namespace-uri(/book:book)
namespace-uri(/mybook:book)
```

The document being evaluated by the expression needn't use either of those two prefixes in the element name, as long as whatever prefix it *does* use is bound to the "http://mynamespace/uri" URI.

### name(nodeset?)

If your applications must refer to nodes in a namespace-aware fashion (as most applications do), the name( ) function will probably be the node-name function you'll use least often. That's because it returns the QName of the node-set passed (or defaulted) as its sole argument—the "intuitive" name, including both the namespace prefix and the local-name portion. Therefore, name( ) is truly reliable only when processing elements and attributes in no namespace at all. As in the other name-related functions, passing no argument at all causes name( ) to operate on a node-set consisting of just the context node; if the node-set argument includes more than one node, the function operates on only the first.

On the face of it, using a function such as name( ) might seem superfluous. After all, the most common form of a location step includes an explicit node name, and if you already know the node's name, there's no need for a function to return it.

Where it comes in handy is when you *don't* (for one reason or another) know the name of the node in question or simply need to test the name (particularly of an attribute) against a string. For instance, you might need to isolate the *n*th child of a particular element, displaying its name and the names and values of all its attributes. Here's another example from XSLT using nested xsl:for-each elements:

```
<!-- Process the first child of each book:section element -->
<xsl:template match="/
   <xsl:for-each select="book:section/*[1]">
      <!-- Display this child's name... -->
      The first child's name is <xsl:value-of select="name( )"/>,
      and it has the following attributes:<br/>
      <xsl:for-each select="@*">
         <!-- ...and the name and value of each attribute -->
         <xsl:value-of select="name( )"/> = <xsl:value-of select="."/><br/>
      </xsl:for-each>
   </xsl:for-each>
</xsl:template>
```

Applied to the sample XML document for this section, this template rule generates the text:

```
The first child's name is book:para, and it has the following attributes:
id = para_01
```

A special case of "not knowing the name of the node in question" occurs in generic XSLT stylesheets whose purpose is to *describe* the documents they process, displaying the names of the various nodes and their values. A portion of such a stylesheet might look something like the following:

```
<!-- Process all element children of the context node -->
<xsl:template match="*">
   <!-- Display the child element's name -->
   Child's name: <xsl:value-of select="name( )"/>
   <!-- Display the child element's (string) value  -->
   Child's value: <xsl:value-of select="."/>
</xsl:template>
```

What makes this a special case is not necessarily that you really don't know the node's name—you may know very well what element names occur in your source document—rather, the general-purpose code doesn't *care* what the element's name is at this point; it treats all (child) elements the same way.

 In Chapter 2, you saw something called an "expanded-name" for the various node types. I described an algorithm there for computing an expanded-name, consisting of the namespace URI, a plus sign, and the local-name of the node. You can use the same algorithm for computing the expanded-name with an XPath expression, by concatenating for a given name the value returned by the namespace-uri( ) function, the +, and the value returned by the local-name( ) function. I'll show you how to do this concatenation in the next section, in the discussion of the concat( ) string function.

## String Functions

The set of XPath functions that operate on string arguments and/or return strings is extensive. Used in XSLT stylesheets, these functions give you enormous flexibility in terms of generating new content based on content in the source tree. In XPointers, you'll find yourself using them most often in the predicate of XPath location steps.

Examples in this section all assume that the following XML document is being navigated via XPath:

```
<dated_relics xmlns="http://mynamespace">
    <relic>
        <name>Smurf</name>
        <price currency="USD">9.00</price>
    </relic>
```

```
<relic>
    <name>lava lamp</name>
    <price currency="GBP">39.95</price>
</relic>
<relic>
    <name>beanbag chair</name>
    <price currency="EU">70.75</price>
</relic>
<relic>
    <name>love bead bracelet</name>
    <price currency="GBP">.37</price>
</relic>
<relic>
    <name>blacklight</name>
    <price currency="USD">323.65</price>
</relic>
<relic>
    <name>VW mini-bus</name>
    <price currency="USD">8500.00</price>
</relic>
<relic>
    <name>open-hand chair</name>
    <price currency="JPY">16865.78</price>
</relic>
</dated_relics>
```

Table 4-2 summarizes the XPath string functions. A detailed discussion of each follows the table.

*Table 4-2. String functions*

| Function prototype | Returns | Description |
|---|---|---|
| string(anytype?) | String | Returns the value of the anytype argument converted to a string |
| concat(string1, string2, ...) | String | Concatenates the values of the passed arguments into a single string and returns that string's value |
| starts-with(string1, string2) | boolean | Returns true if string1 begins with string2, false otherwise |
| contains(string1, string2) | boolean | Returns true if string1 contains string2, false otherwise |
| substring(string, number1, number2?) | String | Returns the portion of string starting at character number1, for a length of number2 characters |
| substring-before(string1, string2) | String | Returns the portion of string1 occurring before string2 |
| substring-after(string1, string2) | String | Returns the portion of string1 following string2 |
| string-length(string?) | Number | Returns the number of characters in string |

*Table 4-2. String functions (continued)*

| Function prototype | Returns | Description |
|---|---|---|
| normalize-space(string?) | String | Returns the whitespace-normalized value of string (that is, stripped of leading and trailing spaces, with multiple consecutive occurrences of whitespace replaced by a single space) |
| translate(string1, string2, string3) | String | Replaces individual characters appearing in both string1 and string2 with corresponding characters in string3 |

## string(anytype?)

As you might guess from its name, the string() function converts the optional argument to a string of characters. There's a set of rules for the way in which this conversion takes place, dependent on the data type of the argument:

**When anytype is a node-set.** When the argument is a node-set (for example, one returned by a location path), string() returns the string-value of the first node in the node-set. If the indicated node-set is empty, the returned value is an empty string. If the argument is missing, it defaults to a node-set whose only member is the context node at the point of the call to string().

**When anytype is a number.** If you pass string() an integer numeric argument, results are pretty much what you'd expect: you get back the number in the form of a string (e.g., "365" instead of 365). A fixed- or floating-point number is converted to a string including a decimal point, at least one number to the left and one to the right of the decimal point, and an optional minus sign (for negative numbers only, obviously). The spec says that the number of trailing zeros in the latter case will always be sufficient only to distinguish the number from all other legal (IEEE 754) numeric values.

Refer back to the sample XML document. Passing string() the value of a price element should produce different results, depending on the price element. Consider:

```
string(number(price))
```

Here, the price of a Smurf should be returned as the string "9" (no leading or trailing zeros, because none are needed to distinguish this or any other integer from all other legal numeric values), the price of a love bead bracelet as the string "0.37" (including a leading zero), and the price of any of the other relics in the document as simply the string-value of the element's text node (e.g., the string "39.95" for the lava lamp).

Any form of the number 0, including positive and negative 0, is converted to the string "0." Positive infinity* is represented as the string "Infinity"; negative infinity is represented the same way, prepended with a minus sign: "-Infinity."

---

* Which I think of as one more than a gazillion.

You may encounter one other oddball condition when passing string( ) a numeric argument, which arises when the argument is only *supposedly* a number, but for one reason or another is not. As mentioned in Chapter 2 in the discussion of data types, XPath represents a number-that-isn't-a-number with the special value, NaN; if NaN (either literally or as the result of some calculation or function call) is passed to string( ), the returned value is the *string* "NaN."

 The XPath Recommendation points out that passing numeric values to the string( ) function is not intended to solve the general problem of formatting numbers as strings—for example, grouping every three positions with commas, forcing specific numbers of leading zeros, and so on. If you're using XSLT, you can do all this with the format-number( ) function and the xsl:number element.

**When anytype is a Boolean.**  A Boolean argument to string( ) returns either the value "true" or "false," depending on the value of the argument.

**When anytype is a string.**  A string argument passed to string( ) returns the same string.

**When anytype is any other data type.**  In a burst of involuted prose, the XPath spec says, "An object of a type other than the four basic types is converted to a string in a way that is dependent on that type." Let's see, the data types allowed under XPath are string, numeric, node-set, Boolean, and, uh....

This clause has been added to future-proof XPath against the introduction of new data types. In theory, the specifier (W3C or otherwise) of such a new data type would be obliged to provide some statement of how its values are to be represented as strings: how to derive their string-values, in short.

For instance, some future version of XPath (or an XPath-aware spec) might include a currency data type. This hypothetical spec might then say something like, "When represented as a string, values of the currency data type will include at least one integer (possibly 0) to the left of the decimal point, the decimal point itself, and at least a two-digit integer to the right of the decimal point, preceded by an optional minus sign and preceded or followed by an optional currency symbol." And there would be your definition of how to expect string( ) to behave when passed a currency value.

(How, exactly, an XPath function such as string( ) is to know all these outside-of-XPath data conversion rules is a tricky question wisely sidestepped by the XPath spec.)

### concat(string1, string2, ...)

The concat( ) function takes at least two arguments and forges them into a single string. The function provides no padding with whitespace, so if you're constructing (say) a list of tokens, or a set of words into a phrase or sentence, you've got to include the " " characters and perhaps punctuation separating one from the other.

For instance, assume that the context node at a given point is any of the relic elements in the sample XML document. Then:

```
concat(price, " (", price/@currency, ")")
```

builds a string consisting of that relic's price, a space an opening parenthesis, the currency in which the price is represented, and a closing parenthesis. Given our sample document, for the seven relics in question, this would yield the strings (respectively):

9.00 (USD)
39.95 (GBP)
70.75 (EU)
.37 (GBP)
323.65 (USD)
8500.00 (USD)

Note that the figures 9.00, .37, and 8500.00 do not follow the rules outlined above for representing numeric values as strings. If for some reason you want to force this representation, you need to explicitly convert the price element nodes' string-values to numbers (using the number( ) function discussed later), pass this result to string( ), and finally, pass that function's result to concat( ) as its first argument. Like this:

```
concat(string(number(price)), " (",
    price/@currency, ")")
```

Also note in this case that the call to string( ) is optional. Because concat( ) expects a string-type argument, it does any necessary conversion automatically.

Earlier in this chapter, in the discussion of name-related node-set functions, I mentioned that the concat( ) function could be used to build an expanded-name for a given element. Following the logic of James Clark's algorithm for this process, you can build an expanded-name for a given name using:

```
concat(namespace-uri(node), "+", local-name(node))
```

Thus, if node is a relic element from our sample XML document, the function call returns the string "http://mynamespace+relic."

### starts-with(string1, string2)

The starts-with( ) function takes two arguments, returning either the Boolean value true if the first argument starts with the value of the second, or false otherwise.

Returning Boolean values makes starts-with() useful primarily in a location step's predicate. Thus:

```
//price[starts-with(., ".")]
```

selects all the price elements whose string-values start with decimal points (i.e., no leading zeros or other digits). For our sample document, the resulting node-set consists of a single price element: the one for the love bead bracelet, with a string-value of ".37."

---

## contains(string1, string2)

Like starts-with( ), the contains( ) function returns a Boolean true or false and, hence, is most commonly used in a predicate. And it too takes two arguments. The value returned by the function is true if the first argument contains the second, or false otherwise.

In our sample document, we could extract a node-set consisting of all relics that are chairs using a location path such as:

```
//relic[contains(name, "chair")]
```

This would locate a two-node node-set: the relic node representing a beanbag chair and the relic node representing an open-hand chair.

## substring(string, number1, number2?)

Like most programming languages, XPath provides a substring( ) function for extracting a portion of a larger string. (Some languages, notably those derived from BASIC, call this the mid( ) function instead.) It takes at least two arguments: the larger string from which you want to select a portion and the starting point for the selection. A third optional argument can specify the number of characters to be extracted; if this argument isn't supplied, the extraction starts at character number1 and goes to the end of first string.

If you're coming to XPath from a programming language that uses 0-based indexing (such as Java), in which the first item is #0, the second #1, and so on, be aware that XPath is 1-based: the first item is #1, and so on. That is, to select the first character of a string, use:

```
substring(string, 1, 1)
```

not:

```
substring(string, 0, 1)
```

What happens when the number passed as the third argument exceeds the length of the string in question? This is not an error; the function behaves as though you hadn't passed a third argument at all. If the value of the *second* argument is greater than the length of the string, you'll get back an empty string as a result.

One way in which I occasionally use the substring( ) function is during testing of an XSLT stylesheet. At this point, I really don't care to see the complete contents of text nodes, particularly lengthy ones. All I care to see is that the correct text nodes are showing up in the right places. So I use substring( ) to return, say, just the first five characters of a text node, with an ellipsis (. . .) appended. Something like this:

```
concat(substring(node, 1, 5), "...")
```

Given the sample XML document used in this section, when iterating through a node-set consisting of all the name elements, this returns a series of substrings such as the following:

Smurf...
lava ...
beanb...
love ...
black...
VW mi...
open-...

### substring-before(string1, string2) and substring-after(string1, string2)

These two functions work very similarly. They each take two arguments: a string from which you want a portion of text extracted and a string where you want the extraction terminated or begun, respectively. In either case, the string2 argument doesn't appear in the result returned by the function; it's simply used as a breakpoint. If string2 doesn't appear in string1 at all, the function returns an empty string.

Consider a check-writing application using the values of the price elements from this section's sample XML document. Such an application takes a number such as "12.34" (assuming that what is represented is in U.S. dollars) and converts it to a phrase like "12 dollars and 34 cents." You could use the decimal point in the price element as the string2 breakpoint for calling both substring-before( ) and substring-after( ), like this:

```
concat(substring-before(price, "."), " dollars and ",
    substring-after(price, "."), " cents")
```

This would naturally have to be tweaked in various ways to be perfectly workable. You'd have to come up with alternative phrasing for non-U.S. currency and also provide for the likelihood that a given price (such as that of the love beads) lacks anything at all to the left of its decimal point. But as a demonstration of the two functions in action, it works just fine.

### string-length(string?)

Given a passed string argument, the string-length( ) function returns the number of characters it contains. If no argument is passed, the function operates on the context node's string-value.

This function is sometimes directly useful in its own right. For example, you can use it to tell you whether one string is longer than another (apply it to the two strings and compare the two values returned). More often, though, you'll see string-length( ) used as an argument passed to another function—or the values returned by other functions as arguments passed to *it*. For instance:

```
string-length(substring-before(price, "."))
```

This returns the number of digits to the left of the decimal point in a price element's string-value, which might be useful information in formatting the number a certain way.

### normalize-space(string?)

If you've spent any time at all poking around XML-related specifications, you've probably come across the verb "normalize" and its variants. The issue here is that an XML parser is required to preserve whitespace found in a source document—to pass it unchanged to a downstream application. To normalize content is to remove extraneous whitespace—to trim leading and trailing whitespace from strings (such as text nodes) and replace multiple successive occurrences of whitespace *within* a string with a single blank space.

That's what the normalize-space( ) function does, cleaning up the extraneous whitespace in a string so that what's left is "pure content." Why would you want to do this? Because if the text content of a document has been hand-entered, you want to be sure that no extra space has crept in as a result of keyboard errors. This extra space can make comparing one string-value to another fail, even when the two nodes are apparently identical. For instance:

```
item1
```

and:

```
item1
```

are not "equal," although they may appear so to a casual human observer; the second item1 is preceded and followed by newlines. That is, their *normalized* values—as returned by normalize-space( ), say—are equal, but their "raw" values are not.

Note that fixing up extraneous whitespace within a string isn't the same as removing whitespace-only text nodes. Needing to do *that* isn't necessarily a problem in its own right, but can be a very big problem in XSLT applications, where the extra text nodes can play havoc with operations, such as processing even-numbered nodes one way and odd-numbered nodes a different way. This is such a big issue in XSLT that the specification includes some of its own facilities for handling such text nodes. For example, there are both xsl:strip-space and xsl:preserve-space elements for identifying the whitespace-only text nodes you want collapsed or preserved, respectively.

The normalize-space( ) function addresses this potential problem by ensuring that you're dealing only with the true #PCDATA content in a complete document or any of its nodes: pass it a string, get back the normalized result; pass it any other data type, get back the normalized corresponding string-value; and pass it nothing at all to get back the normalized string-value of the context node.

### translate(string1, string2, string3)

The `translate()` function replaces individual characters in one string with *different* individual characters. The `string1` argument is the string whose characters you want to replace; `string2` includes the specific characters in `string1` that you want to replace; and `string3` includes the characters with which you want to replace those `string2` characters. So:

```
translate("1234567890", "126", "ABX")
```

replaces each occurrence of any of the single characters "1," "2," or "6," with the single character "A," "B," or "X," respectively. The value returned from this function call would thus be the string "AB2345X7890."

Like `normalize-space()`, the `translate()` function can be valuable in ensuring that two strings are equal, especially when their case—upper vs. lower—is possibly different, even though they're otherwise apparently identical. Instead of comparing the two strings directly, compare their case-folded values using `translate()`. Thus:

```
translate(somestring,
    "abcdefghijklmnopqrstuvwxyz",
    "ABCDEFGHIJKLMNOPQRSTUVWXYZ")
```

Every lowercase "a" in `somestring` is replaced with a capital "A," every "b" with a "B," and so on. Characters in `somestring` that don't match any characters in `string2` appear unchanged in the result.

Note that the lengths of `string2` and `string3` are usually identical but don't need to be. If `string2` is longer than `string3`, `translate()` serves to *remove* characters from `string1`. So:

```
translate(somestring,
    "abcdefghijklmnopqrstuvwxyz",
    "")
```

removes from `somestring` all lowercase letters, while:

```
translate(somestring,
    "abcdefghijklmnopqrstuvwxyz",
    "ABCDEFGHIJKLM")
```

uppercases all lowercase letters in `somestring` in the first half of the alphabet and removes all those appearing in the second half. If `somestring` is "VW mini-bus," this returns the string "VW MII-B": the uppercase letters "VW" (uppercase letters don't appear in `string2`, so they're passed unchanged), a space, the uppercased "mi" and "i" from "mini," the hyphen, and the uppercased "b" from "bus." The "n" in "mini" and the "us" in "bus" are suppressed.

If for some reason it's desirable, `string3` may be longer than `string2`. This is not necessary, because the function considers only those characters in `string3` up to the length of `string2`; it's just like you omitted those characters from `string3` in the first place.

---

One interesting use of translate( ), in conjunction with normalize-space( ), is to "depunctuate" a string. Thus, you can turn the string "Eek!!! Is that a mouse, or what?" into "Eek Is that a mouse or what" using:

```
normalize-space(translate("Eek!!! Is that a mouse, or what?", "!,?",
    "   "))
```

Here, the translate( ) function itself replaces each occurrence of the exclamation mark, comma, and question mark characters with a blank space; the outer call to normalize-space( ) then squashes all the resulting multiple blank spaces between words into one. (If you need to do this, be sure that the length of string3—the blank spaces—matches the number of characters in string2 exactly.)

While translate( ) can be useful for limited cases, it's not really a good general-purpose "search-and-replace" tool—particularly because you can use it only to do single-character matches and replacements. If you need to replace a single character with two or more characters, two or more characters with a single one, or two or more characters with a different set of characters—or a word or phrase with an entirely different one—translate( ) won't help much, if at all.

In this case, you'll have to do more exotic string manipulation, perhaps with XSLT or a programming language.

## Boolean Functions

As the term implies, the XPath Boolean functions all return Boolean true or false values. (And when you hear the word Boolean in an XPath context, a little flag should go up in your head as you think, "Predicate." Hold that thought.)

These functions are all quite simple, with few little gotchas or complications. Thus, I don't think it's necessary to provide a sample XML document for them. But following Table 4-3, which summarizes the Boolean functions, I will provide discussion and examples of each.

*Table 4-3. Boolean functions*

| Function prototype | Returns | Description |
| --- | --- | --- |
| boolean(anytype) | boolean | Converts anytype to a Boolean true or false value |
| not(boolean) | boolean | Returns true if boolean is false, and false if boolean is true |
| true( ) | boolean | Returns the value true |
| false( ) | boolean | Returns the value false |
| lang(string) | boolean | Returns true or false, depending on whether the language in which the context node is presented matches the value of the string argument |

### boolean(anytype)

The boolean( ) function is similar to the string( ) function introduced in the last section: it examines the argument passed to it and returns a value (true or false) depending on the argument's value and data type. Also like the string( ) function, you will almost never need to use boolean( ) explicitly: in contexts (particularly predicates) where a logical true or false is expected, the anytype argument will be converted implicitly, according to the type (string, numeric, node-set, or Boolean) of the argument. Thus, each of the following subsections describes these implicit conversions as well as the result of explicit calls to boolean( ).

**When anytype is a string.** If anytype is at least one character long, the call to boolean( ) returns true; otherwise, it returns false. Thus, the following two XPath expressions are functionally identical (the value true):

```
boolean("some string")
string-length("some-string") > 0
```

Remember that a text node may consist entirely of whitespace, as discussed earlier. This whitespace may fool the human eye but won't fool the boolean( ) function; newlines, spaces, tabs, and so on each count as a string with a length greater than 0.

**When anytype is numeric.** A call to boolean( ) with a numeric argument returns true if the argument is a legitimate number (i.e., not the special NaN value) and does not equal either positive or negative zero.

---

### Positive and Negative Zero?

This positive-or-negative-zero business is consistent with Java and other specifications, although it seems to fly in the face of common sense. (After all, isn't a number either positive *or* negative *or* zero? What does it mean when a number is both positive and zero, or both negative and zero?)

In general, the plain-old number 0 is "positive" (but unsigned) zero. Using this in numeric operations with negative numbers can result in what's called "negative" 0; for instance, -2 times 0 equals "negative zero." The rule is that for multiplication and division, if the operands share the same (perhaps implicit) sign, then the result is positive; otherwise, the result is negative.

In other words, while you may be called upon to know the formal distinction between positive and negative zero, in practice, they're both plain old 0. Also in practice, don't expect to be called upon to know the formal distinction (unless you're taking an exam or writing a spec yourself).

---

In discussing the behavior of boolean( ) with a string argument, I showed you two expressions that produced the same result. To these two we can now add a third:

```
boolean(string-length("some string"))
```

The nested call to string-length( ) returns a number, which is then passed to boolean( ). If the number passed is 0—that is, if the string is empty—boolean( ) returns false, otherwise true.

**When anytype is a node-set.** You already know, from the previous chapter, that you can use a location path in a predicate to test for a particular node's existence. For example:

```
//employee[emp_address]
```

selects only those employee elements that have at least one emp_address child.

This form of the predicate is essentially a shortcut for using the boolean( ) function with a node-set argument. It returns true if the node-set has at least one member, or false otherwise. That is, the following is equivalent to the short form just presented:

```
//employee[boolean(emp_address)]
```

**When anytype is a Boolean value.** If anytype is itself a Boolean value, the value returned by boolean( ) is identical to the value of anytype itself. If anytype is true, boolean( ) returns true; if false, it returns false.

### not(boolean)

The not( ) function simply flips the value of its passed argument. If the value of boolean is true, not( ) returns false and vice versa.

This function is rarely useful in its own right; rather, you pass as an argument some other expression returning a true or false value, enabling not( ) to test for the negation of the other expression's value. So you can select all employee elements that do *not* have at least one emp_address child using an expression such as:

```
//employee[not(emp_address)]
```

Many comparison operations in XPath look and behave peculiarly, and a particular trap to watch out for when using not( ) is how it behaves differently from the ! (exclamation point) Boolean operator in comparisons. Consider the following two location paths:

```
//employee[@id != "emp1002"]
//employee[not(@id = "emp1002")]
```

The first example selects all employee element nodes whose id attributes' values do not equal emp1002 (or that do not have an id attribute at all); the second selects all employee element nodes that do not have an id attribute whose value is emp1002. If you read those two clauses carefully, you'll realize that the two location paths produce different results when encountering an element such as:

```
<employee>...</employee>
```

This employee element *will not* be located by the first example, because it has no id attribute at all; it *will* be located by the second example, though, because it has no id attribute with a value of emp1002.

### true() and false( )

These two Boolean functions are of rather limited utility. You pass them no arguments, and they always return the Boolean value corresponding to their names: true( ) always returns the value true, and false( ) always returns false. I've found them useful in making explicit—documenting, as it were—the purpose of some other Boolean test. Something like this:

```
//book/title[contains(., "XML") = true()]
```

selects a book element only if the string-value of its title child contains the string "XML." Including the = true( ) doesn't change the test at all, it simply clarifies what you're testing for.

Maybe the most common use of true( ) and false( ), though, is in XSLT. While I don't want to plunge further here into the details of that language, it's possible to build XSLT-based "subroutines" called *named templates*. You can pass parameters to a named template in a manner similar to passing arguments to a function; if the named template is driven by parameters whose values it expects to be true or false, the simplest way to pass it either of those values is with the true( ) or false( ) function.

### lang(string)

Use of this function depends on the use of an xml:lang attribute (either directly, in an instance document, or indirectly, via its DTD). If there is no such attribute in scope at the point of the call to lang( ), the function returns false.

However, if there is such an attribute in scope, lang( ) returns true if the context node is "in" the language specified by the string argument passed to it. Consider this code fragment:

```
<word xml:lang="EN">tarradiddle</word>
```

Assuming that this element or its text-node child is the context node, the following function call returns true:

```
lang("EN")
```

More subtly, lang( ) also returns true in a case-*in*sensitive way; you could also use:

```
lang("en")
lang("En")
```

and so on, all of which would return true.

Now, the language codes the xml:lang attribute uses needn't specify major languages only, such as "EN" for English or "DE" for German. They can also specify sublanguages, or language groups, using a hyphen to separate the major language code from the one for the sublanguage. English, for example, can be represented as American English or British English using xml:lang values such as "en-us" and "en-uk." Suppose the code fragment above specified an xml:lang attribute as follows:

```
<word xml:lang="EN-UK">tarradiddle</word>
```

In this case, both of the following would return true:

```
lang("EN")
lang("en-uk")
```

The inverse is *not* true. Whether lang( ) returns true or false, according to the spec, depends on whether the xml:lang value in force for the context node "is the same as or is a sublanguage of the language specified by the argument string." Thus, if you pass lang( ) a string that itself identifies a sublanguage, lang( ) will *not* return true when the xml:lang value in force is a major language. That is:

```
lang("en-uk")
```

returns false when applied to the following code fragment:

```
<word xml:lang="EN">tarradiddle</word>
```

## Numeric Functions

Numeric functions operate on their arguments to produce numeric results. Table 4-4 summarizes these functions; each is discussed separately following the table.

Examples in this section refer to the following simple XML document:

```
<weights>
    <weight label="1kg">1</weight>
    <weight label="2.5kg">2.5</weight>
    <weight label="1ton">1016.0469</weight>
</weights>
```

*Table 4-4. Numeric functions*

| Function prototype | Returns | Description |
| --- | --- | --- |
| number(anytype?) | Number | Converts anytype to numeric value |
| sum(nodeset) | Number | Returns the sum of all nodes in nodeset, after converting each to a number |
| floor(number) | Number | Returns the largest integer that is less than or equal to number |
| ceiling(number) | Number | Returns the smallest integer that is greater than or equal to number |
| round(number) | Number | Returns the integer nearest in value to number (rounds up if number has a decimal portion of .5) |

### number(anytype?)

Like the string( ) and boolean( ) functions discussed earlier, number( ) converts an optional argument to some basic XPath data type—numeric, in this case—based on the data type of the passed argument. If no argument is supplied, the function by default converts the context node's string-value to a number.

***When anytype is a string.*** To be converted to a number, a string argument must consist of optional whitespace, followed by an optional minus sign (-), followed by the numeric value itself, followed by optional whitespace. Any other kind of string is converted to the special value NaN. Note in particular that the string may not include a leading plus sign (+) or formatting characters, such as grouping commas or currency symbols. Among other effects, this also causes "strings" expressing numbers as scientific notation (such as "3.296E3") to be converted to NaN.

***When anytype is a Boolean value.*** If the Boolean value is true, the value returned by number( ) is 1; if false, number( ) returns 0. Thus, in this location step:

```
weight[number(contains(@label, "kg"))]
```

number( ) returns 1 for both the first and second weight elements, and 0 for the third.

***When anytype is a node-set.*** In this case, the argument is first converted to a string as if it had been passed to the string( ) function discussed earlier in this chapter, and then converted to a number according to the rules for converting strings to numbers. This follows common sense; using the sample XML document in this section, for example, this expression:

```
number((//weight)[3])
```

first locates the third weight element in the document, then returns the numeric value 1016.0469.

***When anytype is numeric.*** Passing the number( ) function a numeric argument simply returns the value of that argument.

### sum(nodeset)

You can do simple summations across a node-set using the sum( ) function; just pass it the node-set in question. Each node is first converted to a number using the rules of conversion laid out for the number( ) function, then the summation is performed. We could sum up the values of all the weight elements in the sample document with an expression like:

```
sum(//weight)
```

which would return the value 1 + 2.5 + 1016.0469, or 1019.5469.

Be careful when using sum( ) to ensure that you don't run into a not-a-number wall; it takes only a single node with a non-numeric value to make the sum non-numeric as well. Applied to our sample document, this expression:

```
sum(//weight/@label)
```

returns NaN, because not all of the label attributes in the selected node-set are numeric. (*Any* node failing the numeric test is sufficient to produce a NaN result.)

## floor(number) and ceiling(number)

The floor( ) and ceiling( ) functions perform similar operations on their arguments. Both return integers nearest in value to that of the argument. For floor( ), the result is the largest integer less than or equal to the argument; for ceiling( ), the smallest integer greater than or equal to the argument. So:

```
floor(//weight[3])
```

returns 1016, while:

```
ceiling(//weight[3])
```

returns 1017.

Note that these are not exactly rounding-down and up functions. Although they consider the fractional part of the passed argument, they simply check that it's greater than 0. If so, floor( ) returns the integer portion of the argument and ceiling( ), the integer portion plus 1. If not, floor( ) and ceiling( ) both return the same result: the integer portion of the argument.

Be careful when using floor( ) and ceiling( ) with negative arguments. A function call like:

```
floor(3.2)
```

returns 3, but:

```
floor(-3.2)
```

returns -4.

## round(number)

Unlike floor( ) and ceiling( ), round( ) rounds the argument up or down, depending on which direction the nearest integer lies. Thus, the result will always be identical to that of either floor( ) or ceiling( ):

```
round(//weight[3])
```

returns 1016, for example (the same result obtained using floor( )).

If the fractional part of the passed argument is exactly .5, the round( ) function rounds up, consistent with common use (and therefore always behaving just like ceiling( )). So:

```
round(//weight[2])
```

returns 3.

As with floor( ) and ceiling( ), round( ) can produce unexpected effects when passed a negative argument. (At least, they're unexpected until you think a little about them.)

The calls:

```
round(-3.4)
round(-3.5)
round(-3.8)
```

Return the values -3, -3, and -4, respectively.

# XPath Numeric Operators

XPath includes a set of numeric operators for performing basic arithmetic operations. Don't go looking for net-present-value or square-root operators; they don't exist. But if you simply need to add, subtract, multiply, divide, or find a remainder of two numeric values, here's your answer. Table 4-5 summarizes these numeric operators.

*Table 4-5. XPath numeric operators*

| Operator | Description | Example |
|---|---|---|
| + | Adds two values | `(//weight)[1] + (//weight)[2]` |
| - | Subtracts one value from another | `(//weight)[3] - (//weight)[1]` |
| * | Multiplies one value times another | `(//weight)[3] * 5` |
| div | Divides one value by another | `(//weight)[3] div 1016.0469` |
| mod | Returns the remainder after dividing one value by another | `(//weight)[3] mod 1016.0469` |

Most of these are straightforward, not requiring any further explanation; however, both the div and mod operators could use bit more explanation.

## div

Why use a special div operator at all? Why not just use the more familiar forward slash character, /, to divide one value by another?

The answer is that a slash in an XPath expression is already freighted with meaning: it operates as a delimiter between location steps. (A good analogy, in XML terms, might be the required use of entity references, such as &lt; instead of the literal < character.)

## mod

Unlike div, the mod operator is common in other application languages as well as in XPath. The term "mod" comes from modulus or modulo—the formal arithmetic term for the remainder following a division. (Some languages use a single character, like the percent sign, %, to perform the same operation.)

I promised, earlier in this chapter, to show you how to use mod with the position() function to process every *n*th node in a given node-set.

The basic idea is first to isolate what *n* is, then compare the remainder of dividing a given node's position in the node-set by *n*. If the remainder is 0, the node in question gets the special "every nth node" processing, otherwise it doesn't.

Suppose we have a list of employees in an XML document, coded something like this (irrelevant details omitted):

```
<employees>
    <employee>...</employee>
    <employee>...</employee>
    <employee>...</employee>
    <employee>...</employee>
    <employee>...</employee>
    <employee>...</employee>
</employees>
```

As you can see, this document includes six employee elements within the employees container element. If we want to perform some particular operation just for the employee elements in even-numbered positions within the node-set, we could use an XPath expression such as:

```
//employee[position( ) mod 2 = 0]
```

If we want this operation to occur on every odd-numbered employee in the list, we change the predicate as in this example:

```
//employee[position( ) mod 2 = 1]
```

If we want to select every third employee, change the 2 in the above examples to 3; for every fourth, change it to 4; and so on.

The mod( ) function is also useful for certain conversion-type operations, such as converting raw quantities of something to dozens-of-something-plus-leftover-units and four-digit years to their two-digit values. For instance:

```
1960 mod 100
```

returns the value 60.

# CHAPTER 5

# XPath in Action

Taken on its own terms, as a teaching tool, XPath might not seem to meet the test for a practical standard: it's useful only in the context of some *other* standard. How do you demonstrate something like XPath without requiring the novice to learn that other standard as well? Luckily, several tools have emerged to simplify this task. These tools allow you to enter and modify an XPath expression—typically, a full location path—returning to you in some highlighted form a selected portion of a target document. (The portion in question might or might not be contiguous, of course, depending on how exotic the location path is.) In this chapter, I'll demonstrate XPath using a tool called XPath Visualiser, developed by Dmitre Novatchev.

 XPath Visualiser can be downloaded from the VBXML site, at *http://www.vbxml.com/downloads/files/xpathvisualiserseptember.zip*.

## XPath Visualiser: Some Background

XPath Visualiser runs under Microsoft Windows, from Windows 95 on up, and is built on top of the Microsoft MSXML XML/XSLT processor included with the Internet Explorer browser. This operating environment for the tool implies some advantages and disadvantages to its use.

An important practical advantage of this tool is that the results are *visual*. As we go through the examples in this chapter, you'll be able instantly to see the effects—subtle or grand—of changes in XPath expressions. (You don't even need to use Windows, let alone XPath Visualiser itself, because all these effects are captured in screen shots for you.) Trying to explain verbally what an XPath expression "does" is a convenient way to extend a book's length, but it's not simple, and it's prone to misinterpretation. (A picture of an XPath expression is worth a thousand words of description.)

Next, because XPath Visualiser uses a current version of the MSXML processor, its "understanding" of the XPath Recommendation is complete. If an expression is legal under the terms of that standard, you can illustrate it with XPath Visualiser.

Interestingly, though, a significant disadvantage of using XPath Visualiser is *also* that it's based on MSXML. That's because MSXML supports not only the current versions of XPath and XSLT, but also an early version of XSLT (called plain-old XSL). I described this early version in Chapters 1 and 2. Among the differences in this "backward-compatible" XSL processor is that it included numerous Microsoft-only capabilities; for example, you could use their version of what became XPath to select a valid document's document type declaration. (Note that this isn't a problem with XPath Visualiser itself, which deals only with true-blue XPath; it may be something to consider if you're planning to use MSXML for other purposes of your own.)

XPath Visualiser is not a "program" per se. It's a plain-old frames-based set of HTML documents and a customized version of Microsoft's default XSL(T) stylesheet, which work only when viewed through Internet Explorer Versions 5 and up. (More precisely, it works only with MSXML Versions 3 and up. Internet Explorer 5 and 5.5 do not come with MSXML 3, although you could download and install MSXML 3 to run under them. Internet Explorer 6 comes with the next version of MSXML, Version 4.) Figure 5-1 shows a portion of how the browser window appears when you first open this frameset.

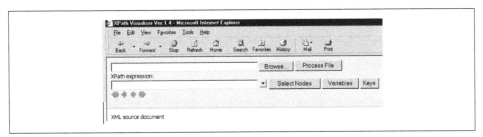

*Figure 5-1. Startup view of XPath Visualiser*

I've suppressed all toolbars except the standard one, to give me as much screen real estate as possible for displaying actual documents. (I've also tweaked the XPath Visualiser default stylesheet; as distributed, the tool displays the document's contents against a pale-blue background, which reproduces poorly in grayscale screen shots.) As you can see, the upper frame includes a number of user-interface controls for specifying the document to be viewed and the location path to be tested or demonstrated. By default, the location path is:

    //*

which selects all element nodes in the loaded document. When you've loaded a document using the controls at the top of this frame and clicked on the Select Nodes button, the nodes your location path has selected are highlighted in any of various ways. (The buttons labeled Variables and Keys have to do with XSLT processing and will not be covered here.) The document itself appears in the bottom frame; its display is an enhanced version of the default MSXML/Internet Explorer view of XML documents, showing the document as an expandable/collapsible "tree" of nodes.

Because there's no document loaded when you first fire up XPath Visualiser, the main document window initially displays the simple text "XML source document." Once you load a document and specify a location path, the lower frame changes in a manner resembling Figure 5-2.

Figure 5-2. A document loaded into XPath Visualiser

The lower frame of the window in Figure 5-2 contains an XML document used in Chapter 3. There are a couple important things to observe about this changed display. First, XPath Visualiser's interface includes a series of "VCR buttons" (the series of arrowheads beneath the location path in the top frame), which you can use to step through a selected node-set. These VCR buttons are labeled to indicate which node in the node-set is currently selected and how many nodes are in the node-set altogether ("0 of 22/22 matches," in this case). Second, the node(s) selected by the location path in the top frame are highlighted in the lower frame. This highlighting appears in Figure 5-2 and throughout the rest of this chapter, as a bordered pale gray background. (In the case of elements, as you can see, only the start tags are highlighted.) Finally, note the small vertical black bars to the left of certain elements' start tags. On screen, these are simply shaded + and - signs, placed there to expand and collapse the tree of nodes descending from elements that have descendants. (As you can see, the name and price elements' start tags don't have these black bars, since they don't have expandable/collapsible sub trees.)

For the remainder of the screen shots in this chapter, I'll simply show portions of the lower frame, preceded by the location path in regular code-style font such as:

```
//elementname
```

This will enable me to show larger portions of the document.

# Sample XML Document

To keep a consistent base for all the example location paths in this chapter, I'll refer to the same XML source document. This document is short but contains at least one of every XPath node type:

```
<!-- Basic astrological data for T's and J's signs -->
<?xml-stylesheet type="text/xsl" href="astro.xsl"?>
<astro xmlns:xlink="http://www.w3.org/1999/xlink">
    <sign start-date="12-22" end-date="01-20">
        <name type="main">Capricorn</name>
        <name type="alt">The Sea-Goat</name>
        <!-- capricorn.gif corresponds to Unicode 3.0 #x2651 -->
        <symbol xlink:type="simple" xlink:href="capricorn.gif"/>
        <ruling_planet>Saturn</ruling_planet>
        <element>Earth</element>
        <energy>Feminine</energy>
        <quality>Cardinal</quality>
        <anatomy>
            <part>Bones</part>
            <part>Knees</part>
        </anatomy>
    </sign>
    <sign start-date="05-21" end-date="06-22">
        <name type="main">Gemini</name>
        <name type="alt">The Twins</name>
        <!-- gemini.gif corresponds to Unicode 3.0 #x264A -->
        <symbol xlink:type="simple" xlink:href="gemini.gif"/>
        <ruling_planet>Mercury</ruling_planet>
        <element>Air</element>
        <energy>Feminine</energy>
        <quality>Mutable</quality>
        <anatomy>
            <part>Hands</part>
            <part>Arms</part>
            <part>Shoulders</part>
            <part>Lungs</part>
        </anatomy>
    </sign>
</astro>
```

The document in question describes elementary properties of two of the Western-style astrological signs, Capricorn and Gemini. When first loaded into XPath Visualiser with the default "all elements" location path selected, it appears as shown in Figure 5-3.

# General to Specific, Common to Far-Out

I'll start out with some fundamental location paths, such as those selecting elements of a particular name, and move on to some special cases (such as examples using axes and predicates). The chapter will include a number of bizarre location paths probably unlike any you'd actually use, but at least theoretically (if not practically!)

```
                    <!-- Basic astrological data for T's and J's signs -->
                <?xml-stylesheet type="text/xsl" href="astro.xsl" ?>
                ▌<astro xmlns:xlink="http://www.w3.org/1999/xlink">
                  ▌<sign start-date="12-22" end-date="01-20">
                      <name type="main">Capricorn</name>
                      <name type="alt">The Sea-Goat</name>
                        <!-- capricorn.gif corresponds to Unicode 3.0 #x2651 -->
                      <symbol xlink:type="simple" xlink:href="capricorn.gif" />
                      <ruling_planet>Saturn</ruling_planet>
                      <element>Earth</element>
                      <energy>Feminine</energy>
                      <quality>Cardinal</quality>
                    ▌<anatomy>
                        <part>Bones</part>
                        <part>Knees</part>
                    </anatomy>
                  </sign>
                  ▌<sign start-date="05-21" end-date="06-22">
                      <name type="main">Gemini</name>
                      <name type="alt">The Twins</name>
                        <!-- gemini.gif corresponds to Unicode 3.0 #x264A -->
                      <symbol xlink:type="simple" xlink:href="gemini.gif" />
                      <ruling_planet>Mercury</ruling_planet>
                      <element>Air</element>
                      <energy>Feminine</energy>
                      <quality>Mutable</quality>
                    ▌<anatomy>
```

*Figure 5-3. Sample astrological document loaded into XPath Visualiser*

legitimate. Along the way, I'll poke into XPath functions, numeric operators, and so on. Each screen shot of XPath Visualiser's lower frame is accompanied by a brief English-language description of what's depicted.

(If you're feeling sufficiently adventurous, you might want to guess what the location paths select before looking at the corresponding screen shots.)

## The Node Test

As a reminder, XPath is capable of locating the following seven *types* of nodes: root; element, attribute, comment, PI, namespace, and text. There's also a special node( ) "node test," which locates nodes of *any* type along the selected axis. I'll cover the attribute and namespace node types in a moment, but for now, here's how XPath (via XPath Visualiser) selects on the other types.

The simplest of these is, of course, the root node itself. The location path to the root node consists of a single slash:

/

XPath Visualiser depicts the result as shown in Figure 5-4.

 Actually, the first thing you see when selecting on the simple / location path is an error message; only after clearing this error message are you greeted by the above. XPath Visualiser seems not to know how to visually represent the root node—not that *I* know how to, either!

```
<!-- Basic astrological data for T's and J's signs -->
<?xml-stylesheet type="text/xsl" href="astro.xsl" ?>
-<astro xmlns:xlink="http://www.w3.org/1999/xlink">
  -<sign start-date="12-22" end-date="01-20">
    <name type="main">Capricorn</name>
    <name type="alt">The Sea-Goat</name>
    <!-- capricorn.gif corresponds to Unicode 3.0 #x2651 -->
    <symbol xlink:type="simple" xlink:href="capricorn.gif" />
    <ruling_planet>Saturn</ruling_planet>
    <element>Earth</element>
    <energy>Feminine</energy>
    <quality>Cardinal</quality>
    -<anatomy>
      <part>Bones</part>
      <part>Knees</part>
    </anatomy>
  </sign>
  -<sign start-date="05-21" end-date="06-22">
    <name type="main">Gemini</name>
    <name type="alt">The Twins</name>
    <!-- gemini.gif corresponds to Unicode 3.0 #x2648 -->
    <symbol xlink:type="simple" xlink:href="gemini.gif" />
    <ruling_planet>Mercury</ruling_planet>
    <element>Air</element>
    <energy>Feminine</energy>
    <quality>Mutable</quality>
    -<anatomy>
```

*Figure 5-4. "Locating" the root node*

Of course, as in Figures 5-2 and 5-3, you've already seen the results of selecting all elements in the document. Figure 5-5 is based on a location path identifying *specific* elements: the part elements, in this case:

```
//part
```

```
<?xml-stylesheet type="text/xsl" href="astro.xsl" ?>
<astro xmlns:xlink="http://www.w3.org/1999/xlink">
  <sign start-date="12-22" end-date="01-20">
    <name type="main">Capricorn</name>
    <name type="alt">The Sea-Goat</name>
    <!-- capricorn.gif corresponds to Unicode 3.0 #x2651 -->
    <symbol xlink:type="simple" xlink:href="capricorn.gif" />
    <ruling_planet>Saturn</ruling_planet>
    <element>Earth</element>
    <energy>Feminine</energy>
    <quality>Cardinal</quality>
    <anatomy>
      <part>Bones</part>
      <part>Knees</part>
    </anatomy>
  </sign>
  <sign start-date="05-21" end-date="06-22">
    <name type="main">Gemini</name>
    <name type="alt">The Twins</name>
    <!-- gemini.gif corresponds to Unicode 3.0 #x2648 -->
    <symbol xlink:type="simple" xlink:href="gemini.gif" />
    <ruling_planet>Mercury</ruling_planet>
    <element>Air</element>
    <energy>Feminine</energy>
    <quality>Mutable</quality>
    <anatomy>
      <part>Hands</part>
      <part>Arms</part>
```

*Figure 5-5. Locating all elements with the same name*

Notice how the highlighting has shifted; only those element nodes whose names are "part" are now selected. The sample document contains three comments. To select them, use the following (the results are as shown in Figure 5-6):

```
//comment( )
```

```
<!-- Basic astrological data for T's and J's signs -->
<?xml-stylesheet type="text/xsl" href="astro.xsl" ?>
<astro xmlns:xlink="http://www.w3.org/1999/xlink">
  -<sign start-date="12-22" end-date="01-20">
    <name type="main">Capricorn</name>
    <name type="alt">The Sea-Goat</name>
    <!-- capricorn.gif corresponds to Unicode 3.0 #x2651 -->
    <symbol xlink:type="simple" xlink:href="capricorn.gif" />
    <ruling_planet>Saturn</ruling_planet>
    <element>Earth</element>
    <energy>Feminine</energy>
    <quality>Cardinal</quality>
    -<anatomy>
      <part>Bones</part>
      <part>Knees</part>
    </anatomy>
  </sign>
  -<sign start-date="05-21" end-date="06-22">
    <name type="main">Gemini</name>
    <name type="alt">The Twins</name>
    <!-- gemini.gif corresponds to Unicode 3.0 #x264A -->
    <symbol xlink:type="simple" xlink:href="gemini.gif" />
    <ruling_planet>Mercury</ruling_planet>
    <element>Air</element>
    <energy>Feminine</energy>
    <quality>Mutable</quality>
    -<anatomy>
```

*Figure 5-6. Locating all comments*

There's only one PI in the sample document, which is the xml-stylesheet PI in the document's prolog. You can select it using either of the following two location paths. In either case, the result is the same, as shown in Figure 5-7.

```
//processing-instruction( )
//processing-instruction("xml-stylesheet")
```

```
<!-- Basic astrological data for T's and J's signs -->
<?xml-stylesheet type="text/xsl" href="astro.xsl" ?>
-<astro xmlns:xlink="http://www.w3.org/1999/xlink">
  -<sign start-date="12-22" end-date="01-20">
    <name type="main">Capricorn</name>
    <name type="alt">The Sea-Goat</name>
    <!-- capricorn.gif corresponds to Unicode 3.0 #x2651 -->
    <symbol xlink:type="simple" xlink:href="capricorn.gif" />
    <ruling_planet>Saturn</ruling_planet>
    <element>Earth</element>
    <energy>Feminine</energy>
    <quality>Cardinal</quality>
    -<anatomy>
      <part>Bones</part>
      <part>Knees</part>
    </anatomy>
  </sign>
  -<sign start-date="05-21" end-date="06-22">
    <name type="main">Gemini</name>
    <name type="alt">The Twins</name>
    <!-- gemini.gif corresponds to Unicode 3.0 #x264A -->
    <symbol xlink:type="simple" xlink:href="gemini.gif" />
    <ruling_planet>Mercury</ruling_planet>
    <element>Air</element>
    <energy>Feminine</energy>
    <quality>Mutable</quality>
    -<anatomy>
```

*Figure 5-7. Locating a PI*

To select all text nodes, use:

```
//text( )
```

## Path Efficiency

It might pay to heed the relative efficiency of one location path over another. While starting off a location path with the // shortcut certainly *works*, it forces the processor to navigate through the entire document tree even though the PI we're after is right there in the prolog. Thus, it'd be a much better use of processor resources to replace the double slash with a single one, as in these two examples:

```
/processing-instruction( )
/processing-instruction("xml-stylesheet")
```

Of course, if what you're really after is either all PIs in the document, or all xml-stylesheet PIs, the double slashes do just that.

This isolates all text nodes in the document; see Figure 5-8 for XPath Visualiser's depiction.

*Figure 5-8. Locating text nodes*

Finally, to select all element, comment, PI, and text nodes in a single step, use the node( ) special node type:

```
//node( )
```

See Figure 5-9 for the result.

One interesting note about these results is that—as discussed in Chapter 3—neither attribute nor namespace nodes are "visible" (or highlighted in Figure 5-9) along the

```
<!-- Basic astrological data for T's and J's signs -->
<?xml-stylesheet type="text/xsl" href="astro.xsl" ?>
<astro xmlns:xlink="http://www.w3.org/1999/xlink">
  <sign start-date="12-22" end-date="01-20">
    <name type="main">Capricorn</name>
    <name type="alt">The Sea-Goat</name>
    <!-- capricorn.gif corresponds to Unicode 3.0 #x2651 -->
    <symbol xlink:type="simple" xlink:href="capricorn.gif" />
    <ruling_planet>Saturn</ruling_planet>
    <element>Earth</element>
    <energy>Feminine</energy>
    <quality>Cardinal</quality>
    <anatomy>
      <part>Bones</part>
      <part>Knees</part>
    </anatomy>
  </sign>
  <sign start-date="05-21" end-date="06-22">
    <name type="main">Gemini</name>
    <name type="alt">The Twins</name>
    <!-- gemini.gif corresponds to Unicode 3.0 #x264A -->
    <symbol xlink:type="simple" xlink:href="gemini.gif" />
    <ruling_planet>Mercury</ruling_planet>
    <element>Air</element>
    <energy>Feminine</energy>
    <quality>Mutable</quality>
```

*Figure 5-9. Locating all elements, comments, PIs, and text nodes*

default child:: axis. To access either, you must employ the attribute:: or namespace:: axis, respectively. For instance, either of the following works to select all attributes in the sample document:

```
//attribute::*
//@*
```

As you can see in Figure 5-10, XPath Visualiser selects the attributes as complete name-value pairs.

```
<!-- Basic astrological data for T's and J's signs -->
<?xml-stylesheet type="text/xsl" href="astro.xsl" ?>
<astro xmlns:xlink="http://www.w3.org/1999/xlink">
  <sign start-date="12-22" end-date="01-20">
    <name type="main">Capricorn</name>
    <name type="alt">The Sea-Goat</name>
    <!-- capricorn.gif corresponds to Unicode 3.0 #x2651 -->
    <symbol xlink:type="simple" xlink:href="capricorn.gif"/>
    <ruling_planet>Saturn</ruling_planet>
    <element>Earth</element>
    <energy>Feminine</energy>
    <quality>Cardinal</quality>
    -<anatomy>
      <part>Bones</part>
      <part>Knees</part>
    </anatomy>
  </sign>
  <sign start-date="05-21" end-date="06-22">
    <name type="main">Gemini</name>
    <name type="alt">The Twins</name>
    <!-- gemini.gif corresponds to Unicode 3.0 #x264A -->
    <symbol xlink:type="simple" xlink:href="gemini.gif"/>
    <ruling_planet>Mercury</ruling_planet>
    <element>Air</element>
    <energy>Feminine</energy>
    <quality>Mutable</quality>
```

*Figure 5-10. Locating attribute nodes*

Namespace nodes are a special case, in XPath Visualiser as in most other contexts. As the README file accompanying the utility says:

> This tool will not display selected nodes that were not explicitly specified in the text of the xml source document. Most notably this is true for (propagated) namespace nodes....
>
> However, the containing nodes are still [highlighted].

That is for namespace nodes, XPath Visualiser does not highlight *all* elements within scope of the element declaring a given namespace, but only the declaration within the declaring element itself. For instance, this location path:

```
//namespace::xlink
```

results in a display like Figure 5-11.

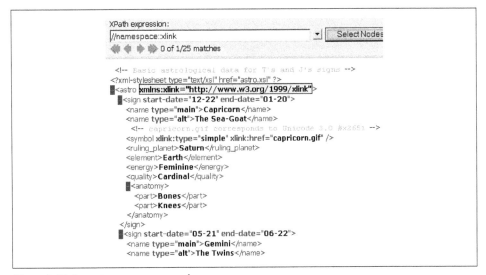

*Figure 5-11. Locating namespace nodes*

In Figure 5-11, I've shown the "X of Y/Z matches" information in the upper frame. For other node types, the Y value in this phrase equals the Z. For namespace nodes, though, XPath Visualiser sets Y equal to the number of namespace-declaring elements matching the location path and Z equal to the number of elements within scope of the selected namespace declarations. If you refer back to the full code listing, you will see that (as Figure 5-11 shows) there are 26 elements, including the astro element itself, within scope of the astro element's declaration of the xlink namespace.

(Remember, by the way, the built-in namespace associated with all XML documents, the one bound to the xml: prefix. If you change the above location path to:

```
//namespace::*
```

XPath Visualiser changes the "Z" in "X of Y/Z" to 52—that is, 26 namespace nodes for the xlink namespace and 26 for the xml namespace.)

Finally, to select a document's entire contents, you'd use a compound location path:

```
//node( ) | //@* | //namespace::*
```

Figure 5-12 depicts the result.

*Figure 5-12. Locating all nodes in a document*

## Axes

Previous examples have already demonstrated some of the simpler axes, that is, the child::, attribute::, and namespace:: axes. (Many of the previous examples also demonstrated, without explicit comment, the use of the descendant-or-self:: axis, as abbreviated //.) Let's take a look at some of the other axes now. Note that to use many of these other "family relationships," we'll typically use one or more location steps to navigate to some particular node-set in the document *followed by* a location step, which "turns the viewpoint" along the axis in question.

The parent:: axis, usually abbreviated .., looks "up" from the context node one level in the document's tree of nodes. A location path like:

```
//part/parent::*
```

locates all parent elements of any elements named "part"—in the case of our sample document, as shown in Figure 5-13, the two anatomy elements.

The parent of an attribute, comment, text node, or PI is the element that contains it (or, for comments and PIs in the document prolog, the root node). So:

```
//comment( )/../@*
```

(as you can see in Figure 5-14) selects all attributes of all elements that are parents of (that is, that contain) any comment nodes.

```
<?xml-stylesheet type="text/xsl" href="astro.xsl" ?>
<astro xmlns:xlink="http://www.w3.org/1999/xlink">
  <sign start-date="12-22" end-date="01-20">
    <name type="main">Capricorn</name>
    <name type="alt">The Sea-Goat</name>
    <!-- capricorn.gif corresponds to Unicode 3.0 #x2651 -->
    <symbol xlink:type="simple" xlink:href="capricorn.gif" />
    <ruling_planet>Saturn</ruling_planet>
    <element>Earth</element>
    <energy>Feminine</energy>
    <quality>Cardinal</quality>
   -<anatomy>
      <part>Bones</part>
      <part>Knees</part>
    </anatomy>
  </sign>
  <sign start-date="05-21" end-date="06-22">
    <name type="main">Gemini</name>
    <name type="alt">The Twins</name>
    <!-- gemini.gif corresponds to Unicode 3.0 #x2643 -->
    <symbol xlink:type="simple" xlink:href="gemini.gif" />
    <ruling_planet>Mercury</ruling_planet>
    <element>Air</element>
    <energy>Feminine</energy>
    <quality>Mutable</quality>
   -<anatomy>
      <part>Hands</part>
```

*Figure 5-13. Locating the parents of any part elements*

```
<!-- Basic astrological data for T's and J's signs -->
<?xml-stylesheet type="text/xsl" href="astro.xsl" ?>
<astro xmlns:xlink="http://www.w3.org/1999/xlink">
 -<sign start-date="12-22" end-date="01-20">
    <name type="main">Capricorn</name>
    <name type="alt">The Sea-Goat</name>
    <!-- capricorn.gif corresponds to Unicode 3.0 #x2651 -->
    <symbol xlink:type="simple" xlink:href="capricorn.gif" />
    <ruling_planet>Saturn</ruling_planet>
    <element>Earth</element>
    <energy>Feminine</energy>
    <quality>Cardinal</quality>
   -<anatomy>
      <part>Bones</part>
      <part>Knees</part>
    </anatomy>
  </sign>
 -<sign start-date="05-21" end-date="06-22">
    <name type="main">Gemini</name>
    <name type="alt">The Twins</name>
    <!-- gemini.gif corresponds to Unicode 3.0 #x2643 -->
    <symbol xlink:type="simple" xlink:href="gemini.gif" />
    <ruling_planet>Mercury</ruling_planet>
    <element>Air</element>
    <energy>Feminine</energy>
    <quality>Mutable</quality>
   -<anatomy>
```

*Figure 5-14. Using the parent:: axis to locate attributes of a comment's parent element*

An important concept this screen shot illustrates is that although a full location path may contain references to many nodes at many levels of the document tree, *only the final location step* in the path identifies the nodes that will actually be selected. Here, neither the comment nodes nor their parents are highlighted by XPath Visualiser. As the final location step in the path indicates, only the attributes of those parents are ultimately selected.

XPath does not define a simple sibling:: axis; to get all siblings of a given node, you must use the preceding-sibling:: and following-sibling:: axes together. Something like this (note that this is a single compound location path wrapped over two lines):

```
//processing-instruction("xml-stylesheet")/preceding-sibling::node() |
//processing-instruction("xml-stylesheet")/following-sibling::node()
```

This selects the siblings of the xml-stylesheet PI, as shown in Figure 5-15.

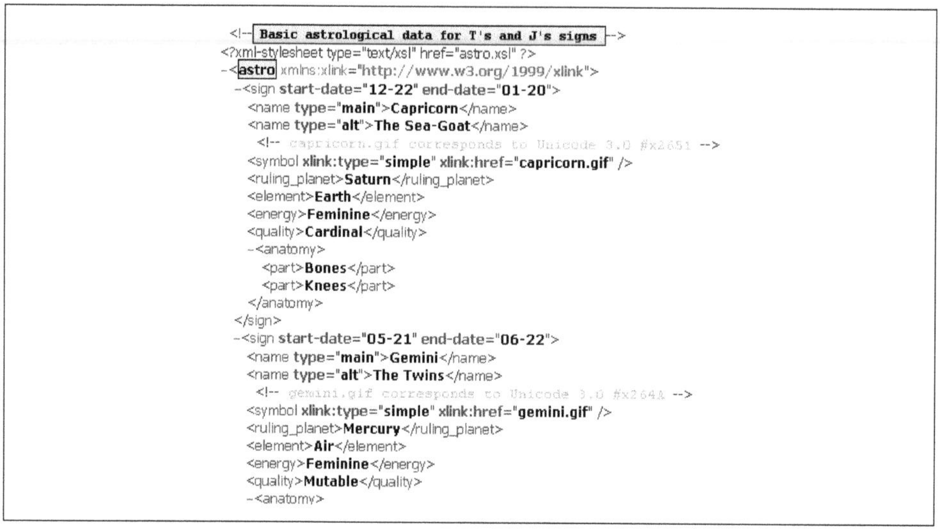

*Figure 5-15. Selecting all siblings of a PI in the prolog*

As the xml-stylesheet PI is located in this document's prolog, it has one preceding sibling (the opening comment) and one following (the document's root astro element).

As discussed in Chapter 3, the preceding:: and following:: axes locate nodes that terminate before or begin after (respectively) the full scope of a given node's markup. They differ from preceding-sibling:: and following-sibling:: in not requiring a "shared parent" condition. The following location path:

```
//quality[.="Cardinal"]/following::*
```

as you can see in Figure 5-16, selects not only that quality element's anatomy sibling, but also that anatomy element's children *and* all the other elements that follow the close of the quality element—even those otherwise unrelated (except distantly) to it.

The ancestor:: and descendant:: axes, of course, restrict the view from a given node to the same branch of the family tree in an up or down direction, respectively. Thus:

```
//part[.="Knees"]/ancestor::*
```

locates (as shown in Figure 5-17) the anatomy parent of that part element, the sign parent of that anatomy element, and the astro parent of that sign element. (It also locates the root node but, as explained earlier, XPath Visualiser has no way to "highlight" the root node.)

```
        <quality>Cardinal</quality>
        <anatomy>
          <part>Bones</part>
          <part>Knees</part>
        </anatomy>
      </sign>
      <sign start-date="05-21" end-date="06-22">
        <name type="main">Gemini</name>
        <name type="alt">The Twins</name>
        <!-- gemini.gif corresponds to Unicode 3.0 #x264A -->
        <symbol xlink:type="simple" xlink:href="gemini.gif" />
        <ruling_planet>Mercury</ruling_planet>
        <element>Air</element>
        <energy>Feminine</energy>
        <quality>Mutable</quality>
        <anatomy>
          <part>Hands</part>
          <part>Arms</part>
          <part>Shoulders</part>
          <part>Lungs</part>
        </anatomy>
      </sign>
    </astro>
```

*Figure 5-16. Locating elements along the following:: axis*

```
      <!-- Basic astrological data for T's and J's signs -->
      <?xml-stylesheet type="text/xsl" href="astro.xsl" ?>
      <astro xmlns:xlink="http://www.w3.org/1999/xlink">
        <sign start-date="12-22" end-date="01-20">
          <name type="main">Capricorn</name>
          <name type="alt">The Sea-Goat</name>
          <!-- capricorn.gif corresponds to Unicode 3.0 #x2651 -->
          <symbol xlink:type="simple" xlink:href="capricorn.gif" />
          <ruling_planet>Saturn</ruling_planet>
          <element>Earth</element>
          <energy>Feminine</energy>
          <quality>Cardinal</quality>
        - <anatomy>
            <part>Bones</part>
            <part>Knees</part>
          </anatomy>
        </sign>
      - <sign start-date="05-21" end-date="06-22">
          <name type="main">Gemini</name>
          <name type="alt">The Twins</name>
          <!-- gemini.gif corresponds to Unicode 3.0 #x264A -->
          <symbol xlink:type="simple" xlink:href="gemini.gif" />
          <ruling_planet>Mercury</ruling_planet>
          <element>Air</element>
          <energy>Feminine</energy>
          <quality>Mutable</quality>
        - <anatomy>
```

*Figure 5-17. Locating an element's ancestors*

Adding the -or-self qualifier to the ancestor:: or descendant:: axis, on the other hand, selects not only that chain of parents but also the context node itself. The location path:

```
//part[.="Knees"]/ancestor-or-self::*
```

thus adds to the node-set selected by the preceding example the indicated part element itself. Figure 5-18 illustrates.

```
<!-- Basic astrological data for I's and J's signs -->
<?xml-stylesheet type="text/xsl" href="astro.xsl" ?>
<astro xmlns:xlink="http://www.w3.org/1999/xlink">
  <sign start-date="12-22" end-date="01-20">
    <name type="main">Capricorn</name>
    <name type="alt">The Sea-Goat</name>
    <!-- capricorn.gif corresponds to Unicode 3.0 #x2651 -->
    <symbol xlink:type="simple" xlink:href="capricorn.gif" />
    <ruling_planet>Saturn</ruling_planet>
    <element>Earth</element>
    <energy>Feminine</energy>
    <quality>Cardinal</quality>
    <anatomy>
      <part>Bones</part>
      <part>Knees</part>
    </anatomy>
  </sign>
  -<sign start-date="05-21" end-date="06-22">
    <name type="main">Gemini</name>
    <name type="alt">The Twins</name>
    <!-- gemini.gif corresponds to Unicode 3.0 #x264A -->
    <symbol xlink:type="simple" xlink:href="gemini.gif" />
    <ruling_planet>Mercury</ruling_planet>
    <element>Air</element>
    <energy>Feminine</energy>
    <quality>Mutable</quality>
    -<anatomy>
```

*Figure 5-18. Adding an element to its ancestor node-set, using the ancestor-or-self:: axis*

## Predicates

Chapter 3 noted that while the axis "turns the view" in a particular direction from the context node, to further refine the list of nodes to be selected from among all those visible in that direction you must use a predicate. For instance:

```
//name[@type="alt"]
```

selects only those name elements whose type attributes have the value alt. As you can see from Figure 5-19, this prunes the node-set of all name elements in the document down to just two—the ones whose string-values are The Sea-Goat and The Twins— and excludes those (string-values Capricorn and Gemini) whose type attributes have some value other than alt.

While on the subject of selecting via attribute values, by the way, this might be a good moment to illustrate the different effects produced by two similar but not identical predicates. First, consider this location path:

```
//*[@type!="alt"]
```

Figure 5-20 shows how this selects all elements in the source document whose type attribute does *not* equal alt.

Only four elements have a type attribute, and of those only two do *not* have the indicated value.

Chapter 4, under the discussion of the not( ) function, described how in some cases it seemed "obviously" to but did not actually perform identically to the != "not equal to" operator. That is, the preceding location path behaves differently from the following:

```
//*[not(@type="alt")]
```

```
<!-- Basic astrological data for T's and J's signs -->
<?xml-stylesheet type="text/xsl" href="astro.xsl" ?>
<astro xmlns:xlink="http://www.w3.org/1999/xlink">
  <sign start-date="12-22" end-date="01-20">
    <name type="main">Capricorn</name>
    <name type="alt">The Sea-Goat</name>
    <!-- capricorn.gif corresponds to Unicode 3.0 #x2651 -->
    <symbol xlink:type="simple" xlink:href="capricorn.gif" />
    <ruling_planet>Saturn</ruling_planet>
    <element>Earth</element>
    <energy>Feminine</energy>
    <quality>Cardinal</quality>
    -<anatomy>
      <part>Bones</part>
      <part>Knees</part>
    </anatomy>
  </sign>
  <sign start-date="05-21" end-date="06-22">
    <name type="main">Gemini</name>
    <name type="alt">The Twins</name>
    <!-- gemini.gif corresponds to Unicode 3.0 #x264A -->
    <symbol xlink:type="simple" xlink:href="gemini.gif" />
    <ruling_planet>Mercury</ruling_planet>
    <element>Air</element>
    <energy>Feminine</energy>
    <quality>Mutable</quality>
    -<anatomy>
```

*Figure 5-19. Trimming a node-set using a predicate*

```
<!-- Basic astrological data for T's and J's signs -->
<?xml-stylesheet type="text/xsl" href="astro.xsl" ?>
<astro xmlns:xlink="http://www.w3.org/1999/xlink">
  <sign start-date="12-22" end-date="01-20">
    <name type="main">Capricorn</name>
    <name type="alt">The Sea-Goat</name>
    <!-- capricorn.gif corresponds to Unicode 3.0 #x2651 -->
    <symbol xlink:type="simple" xlink:href="capricorn.gif" />
    <ruling_planet>Saturn</ruling_planet>
    <element>Earth</element>
    <energy>Feminine</energy>
    <quality>Cardinal</quality>
    -<anatomy>
      <part>Bones</part>
      <part>Knees</part>
    </anatomy>
  </sign>
  <sign start-date="05-21" end-date="06-22">
    <name type="main">Gemini</name>
    <name type="alt">The Twins</name>
    <!-- gemini.gif corresponds to Unicode 3.0 #x264A -->
    <symbol xlink:type="simple" xlink:href="gemini.gif" />
    <ruling_planet>Mercury</ruling_planet>
    <element>Air</element>
    <energy>Feminine</energy>
    <quality>Mutable</quality>
    -<anatomy>
```

*Figure 5-20. Selecting all elements with an attribute whose value does not meet a condition*

As you can see from Figure 5-21, this location path selects all element nodes which do not have a type attribute whose value is alt—including all element nodes with no type attribute at all. Quite a difference!

Arguably the most common predicate test is one that selects nodes from among a candidate node-set based on their positions within that node-set. You can use the position() function for this test; when simply testing for a single specific position,

```
<!-- Basic astrological data for T's and J's signs -->
<?xml-stylesheet type="text/xsl" href="astro.xsl" ?>
<astro xmlns:xlink="http://www.w3.org/1999/xlink">
  <sign start-date="12-22" end-date="01-20">
    <name type="main">Capricorn</name>
    <name type="alt">The Sea-Goat</name>
    <!-- capricorn.gif corresponds to Unicode 3.0 #x2651 -->
    <symbol xlink:type="simple" xlink:href="capricorn.gif" />
    <ruling_planet>Saturn</ruling_planet>
    <element>Earth</element>
    <energy>Feminine</energy>
    <quality>Cardinal</quality>
    <anatomy>
      <part>Bones</part>
      <part>Knees</part>
    </anatomy>
  </sign>
  <sign start-date="05-21" end-date="06-22">
    <name type="main">Gemini</name>
    <name type="alt">The Twins</name>
    <!-- gemini.gif corresponds to Unicode 3.0 #x264A -->
    <symbol xlink:type="simple" xlink:href="gemini.gif" />
    <ruling_planet>Mercury</ruling_planet>
    <element>Air</element>
    <energy>Feminine</energy>
    <quality>Mutable</quality>
    <anatomy>
```

*Figure 5-21. Selecting all elements lacking a particular attribute with a particular value*

you can use the literal position number (or an expression that evaluates to a number) as the predicate. Thus, the following two location paths are identical:

```
//*[position( )=3]
//*[3]
```

Using the sample document as its source, XPath Visualiser displays the result shown in Figure 5-22.

```
<astro xmlns:xlink="http://www.w3.org/1999/xlink">
  <sign start-date="12-22" end-date="01-20">
    <name type="main">Capricorn</name>
    <name type="alt">The Sea-Goat</name>
    <!-- capricorn.gif corresponds to Unicode 3.0 #x2651 -->
    <symbol xlink:type="simple" xlink:href="capricorn.gif" />
    <ruling_planet>Saturn</ruling_planet>
    <element>Earth</element>
    <energy>Feminine</energy>
    <quality>Cardinal</quality>
    -<anatomy>
      <part>Bones</part>
      <part>Knees</part>
    </anatomy>
  </sign>
  <sign start-date="05-21" end-date="06-22">
    <name type="main">Gemini</name>
    <name type="alt">The Twins</name>
    <!-- gemini.gif corresponds to Unicode 3.0 #x264A -->
    <symbol xlink:type="simple" xlink:href="gemini.gif" />
    <ruling_planet>Mercury</ruling_planet>
    <element>Air</element>
    <energy>Feminine</energy>
    <quality>Mutable</quality>
    <anatomy>
      <part>Hands</part>
      <part>Arms</part>
      <part>Shoulders</part>
```

*Figure 5-22. Locating nodes based on their positions*

As you can see, the result is a little surprising. The location path doesn't select simply the third element in the document; it selects the third child element of every element in the document. (As long as the parent element has at least three children, of course. Elements with fewer than three children have none of their children selected. The location path //*[3] might be read as, "Locate all elements in the document whose position along the (default) child:: axis equals 3.")

Also remember that a node's position along a given axis depends on the axis's *direction*, forward or reverse. In particular, the ancestor::, ancestor-or-self::, preceding::, and preceding-sibling:: axes are *reverse* axes. All others (except the special case self:: axis, for obvious reasons) are forward axes. The position is counted starting at the context node and proceeding in the direction of the axis towards the beginning of the document (reverse axes) or the end of the document (forward axes). Consider this location path:

```
//quality[.="Mutable"]/preceding-sibling::*[1]
```

XPath Visualiser selects the first preceding sibling of the Mutable quality element in reverse document order, as you can see in Figure 5-23.

```
<?xml-stylesheet type="text/xsl" href="astro.xsl" ?>
<astro xmlns:xlink="http://www.w3.org/1999/xlink">
  -<sign start-date="12-22" end-date="01-20">
    <name type="main">Capricorn</name>
    <name type="alt">The Sea-Goat</name>
    <!-- capricorn.gif corresponds to Unicode 3.0 #x2651 -->
    <symbol xlink:type="simple" xlink:href="capricorn.gif" />
    <ruling_planet>Saturn</ruling_planet>
    <element>Earth</element>
    <energy>Feminine</energy>
    <quality>Cardinal</quality>
    -<anatomy>
      <part>Bones</part>
      <part>Knees</part>
    </anatomy>
  </sign>
<sign start-date="05-21" end-date="06-22">
    <name type="main">Gemini</name>
    <name type="alt">The Twins</name>
    <!-- gemini.gif corresponds to Unicode 3.0 #x264A -->
    <symbol xlink:type="simple" xlink:href="gemini.gif" />
    <ruling_planet>Mercury</ruling_planet>
    <element>Air</element>
    <energy>Feminine</energy>
    <quality>Mutable</quality>
    -<anatomy>
      <part>Hands</part>
```

*Figure 5-23. Node position on a reverse-direction axis*

If all axes were in the forward direction only, the preceding location path would have located the first Gemini name element—that is, the first preceding sibling in document order of the Mutable quality element. If you want to get the first node in document order when using a reverse axis, don't use the absolute position 1 in the predicate; use the last( ) function, as here:

```
//quality[.="Mutable"]/preceding-sibling::*[last()]
```

Now XPath Visualiser (or any other XPath 1.0-compliant processor) will indeed select that first Gemini name element, as shown in Figure 5-24.

*Figure 5-24. Using last( ) on a reverse-direction axis*

## Functions

For the most part, as explained in Chapter 4, XPath functions are useful primarily in the predicates of location steps. They serve to narrow the focus to particular nodes in a candidate node-set in ways that can't be tested directly, for example, by checking the nodes' string-values.

Among the node-set functions, the most esoteric are probably those having to do with namespaces. Still, these can be useful in ways completely unapproachable by any other means. In our sample document, we've got both an href pseudoattribute (on the xml-stylesheet PI) and a couple of xlink:href attributes (on the symbol elements). Because the strings "href" and "xlink:href" are clearly not equal—and because a PI's pseudoattributes are invisible along the regular attribute:: axis—it might seem impossible to construct a location path that locates all hyperlink references in the document (assuming all such references appear either in a PI or as values of xlink:href attributes) with a compound location path such as:

```
//@*[local-name()="href"]/.. | //processing-instruction( )[contains(., "href")]
```

This location path, applied to our sample document, locates the nodes shown in Figure 5-25.

Note in Figure 5-25 that the local-name( ) function serves to strip the namespace prefix from the attributes associated with the xlink: namespace. Testing for some value in the PI requires use of a string function, like contains( ) here, because everything except the PI's name itself is considered (in XPath terms) one big string-value.

---

```
<!-- Basic astrological data for I's and J's signs -->
<?xml-stylesheet type="text/xsl" href="astro.xsl"?>
<astro xmlns:xlink="http://www.w3.org/1999/xlink">
  <sign start-date="12-22" end-date="01-20">
    <name type="main">Capricorn</name>
    <name type="alt">The Sea-Goat</name>
      <!-- capricorn.gif corresponds to Unicode 3.0 #x2651 -->
    <symbol xlink:type="simple" xlink:href="capricorn.gif" />
    <ruling_planet>Saturn</ruling_planet>
    <element>Earth</element>
    <energy>Feminine</energy>
    <quality>Cardinal</quality>
    -<anatomy>
       <part>Bones</part>
       <part>Knees</part>
    </anatomy>
  </sign>
  <sign start-date="05-21" end-date="06-22">
    <name type="main">Gemini</name>
    <name type="alt">The Twins</name>
      <!-- gemini.gif corresponds to Unicode 3.0 #x264A -->
    <symbol xlink:type="simple" xlink:href="gemini.gif" />
    <ruling_planet>Mercury</ruling_planet>
    <element>Air</element>
    <energy>Feminine</energy>
    <quality>Mutable</quality>
    -<anatomy>
       <part>Hands</part>
```

*Figure 5-25. Locating href pseudoattributes and xlink:href attributes with a single location path*

The Boolean XPath functions, boolean( ) can be used to explicitly test for the very existence of a node, especially relative to the context node. For instance:

```
//*[boolean(child::*)]
```

selects all elements in the document that have any child elements at all. This can also be abbreviated, taking advantage of various defaults and shortcuts, to the more enigmatic form:

```
//*[*]
```

In either case, the result of applying this location path to our sample document is as shown in Figure 5-26.

When you turn to XPath string functions, you really start to open up the doors to fine-tuned (sometimes almost bizarrely so) location paths. If for some reason you wanted to locate all elements whose string-values began with a capital "M" or ended with a lowercase "e," you could use this location path:

```
//node()[starts-with(., "M") or substring(., string-length( ), 1)="e"]
```

(Note that because there's no ends-with( ) function available under XPath 1.0, we have to simulate its purpose using the substring( ) function, starting with position $N$ in an $N$-length string for a length of one character.)

This location path, applied to our sample document, is processed by XPath Visualiser as shown in Figure 5-27.

```
<?xml-stylesheet type="text/xsl" href="astro.xsl" ?>
<astro xmlns:xlink="http://www.w3.org/1999/xlink">
  <sign start-date="12-22" end-date="01-20">
    <name type="main">Capricorn</name>
    <name type="alt">The Sea-Goat</name>
      <!-- capricorn.gif corresponds to Unicode 3.0 #x2651 -->
    <symbol xlink:type="simple" xlink:href="capricorn.gif" />
    <ruling_planet>Saturn</ruling_planet>
    <element>Earth</element>
    <energy>Feminine</energy>
    <quality>Cardinal</quality>
    -<anatomy>
      <part>Bones</part>
      <part>Knees</part>
    </anatomy>
  </sign>
  <sign start-date="05-21" end-date="06-22">
    <name type="main">Gemini</name>
    <name type="alt">The Twins</name>
      <!-- gemini.gif corresponds to Unicode 3.0 #x264A -->
    <symbol xlink:type="simple" xlink:href="gemini.gif" />
    <ruling_planet>Mercury</ruling_planet>
    <element>Air</element>
    <energy>Feminine</energy>
    <quality>Mutable</quality>
    -<anatomy>
      <part>Hands</part>
```

*Figure 5-26. Using boolean() to locate all elements that are parents of other elements*

```
  <!-- Basic astrological data for T's and J's signs -->
<?xml-stylesheet type="text/xsl" href="astro.xsl" ?>
<astro xmlns:xlink="http://www.w3.org/1999/xlink">
  <sign start-date="12-22" end-date="01-20">
    <name type="main">Capricorn</name>
    <name type="alt">The Sea-Goat</name>
      <!-- capricorn.gif corresponds to Unicode 3.0 #x2651 -->
    <symbol xlink:type="simple" xlink:href="capricorn.gif" />
    <ruling_planet>Saturn</ruling_planet>
    <element>Earth</element>
    <energy>Feminine</energy>
    <quality>Cardinal</quality>
    -<anatomy>
      <part>Bones</part>
      <part>Knees</part>
    </anatomy>
  </sign>
  <sign start-date="05-21" end-date="06-22">
    <name type="main">Gemini</name>
    <name type="alt">The Twins</name>
      <!-- gemini.gif corresponds to Unicode 3.0 #x264A -->
    <symbol xlink:type="simple" xlink:href="gemini.gif" />
    <ruling_planet>Mercury</ruling_planet>
    <element>Air</element>
    <energy>Feminine</energy>
    <quality>Mutable</quality>
    -<anatomy>
```

*Figure 5-27. Using XPath string functions*

## Sublimely Ridiculous

As I've said, it's nearly impossible to theorize a portion of an XML document's content that *cannot* be located with XPath. That said, even some straightforward English-language questions can be answered only by very complex, even bizarre, XPath location steps. And even when the questions can be answered simply, it's possible—if your inclinations run to the perverse—to come up with incredible convolutions of syntax. Here are a couple of examples.

For starters, look back at the sample document of astrological data, particularly at the contents of the part elements (within the two anatomy elements). Note that for any given astrological sign, the text nodes contained by the part elements identify either singular or plural body parts. (Our sample document, as it happens, includes only plurals, such as Bones and Shoulders.) So let's start by asking this English-language question:

What are the main names of all astrological signs with at least one plural part element?

The easiest way to build up a long XPath location path is step by step, confirming that each step along the way does what it needs to do. In this case, the place to start might be at the *end* of the question: which part elements have plural text nodes? A location path to accomplish this might look something like this:

```
//part[substring(., string-length(),1)="s"]
```

That is: locate all part descendants of the root node, substring the last character in each of their string-values, and select only those for which that substring equals "s." (Of course, this would fail to locate any part element whose string-value is "Teeth." This is not an issue given the two astrological signs in question but be aware of such little wrinkles in making assumptions about your own documents' contents.) Applied to our sample document, XPath Visualiser comes up with the selection shown in Figure 5-28.

*Figure 5-28. Locating all "plural body parts"*

Working backwards through our English-language question and comparing it to the sample document structure, the next thing we're evidently seeking is the sign element corresponding to any of the selected "plural body parts" located by the existing location path. As is usual with XPath, there are a number of ways to locate such a sign element. One way would be to use the ancestor:: axis, as here (additional location step boldfaced):

```
//part[substring(., string-length(.),1)="s"]/ancestor::sign
```

As Figure 5-29 illustrates, the location path now walks the selection back up the document tree to the corresponding sign elements.

*Figure 5-29. Locating the sign elements with "plural body parts"*

The English-language question now says we need to locate the "main names" of all these signs. In terms of the document's structure, this can be interpreted as "all child name element(s) of the selected sign element(s) that have a type attribute whose value is main." Now the location path looks as follows:

```
//part[substring(., string-length(.),1)="s"]/ancestor::sign/name[@type="main"]
```

Figure 5-30 shows how this location path works in practice.

One further refinement: as you can see from Figure 5-30, the location path as it stands locates the desired name element(s) (with their start tags highlighted by XPath Visualiser). If we really want to locate the main *names* of the selected signs, we need to locate not the elements themselves, but rather the text nodes that make up their string-values. So our full location path would be:

```
//part[substring(., string-length(.),1)="s"]/ancestor::sign/name[@type="main"]
/text()
```

(Note that this location path breaks across two lines here, but actually is a single line for XPath Visualiser's purposes; in XPath's own terms, breaking this expression across two lines like this is quite acceptable.)

```
<?xml-stylesheet type="text/xsl" href="astro.xsl" ?>
<astro xmlns:xlink="http://www.w3.org/1999/xlink">
  <sign start-date="12-22" end-date="01-20">
    <name type="main">Capricorn</name>
    <name type="alt">The Sea-Goat</name>
    <!-- capricorn.gif corresponds to Unicode 3.0 #x2651 -->
    <symbol xlink:type="simple" xlink:href="capricorn.gif" />
    <ruling_planet>Saturn</ruling_planet>
    <element>Earth</element>
    <energy>Feminine</energy>
    <quality>Cardinal</quality>
    -<anatomy>
      <part>Bones</part>
      <part>Knees</part>
    </anatomy>
  </sign>
  <sign start-date="05-21" end-date="06-22">
    <name type="main">Gemini</name>
    <name type="alt">The Twins</name>
    <!-- gemini.gif corresponds to Unicode 3.0 #x264A -->
    <symbol xlink:type="simple" xlink:href="gemini.gif" />
    <ruling_planet>Mercury</ruling_planet>
    <element>Air</element>
    <energy>Feminine</energy>
    <quality>Mutable</quality>
    -<anatomy>
      <part>Hands</part>
```

*Figure 5-30. Locating the main name element for each sign with "plural body parts"*

In Figure 5-31, as you can see, XPath Visualiser finally answers our original question. It locates that actual name for which we're looking.

```
<?xml-stylesheet type="text/xsl" href="astro.xsl" ?>
<astro xmlns:xlink="http://www.w3.org/1999/xlink">
  <sign start-date="12-22" end-date="01-20">
    <name type="main">Capricorn</name>
    <name type="alt">The Sea-Goat</name>
    <!-- capricorn.gif corresponds to Unicode 3.0 #x2651 -->
    <symbol xlink:type="simple" xlink:href="capricorn.gif" />
    <ruling_planet>Saturn</ruling_planet>
    <element>Earth</element>
    <energy>Feminine</energy>
    <quality>Cardinal</quality>
    -<anatomy>
      <part>Bones</part>
      <part>Knees</part>
    </anatomy>
  </sign>
  <sign start-date="05-21" end-date="06-22">
    <name type="main">Gemini</name>
    <name type="alt">The Twins</name>
    <!-- gemini.gif corresponds to Unicode 3.0 #x264A -->
    <symbol xlink:type="simple" xlink:href="gemini.gif" />
    <ruling_planet>Mercury</ruling_planet>
    <element>Air</element>
    <energy>Feminine</energy>
    <quality>Mutable</quality>
    -<anatomy>
      <part>Hands</part>
```

*Figure 5-31. Locating the true name of each sign with "plural body parts"*

One more example, this one based on (perhaps quite unreasonable!) assumptions about the way this document (and any other in the same vocabulary) is structured: each symbol element is immediately preceded by a comment identifying the Unicode 3.0 character corresponding to the image file for that sign's symbol. Also note that a sign may have one or more body parts (Bones and Knees for Capricorn; Hands, Arms, Shoulders, and Lungs for Gemini). Given these assumptions, we might frame a question such as the following:

> What is the name of the image file *and* the Unicode character equivalent for the symbol of each sign with more than two body parts?

As with the previous example, let's begin at the end of the question by locating all the signs with more than two body parts:

```
//sign[count(descendant::part) > 2]
```

Figure 5-32 shows that this selects only one sign element (Gemini).

*Figure 5-32. Locating signs with more than two body parts*

How to proceed next may seem a little complicated, thanks to the presence in our question of the word "and." All it really means, though, is that we'll be constructing a compound location path. We can work on either the "image file" or the "Unicode character" subordinate location path first; however, because we're going for baroque (sorry) here, let's assume that we want to get to the Unicode character *by way of* the corresponding image. The image for this sign element can be singled out thus:

```
//sign[count(descendant::part) > 2]/symbol/@xlink:href
```

That is, from the selected signs, walk down to their symbol children and then select each symbol's xlink:href attribute. Figure 5-33 illustrates the result.

Now we've got to add a second location path, joined to the first by the union (|, vertical bar or pipe symbol). For this second location path, we're going to navigate down to the same point as the first, but then go back to the preceding comment node:

```
//sign[count(descendant::part) > 2]/symbol/@xlink:href |
//sign[count(descendant::part) > 2]/symbol/@xlink:href/../preceding-sibling::comment(
)
```

```
-<sign start-date="12-22" end-date="01-20">
   <name type="main">Capricorn</name>
   <name type="alt">The Sea-Goat</name>
    <!-- capricorn.gif corresponds to Unicode 3.0 #x2651 -->
   <symbol xlink:type="simple" xlink:href="capricorn.gif" />
   <ruling_planet>Saturn</ruling_planet>
   <element>Earth</element>
   <energy>Feminine</energy>
   <quality>Cardinal</quality>
   -<anatomy>
      <part>Bones</part>
      <part>Knees</part>
   </anatomy>
 </sign>
 <sign start-date="05-21" end-date="06-22">
   <name type="main">Gemini</name>
   <name type="alt">The Twins</name>
    <!-- gemini.gif corresponds to Unicode 3.0 #x264A -->
   <symbol xlink:type="simple" xlink:href="gemini.gif"/>
   <ruling_planet>Mercury</ruling_planet>
   <element>Air</element>
   <energy>Feminine</energy>
   <quality>Mutable</quality>
   -<anatomy>
      <part>Hands</part>
      <part>Arms</part>
      <part>Shoulders</part>
      <part>Lungs</part>
```

*Figure 5-33. Locating the image file for the symbol of each sign with more than two body parts*

An important part of this second location path is the /.. buried within it, which shifts the context for succeeding location steps back up the document tree from the xlink: href attribute, to its parent symbol element. If you omit this location step, the location path attempts to select all preceding siblings *of the attribute itself*—which is almost never what you want (in answering this question or any other: it always returns an empty node-set).

As you can see in Figure 5-34, we've succeeded in locating all information in the document about the symbols of all signs with more than two body parts.

```
-<sign start-date="12-22" end-date="01-20">
   <name type="main">Capricorn</name>
   <name type="alt">The Sea-Goat</name>
    <!-- capricorn.gif corresponds to Unicode 3.0 #x2651 -->
   <symbol xlink:type="simple" xlink:href="capricorn.gif" />
   <ruling_planet>Saturn</ruling_planet>
   <element>Earth</element>
   <energy>Feminine</energy>
   <quality>Cardinal</quality>
   -<anatomy>
      <part>Bones</part>
      <part>Knees</part>
   </anatomy>
 </sign>
 <sign start-date="05-21" end-date="06-22">
   <name type="main">Gemini</name>
   <name type="alt">The Twins</name>
    <!-- gemini.gif corresponds to Unicode 3.0 #x264A -->
   <symbol xlink:type="simple" xlink:href="gemini.gif"/>
   <ruling_planet>Mercury</ruling_planet>
   <element>Air</element>
   <energy>Feminine</energy>
   <quality>Mutable</quality>
   -<anatomy>
      <part>Hands</part>
      <part>Arms</part>
      <part>Shoulders</part>
      <part>Lungs</part>
```

*Figure 5-34. Locating all Unicode and image-file representations of the symbols for all signs with more than two body parts*

By the way, although it doesn't matter for this particular sample document, note that the compound location path is susceptible to breaking—returning an incorrect result—in at least one case. If there's more than one comment that is a preceding sibling for a given symbol, the location path will select them all. Thus, to make the location path more robust, you might consider adding a predicate to the final location step, like this:

```
/comment( )[contains(.,"corresponds to Unicode 3.0")]
```

Again, adding this predicate has no effect in the case of this particular document. There are other built-in assumptions in the full location path that may or may not be true in other documents in the "astrology markup language." For example, the location path takes it for granted that each symbol element *will* have an xlink:href attribute; to be even more bullet-proof, the path might choose to ignore symbol elements without that attribute. This depends of course on your application's specific needs. Just remember that as a rule, if you don't cover the unexpected in your location paths, XPath won't cover it for you!

# CHAPTER 6

# XPath 2.0

Even when the W3C promulgates a spec in its final Recommendation form, the spec does not become fixed in stone.* Any product expressed in human language always requires further tweaking—filling gaps, fixing ambiguities, and making room for new developments in related specs and technologies. This is the case with the next, still-upcoming version of XPath: Version 2.0.

The XPath 2.0 spec, as of late 2001, still exists in a very tentative state. Not only is it a Working Draft (one of the very first rungs a spec must negotiate on its way up the ladder to full Recommendation status). It's not yet a specification of syntax, but rather a simple statement of *requirements*. All you'll learn from perusing the XPath 2.0 documentation at this point is what XPath 2.0 may ultimately permit you to accomplish—not the specific means you will use to accomplish those ends.

The XPath 2.0 Requirements document explored in this chapter was issued in February, 2001. You can find it on the W3C web site, at *http://www.w3.org/TR/xpath20req*.

 In December 2001, the W3C finally published a Working Draft of the XPath 2.0 spec. In April 2002, this December WD was followed up by another version. This chapter will make occasional reference to this version of the WD as well as the Requirements document.

## General Goals

The XML 1.0 Recommendation implicitly established something of a precedent for future XML-related standards, particularly in its opening statement of 10 "design principles" from which all the individual details flowed. Likewise, the XPath 2.0

---

* The main exception—and it's a biggie—has been the Extensible Markup Language (XML) 1.0 standard itself, still mostly unchanged (except for minor editorial buffing) after four years. In my opinion, this is a testament to XML 1.0's concise expression of far-reaching goals, especially in contrast to certain other specs' swollen expression of minutiae. On the other hand, some would argue that the minutiae are the "hard part" and therefore warrant all the verbiage.

## XPath 2.0 and XQuery 1.0

XPath 2.0 needs to support not only XSLT 2.0 and XPointer 1.0, but the emerging XML Query (XQuery) standard as well.

XQuery is intended to be a general-purpose "interrogator" of XML content, roughly analogous to the way that Structured Query Language (SQL) behaves in a relational database context. The connections between XPath 2.0 and XQuery 1.0 are so critical that the two languages are being developed in lockstep, so to speak.

Of course, XPath 1.0 already exists and is in wide use, while XQuery is still in its infancy as a W3C spec. This might seem to imply that XPath would be the "favored child" of the two languages, but don't bet on it: XQuery is under development with full knowledge of the recently—finally—approved XML Schema Recommendations, of which XPath 1.0 is entirely ignorant. More on XML Schema, as well as its implications for XPath 2.0, later in this chapter.

An important document for you to consider, in these circumstances, is the "XQuery 1.0 and XPath 2.0 Functions and Operators Version 1.0" Working Draft, at *http://www. w3.org/TR/xquery-operators/*. This document, published in August 2001, provides a first-cut look at what XPath 2.0 syntax may resemble, at least regarding function calls and operators. You'll find much the same and—alas—much different. For instance, function names will now (*possibly*) be qualified with a namespace prefix, xf:, mapped to the URI *http://www.w3.org/2001/08/xquery-operators*. So while the count( ) function will still be present, under this guideline it would be called xf:count( ). (In this chapter, I will omit these namespace prefixes. the namespace prefixing of function names is unlikely to be required, despite the "Functions and Operators" implication that it will be.)

Be prepared to be overwhelmed by this so-called "F&O" document. Using fairly conservative margins and font size, its length sprawls over 165 pages when printed on my laser printer. I'm one of a dwindling minority who remain optimistic that XML as such needn't be rocket science, but specs this long and complex give pause to even us starry-eyed innocents.

Requirements document (which I'll hereafter most often refer to as "XPath 2.0") states eight general goals it hopes to accomplish. The general *goals* are distinct from the five general *requirements* XPath 2.0 lays out in some detail. I'll discuss each of the former briefly, then in the next section, break down the latter.

 Be aware that I'm not a member of the joint Working Group preparing the standard and not privy to their confidential discussions; what follows in this section, therefore, is at best informed interpretation of publicly available documents.

## Simplify Manipulation of XML Schema-Typed Content

Well before the W3C's XML Schema standard acquired Recommendation status, it loomed large in the thinking of other W3C Working Groups preparing—or even having finished—specs of their own.

That's what this general XPath 2.0 goal shoots for: reconciling, in XPath 2.0, the existence of XPath 1.0 with the existence of XML Schema 1.0. For instance, it might be useful for XPath 2.0 processors to locate all of a Schema-based document's dates or integers, ignoring the floating-point values and string-values.

## Simplify Manipulation of String Content

XPath 1.0 provides a core set of string-handling features—particularly the string *functions*. But users coming to XPath from other computing languages are occasionally often frustrated by the things you *can't* do with strings.

For example, the translate( ) function provides easy one-for-one character substitution. What it doesn't provide is the ability to substitute, say, a multicharacter string for a given single character (or for a given pair of characters, or whatever).

## Support Related XML Standards

Aside from XML Schema, XPath 2.0 also needs to take into consideration the requirements of certain other XML-based standards dependent on it. In particular, it needs to address the upcoming XSLT 2.0 and XML Query specifications. The joint W3C Working Group currently responsible for XPath 2.0 is composed of individuals from the two separate Working Groups responsible for those two standards, so this should be (in theory!) an easily achieved goal.

Potentially more problematic is how to continue to support XPointer 1.0, which kind of falls into a crack in the timeline between XPath 1.0 and 2.0.

## Improve Ease of Use

On the whole, I think XPath 1.0 is much easier to use than it seems at first glance. But there's no denying that it's got its share of idiosyncrasies and counterintuitive crotchets, too, and this goal of XPath 2.0 addresses these obstacles.

For instance, as you know, you can use the union operator, |, to construct compound location paths. But—somewhat arbitrarily—you can't use it in a location *step*. XPath 2.0 will let you do that.

# Improve Interoperability

While XPath 2.0 doesn't use the word "interoperability" (or any of its other forms) anywhere else but in the statement of this goal, it seems pretty clear what it's referring to. This is not interoperability among products—XPath-aware processors—but among XPath and other standards.

How does "interoperability among" differ from "support for"? Well, it's conceivable that some hypothetical XPath 2.0 standard might support XSLT, XPointer, and XML Query equally well but use different syntaxes, say, or different data models. This goal mandates the development of *common* solutions to common problems. An XPath 2.0 processor, you might say, should be plug-compatible whether it's used in the context of a larger XSLT application, XPointer application, or XML Query application. That said, there's little likelihood of XPath 2.0's use in an XPointer application—given (as you will see) XPointer's lagging progress through the standards process.

A little more tricky may be that word "improve." XSLT has been around for a while and thus has a fairly large base of processors based on it, which by necessity understand XPath 1.0 expressions. XPointer and XML Query are still in their infancy; hence, in one respect, there wouldn't seem to be much in the way of any interoperability at all, improvable or otherwise. But remember that this isn't a question so much about the interoperability of processing applications as the interoperability of related *standards behind the applications*.

# Improve i18n Support

The term "i18n" is a shorthand expression. To expand it, simply take the initial "i," follow it with 18 other letters, and conclude with the letter "n": the word internationalization. This goal is going to be both important and (I think) rather difficult to meet. Importantly, the goal says that i18n support should be *improved*, not outright *resolved*. Its intention is to facilitate the use of XPath with documents in non-Western languages, particularly those requiring the use of full Unicode-based character sets.

This goal addresses such questions, for instance, as:

- Must an XPath-aware processor be able to perform mathematical operations, particularly with the (explicit or implicit) number( ) function, on non-Arabic representations of the text string "2"?
- What should happen when you convert a character from a caseless language, such as Japanese, to upper- or lowercase?

# Maintain Backward Compatibility

This one's easy to explain, if not necessarily to achieve. One implication of this goal is that a processor that fully supports XPath 1.0 should still be able to operate in an XPath 2.0 context (albeit with a mere subset of the latter's functionality). More importantly, an XPath 1.0 expression should "mean" the same thing to an XPath 2.0 application that it does to an application that's been doing useful work for years. (You might want to recode your XSLT stylesheets to take advantage of new XPath 2.0 features, but you wouldn't expect—let alone want—them to break outright.)

## Enable Improved Processor Efficiency

One of the knocks on using XML as a data-storage format, especially relative to established tools such as database management systems (DBMSs), is that the tool for locating specific content (XPath) is rather cumbersome for processors to implement, let alone to implement efficiently. In a database, for example, you can construct an index on virtually any field or combination of fields; when a new record is added, all the corresponding indexes are added to or updated as well. For a DBMS to work efficiently in this regard, it simply needs to load all indexes up-front, not all *tables*.

XML itself, and particularly XPath 1.0, provide a halfway kind of solution to this problem, by using ID-type attributes to ensure that each element (or at least each element that we particularly care about) has a unique identifier. It's common for XML parsers, or rather the processors built on them, to then build indexes to the uniquely-identified elements for speedy location. XSLT builds further on this, allowing you to construct *non*-unique keys on almost any kind of content in a given document, even one lacking any attributes at all. There's a point of diminishing returns, of course, where it takes longer and is generally less efficient to build a host of indexes (unique or otherwise) than it does to simply hold the document in memory. And still, there's no way for an XML document's "index" to be somehow part and parcel of the document itself; even a document heavily keyed with ID-type attributes still has to be read in from beginning to end to be sure you've collected all the key values.

My reading of this goal might be considered a pessimistic one—not so much that processor efficiency will be outright improved (despite the goal's wording). Rather, processor efficiency should not be *made worse*, even with the addition of new and improved XPath 2.0 features.

# Specific Requirements

XPath 2.0 breaks down a list of 25 specific requirements into five general categories:

1. Must support the XML "family" of standards
2. Must improve ease of use
3. Must support string matching using regular expressions
4. Must add support for XML Schema primitive data types
5. Should add support for XML Schema structures

XPath 2.0 does not explicitly tie these five general categories back to the list of eight overall goals. That said, a careful reading of the spec might result in a grid something like that represented by Table 6-1. To see the general goal(s) addressed by a category of requirements, read down; to see which requirement(s) address a given general goal, read across.

*Table 6-1. XPath 2.0 requirements, by general goal*

| General Goals | Support XML "family" | Improve ease of use | Regular-expression matching | Schema data types | Schema structures |
|---|---|---|---|---|---|
| XML Schema-typed content | yes | | | yes | |
| Simpler string manipulation | | yes | yes | | |
| Support of related standards | yes | | | yes | yes |
| Improve ease of use | yes | yes | yes | yes | yes |
| Improve interoperability | yes | yes | | yes | yes |
| Improve i18n support | yes | | yes | | |
| Backward compatibility | yes | | | | |
| Processor efficiency | yes | yes | | | yes |

One thing about the list of categories is very interesting: the use of the words "must" and "should." Categories 1 through 4 are pretty clearly meant to represent non-optional things XPath 2.0 must achieve; category 5 is a bit more weasel-worded, implying (at the least) a certain amount of ambivalence among the XPath 2.0 authors. The distinction between these two words continues throughout the XPath 2.0 Requirements document.

It's such an important distinction, in fact, that I'm going to depart from the structure of the document itself in discussing the 25 specific requirements. Rather than list them on a category-by-category basis, I'm going to break them down into separate "must-do" and "should-do" sections. Note that within a given category, regardless of the must/should associated with it, specific requirements are must-/should-valued independently. Also note that one of the general categories (#3, "Support string matching with regular expressions") is not further broken down into specific requirements.

Alongside the heading for each specific requirement discussed below, I'll indicate the number assigned to it by the XPath 2.0 Requirements document; you can use this number to trace, via the numbered list of requirements categories above, to which of the five categories it belongs. For instance, the "MUST requirement" headed "Provide a conditional expression" is requirement #2.2, making it one of the "Improve ease of use" categories.

## XPath 2.0 MUSTs

The following sections describe those things that are required by the spec.

### Express its data model in terms of the XML Infoset (1.1)

A data model is a formal expression of the kinds of objects and their properties accessible under the terms of a particular data storage/transmission specification, such as XPath. The XML Infoset is a W3C Recommendation (finalized October 2001) that sets forth the data model—the *information set*—of XML documents. The XML Infoset spec is located at *http://www.w3.org/TR/xml-infoset*.

This information set is defined as a collection of 11 *information items*. An information set is analogous to the tree of nodes in a document; information items, to nodes in the tree.

Most of the information items possible in an XML document conform to what you'd expect: the document itself, elements, attributes, and so on. There are a couple of nonobvious information items, though, such as unexpanded entity references (the "things" that exist in a document when a parser does not, for one reason or another, actually expand the entity references to their full forms) and notations. Also noteworthy are the things you might find in a document that are *not* considered part of the Infoset: content models, whitespace outside the document element and immediately following the target of a PI, and so on. (The complete list of 20 excluded object types appears in Appendix D of the spec.)

What this requirement means for XPath 2.0 is probably that the language used to name various object types and properties will be brought into synch with that used in the XML Infoset spec, to eliminate ambiguities among XPath 2.0 and other XML specifications (such as XML Query and XSLT) that refer to the same object types. It may also result in the introduction of new object types and properties into XPath. For instance, the Infoset defines a "Base URI" property for various information items such as the document entity itself and each element in the document. (Personally, I hope that the language isn't brought *too much* into synch with the Infoset's. Carried to a zealous extreme, this might produce such awful terms as "information item-set" instead of "node-set." I'm all in favor of consistency, but I think reasonable people can be expected to make the intellectual leap, in this case, from "node" to "information item" without having to actually *say* the latter.)

### Provide common core syntax and semantics for XSLT and XML Query (1.2)

As I mentioned, the XPath 2.0 Requirements document is a joint product of two separate W3C bodies: the XSL Working Group (responsible for XSLT 2.0) and the XML Query Working group (XML Query, or XQuery, 1.0). This requirement says that XPath 2.0 will boil down the content-location needs of the two specs into a single common body of features, which may be extended by the separate specs as required to cover their distinct needs. The general idea is illustrated by Figure 6-1.

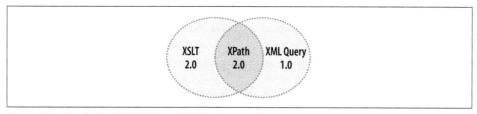

*Figure 6-1. XPath 2.0, XSLT 2.0, and XML Query 1.0*

In this classic Venn-diagram figure, the core syntax and semantics to be provided by XPath 2.0 is the shaded area where the other two specs overlap. Content may also be located by extension features provided by the other two specs—features of no common use. For instance, XSLT 1.0 extended the XPath set of core functions with a document( ) function for accessing the contents of other XML documents (source trees) than the one nominally being processed by a given stylesheet. This function is considered desirable by XML Query as well, and it has accordingly moved into XPath 2.0's set of core functions and out of XSLT 2.0.

> The XPath 2.0 Requirements document asserts that while the XSL Working Group has consensus on this XPath 2.0 requirement, the XML Query WG does not: the latter "is discussing what functionality constitutes a common core."

## Support explicit "for any" and "for all" Boolean operations (1.3)

Here's a typical XPath 1.0 location path with a predicate:

```
//book[price > 5.00]
```

This location path selects all book elements for which the first price child has a numeric value greater than 5.00. Now consider that location path in light of the following document:

```
<books>
    <book>
        <price type="wholesale">12.00</price>
        <price type="retail">16.95</price>
    </book>
    <book>
        <price type="wholesale">4.95</price>
        <price type="retail">6.95</price>
    </book>
    <book>
        <price type="retail">5.25</price>
        <price type="wholesale">4.75</price>
    </book>
</books>
```

Under XPath 1.0, all three of the above book elements would be selected, because XPath 1.0 works in what might be termed "any mode"—selecting the book elements, in this case, for which *any* price child is greater than 5.00. This requirement of XPath 2.0 says it would also be nice to be able to select a book element if *all* its price children are greater than 5.00 (which would select only the first book element in the above document).

## Extend the existing set of aggregate functions (1.4)

The XSLT user community has been especially vocal in its requests (verging on outright demands in some cases) that extra functions be made available for processing across a single selected node-set. Currently there are only two such functions, sum( ) and count( ). Why not min( ) and max( ) functions? Why not avg( )? Why not a distinct( ) function to locate unique nodes?

For meeting this requirement, the XPath 2.0 authors will look primarily to XML Query for inspiration. That spec, which will be informed by its authors' experience with and knowledge of database manipulation languages such as SQL, is almost certain to provide a richer set of aggregate functions than XPath 1.0's.

 That said, there will probably be some difficult decisions ahead on this requirement. For instance, if XML Query defines an npv( ) function for returning the net present value based on a series of arguments, is this of general utility among the core functions of XPath 2.0 and, therefore, available for use in XSLT and XPointer as well?

### Loosen restrictions on location steps (2.1)

XPath 1.0 places some bizarre, seemingly arbitrary constraints on what you can do in a location step:

- You can't use a node-set function itself as a location step. It might be very useful, for example, to retrieve a descendant of an element with a particular ID-type attribute using something like:

  ```
  id("Belkin")/price
  ```

- You can't use the union operator, |, within a location step—only to delimit the components of a compound location path. In the previous chapter, you saw a rather complicated location step that looked like this:

  ```
  //sign[count(ruling_planet) > 1]/symbol/@xlink:href |
  //sign[count(ruling_planet) > 1]/symbol/preceding-sibling::comment()
  ```

  This would be much more naturally coded (and easier to understand!) as:

  ```
  //sign[count(ruling_planet) > 1]/symbol/(@xlink:href |
      preceding-sibling::comment())
  ```

  (Note the parentheses enclosing the alternatives in the final location step.)

- When used in XPointer, a location path cannot end with a node-set function, such as count() or sum(). Thus, the following would be an illegal location path in an XPointer:

  ```
  //last()
  ```

This goal of XPath 2.0 would minimize these kinds of restrictions.

### Provide a conditional expression (2.2)

Many computer languages provide a function that evaluates one argument for a true or false value, returning one value if the result of that evaluation is true or a different value if false. For instance, in a Microsoft Visual Basic program, you might see an expression such as:

```
iif(flasher = "yellow", "slow", "go")
```

The iif() function here tests the value of a variable called flasher; if flasher's value is the string "yellow," the function returns the string "slow," or otherwise returns the string "go." Providing a similar "if condition X, then result A, else result B" logic is the intention behind this goal of XPath 2.0. The April 2002 Working Draft of the spec spells out a syntax that looks as follows:

```
if (expr1) then expr2 else expr3
```

The idea here, as you might expect, is to locate either the content identified by expr2 or expr3, depending on the true or false value of expr1. Thus, you might do something like the following:

```
if (title="Callings" or title="Wishcraft") then title else "Unknown Title"
```

This first evaluates the string-value of the title child of the context node. If the string-value is "Callings" or "Wishcraft," the value of the conditional expression as a whole is that string-value; otherwise, the conditional expression as a whole has the value "Unknown Title."

### Define consistent implicit semantics for collection-valued subexpressions (2.3)

To figure out what this is saying, let's start with that phrase at the end. A *subexpression*, clearly, is a component (or possibly the entirety) of a normal XPath expression. The term *collection-valued* refers to those bits of an expression that are the names of groups of objects—particularly node-sets.

Thus, this goal asserts that any reference to (say) a node-set must always inherently "mean" the same thing, no matter what its syntactic context might be at the moment.

The XPath 2.0 Requirements document provides an example showing how XPath 1.0 fails to meet this requirement. Here's a slight modification of that example. Consider an XML-based library application. In an XPath expression designed to locate content in a document built according to this application, you might do something like this:

```
shelf[books = 31]
```

This selects all shelf elements that have at least one books child with a value of 31. However, if you use the books element in a subexpression, you get a slightly different result:

```
shelf[books + 1 = 32]
```

This returns all shelf elements for which only the *first* books element equals 31. (Slightly different, indeed!) Ironing out this and similar inconsistencies will make XPath 2.0 easier both to learn and use than its predecessor.

### Support string matching with regular expressions (3)

Many computer languages—especially those with a background in the Unix operating system—support the use of *regular expressions* to manipulate string content. You've probably already been exposed to some of the more common types of regular expression, such as wildcard asterisks (meaning "zero or more occurrences of any characters") and question marks ("exactly one occurrence of any character") in listing the contents of a filesystem directory. Being able to use even these simple regular expressions in XPath would make the language terrifically more powerful. For instance:

```
//employee[name = "Simon*" or name = "*Lenz"]
```

would locate all employee elements with a child name element whose string-value *starts* with the string "Simon" or *ends* with the string "Lenz."

But fully supporting regular expressions would go beyond simple wildcard matching. Whole books have been written about the nuances and more exotic forms of regular expressions, and this isn't the place to learn about them. But with them, you could tailor your selections to do things like:

- Search for the strings "Calendar" or "calendar" (upper- and lowercase "C," respectively) in a single step, without using the translate( ) function.
- Locate all strings formatted like a conventional U.S. telephone number (numeric strings separated into three-digit area code, three-digit exchange, and four-digit number, delimited by hyphens)

For more information on regular expressions, you might want to hunt down a copy of O'Reilly's "owl book," *Mastering Regular Expressions*, by Jeffery E.F. Friedl.

### Define the operator matrix and conversions (4.1)

Well, that's the way the requirement is worded in the spec. It's followed by this explanation, evidently meant to be at least as helpful:

> XPath 2.0 MUST support the operators and type-coercion rules defined by the joint XSLT/Schema/Query task force on operators.

You'll search in vain, though, for more information on this joint task force or the "operator matrix." What you can do productively is read further in the spec, looking especially at the four use cases (that is, specific reasons to pursue the requirement): general, DateTime, Boolean, and QName.

The requirement's purpose is given away in the last three use cases. DateTime, Boolean, and QName are all data types supported by XML Schema alone or in concert with XPath. And what all this jargon about the operator matrix and type-coercion rules has to do with is, in short, the selection and manipulation of content on the basis of the content's data type—not simply on the basis of its value.

Consider the DateTime data type, for example. In most fully-featured data systems, knowing that a particular datum is of DateTime type permits operations such as:

- Subtracting one DateTime value from another, yielding an *interval* that is itself of the DateTime type
- Adding an interval to a DateTime, yielding an end-time
- Comparing one DateTime to another, yielding a Boolean true or false

For another example, given content of Boolean type, without meeting this XPath 2.0 requirement the language will still lack a fundamental component of a serious data manipulation language: the ability to test for a *literal* Boolean value, such as true and false (as opposed to strings which have those values).

### Allow scientific notation for numbers (4.2)

This simple requirement—again, intended primarily to bring XPath into XML Schema conformance—fine-tunes the number data type, assuring that any floating-point or double-precision content can be handled properly as long as it's in one of the various numeric formats defined by XML Schema. The Schema language supports not only scientific notation (such as 7.25e2, representing 7.25 times 10 squared, or 725) but also certain exotic forms such as INF and -INF for positive and negative infinity.

### Define cast and constructor functions (4.3)

Cast and constructor functions permit XPath-based applications to force a particular bit of content to a desired data type. Some of these are available already under XPath 1.0, in the form of the number( ), string( ), and boolean( ) functions. To align XPath 2.0 with XML Schema, this requirement mandates the addition of equivalent functions for converting content to XML Schema's URI and DateTime types.

 Early in the chapter, a sidebar discussed a new spec, called XQuery 1.0 and XPath 2.0 Functions and Operators—the "F&O" document. In that spec, constructor and cast functions are defined differently. A cast function will take an expression (such as a location path) as an argument. A constructor function will always operate on literal arguments. (That is, in the latter case, a literal argument, such as 123.45, might be considered a typeless argument; to make it a value of a particular type, the function must *construct* a datum of that type and assign the argument's value to that datum.)

### Support accessing the simple-type values of elements and attributes (4.5)

As with the cast/constructor functions mentioned in the previous item, XPath 1.0 already satisfies part of this requirement by supporting content of the string, numeric, Boolean, and node-set data types. But then along comes XML Schema, which adds quite a few new data types to the stew, including binary, byte, century, double, QName, URI, and so on. XPath 2.0 must be able to address and manipulate these simple data types, as well as the four existing ones, without converting such content to (say) string values.

### Define the behavior of operators for null arguments (4.6)

No matter whether you're dealing with XPath or some other language for locating or otherwise handling data, the language needs to lay out some ground rules for processing data with a null value.

Null values are different from empty-string values. Nulls say something like "nothing at all," as if the content were never assigned in the first place; an empty string, on the other hand, is a string of length 0. The issue with this requirement is that XML Schema allows content to be explicitly assigned a type of null if the content is not provided in the instance document.

What is the value, for example, of an empty element? of a legal attribute that is nei-ther explicitly assigned in a document nor defaulted via a DTD or Schema? You already know what this XPath expression "means":

```
unit_price * qty
```

It calculates the product of the unit_price child of the context node and the qty child of the context node. But what if there is no unit_price child at all and/or no qty child, *and* if unit_price and qty are both explicitly typed as null when unavailable? Should the result of this calculation be some "default" value useful in other computa-tional contexts, like 0, or should the result itself be null?

# XPath 2.0 SHOULDs

The following sections describe those things that are recommended by the spec.

### Maintain backward compatibility with XPath 1.0 (1.5)

This may qualify as the very least surprising of all XPath 2.0 requirements. But it's important that it's made explicit. It says, in effect, "Do *not* break a given XPath 1.0 expression simply, because it's being evaluated in an XPath 2.0 context."

The only surprise may be that this requirement falls into the "SHOULD" category, rather than the "MUST." I don't know but am fairly certain that this simply recog-nizes the pragmatic truth of life in the post-XPath 1.0 world—particularly, the loom-ing XSLT 2.0 and XML Schema. It may very well be possible that satisfying one or more of the MUSTs may make something about XPath 1.0 "break." For instance, consider the last item in the MUST section which has to do with XML Schema-typed null values. Instead of treating an empty (i.e., null) element as having an empty string-value, XPath 2.0 will treat it as if it has the special null value. This may very well cause changes in the way processors treat an expression such as:

```
concat(title, ". ", surname)
```

if a given surname element is empty-and-null as a result of the source document's Schema.

### Provide intersection and difference functions (1.6)

As you know, XPath 1.0 permits you to "union together" two or more node-sets with the union operator, |. For full set-processing functionality, XPath 2.0 should also allow you to extract the *intersection* (overlapping content) and the *difference* (areas of non-overlap) between two node-sets.

Consider a simple XML document such as the following:

```
<animations>
  <short>
    <title>A Grand Day Out</title>
    <character>Wallace</character>
```

```
    <character>Grommit</character>
    <character>Tin Robot</character>
  </short>
  <short>
    <title>The Wrong Trousers</title>
    <character>Wallace</character>
    <character>Grommit</character>
    <character>Feathers McGraw (The Penguin)</character>
    <character>Techno Trousers</character>
  </short>
  <short>
    <title>A Close Shave</title>
    <character>Wallace</character>
    <character>Grommit</character>
    <character>Shawn</character>
    <character>Wendolene</character>
  </short>
</animations>
```

The ability to select by *intersection* would allow you to easily locate all short anima-tions in which Wallace, Grommit, and Wendolene appeared. The ability to select by *difference* would allow you to easily locate all films in which Grommit but not Feath-ers McGraw (The Penguin) appeared. According to the XPath 2.0 WD released in April 2002, the intersection might be accomplished as follows:

```
short[character = 'Wallace'] intersect
  short[character = 'Grommit'] intersect
  short[character = 'Wendolene']
```

The difference operation would be achieved using a special except operator:

```
short[character = 'Grommit'] except
  short[character = 'Feathers McGraw (The Penguin)']
```

### Support the unary plus operator (1.7)

This requirement, if satisfied in XPath 2.0, will simply correct what to my mind is an oversight in XPath 1.0: the failure to recognize a leading + sign as a legitimate por-tion of a numeric value. (A value of -2.0 is already recognized as numeric; +2.0, though, is read as a string—or more exactly, if you pass it to the number( ) function, the result returned is the special NaN value.)

### Simplify string replacement (2.4.1)

I mentioned earlier in this chapter a cardinal limitation of the translate( ) string function: it permits you to replace characters only on a one-by-one basis. (Or, if the third argument is shorter than the second, to *remove* single characters.) This con-stantly frustrates newcomers to XPath, who'd like (along with the rest of us!) to be able to replace single characters with multiples, or vice versa.

As a simple example, consider an XML document of data concerning a company's employees. Such applications frequently make heavy use of single-character codes to represent different employee statuses (full- versus part-time and temporary versus permanent), job categories, and so on. Under XPath 2.0, there's a new replace() function whose syntax is (the slightly scary-looking):

```
replace(string1?, string2?, string3)
```

Here's what the April 2002 WD of the XQuery 1.0/XPath 2.0 Functions and Operators spec says about this function:

> Returns the value of [string1] in which every substring of the value of [string1] that is matched by the regular expression that is the value of [string2], has been replaced by a copy of the value of [string3].

Teased apart into something a little less convoluted (albeit less concise), this says to pass replace() the following arguments:

- string1 is the entire string to be scanned for text to be replaced.
- string2 represents the value to be located within string1. (Note that this is a regular expression, and hence can use various special characters such as an asterisk to represent "any number of any characters.")
- string3 represents the value with which to replace every occurrence, within string1, of string2.

Thus, in our hypothetical employee-information application, we might encounter XPath expressions such as:

```
replace(emp_status, "T", "Temporary Worker")
```

This evaluates the emp_status child of the context node, returning a string in which the single character "T" is replaced with the string "Temporary Worker."

### Simplify string padding (2.4.2)

The issue here is that in many applications, it's useful to know that a particular string always has a length of N characters (or possibly more). If the string is shorter, it should be padded with, for example, spaces or leading zeros.

Note that it's possible to do this kind of string manipulation with XSLT. But it's non-intuitive and, in any case, of no use if an XPointer or XQuery expression requires that the returned string have a particular length.

### Simplify string case conversions (2.4.3)

As with the preceding "should" requirement, there already exists a way to achieve this objective: use the translate() function, specifying the entire uppercase alphabet as the second argument and the lowercase equivalents as the third (or vice versa, if trying to force a string to uppercase). Just as with the preceding requirement, though, it would be much simpler to have a pair of functions—call them upper() and lower(), perhaps—to achieve the same result more simply and intuitively (to say nothing of its virtues in supporting i18n goals!).

### Support aggregation functions over collection-valued expressions (2.5)

Under XPath 1.0, as you know, some functions operate across all members of a node-set. For example:

```
sum(price)
```

This expression totals up the values of all price children of the context node, returning the resulting sum. What you can't do with XPath 1.0, though, is pass to such an aggregation function even a simple, non-node-set *expression*. Assume what you're after isn't a simple sum of a single node-set, but a sum of some set of calculated values. For example:

```
sum(unit_price *qty)
```

You can't do this because the sum( ) function operates only on arguments of the node-set data type—and whatever else it may be, the expression unit_price * qty is definitely not a node-set. This kind of arbitrary (in truth, artificial) limitation on aggregation functions (including any new ones to be added, such as min( ) and max( )) will be lifted if this requirement makes its way into the final version of the XPath 2.0 spec.

### Add a "list" data type (4.4)

Some computer languages, such as Python, include not only simple data types such as Boolean and string, but also a list data type. As the name implies, a list is a sequence of individual data objects that can be treated, alternatively, as a sequence or as separate items, depending on the need.

XPath 2.0 is expected to include a list data type as well. This will simplify the manipulation of such common XML "plural attribute types" as NMTOKENS and IDREFS. It will also permit XPath 2.0 to handle user-defined lists, locate the first or last item in the list, return the range of integers between two adjacent list members, and so on.

### Select elements/attributes based on an explicit XML Schema type (5.1)

Beginning with requirement 5.1, the XPath 2.0 Requirements document trails off into a final set of four SHOULDs, all having to do with support for XML Schema-defined documents.

This requirement in particular seems both very important and very likely to make an appearance in XPath 2.0 in its final form. It will allow a location path to select elements and attributes not on the basis of their values, but on the basis of the *types* of their values. And note that by "type," the selection criteria won't be limited just to simple types such as integer, Boolean, URI, and so on. For instance, with XML Schema you can build up application-specific "type molecules" from the many simple types predefined by the standard. Thus, you could define an ISBN complex type, made up of the various pieces in a full ISBN (each of which would have a simple type like integer or string). Then, with XPath 2.0, you could easily extract all elements and/or attributes of this ISBN type.

### Select elements/attributes based on an XML Schema type hierarchy (5.2)

Not only does XML Schema allow for building application-specific types from simple data types; it allows the designer to build types based on *other* types. (That is, there's a hierarchy of content types analogous to the hierarchy of content nodes in the document tree.) An Address type, for example, might be derived from a Street type or City type. Satisfying this requirement would allow you to locate content of any "subtype" descended from a higher-order one and to locate any content of higher-order type(s) derived from a given subtype.

### Select elements based on XML Schema substitution groups (5.3)

XML Schema provides a feature called substitution groups as a means whereby you can declare a generic element type, such as (say) paragraph, and then declare (in this case) specific kinds of paragraph elements: narrative, blockquote, and so on. The specific element types can be assigned to substitution groups, such that anywhere in an instance document where a paragraph can appear, so can one of the specific types in the substitution group.

Given that freedom, this requirement says that XPath 2.0 should be able to easily select the generic paragraph element *as well as* any member of its substitution group and perhaps simply to test whether a given element is a member of the substitution group for paragraph.

### Support lookups based on XML Schema unique constraints and keys (5.4)

As you already know, you can do a simple lookup of any ID-typed element in XPath 1.0, using the id( ) node-set function.

 XSLT goes a step further, allowing you to construct an index for and then reference any element, even with nonunique values, using a key( ) function.

XML Schema permits multipart keys to be assigned to elements. For instance, in a simple CD-catalog application, the artist's name alone (except in the case of "one-hit wonders") isn't sufficient to locate a particular CD—and in many cases, the CD's title alone wouldn't be enough. But you could define a CDKey key, for example, made up of the Artist and Title elements. Under XPath 2.0, you could then get ID-attribute-like indexing into the document simply by invoking (say) an XPath index( ) function, passing it the name of the key and the value sought:

```
index("CDKey", concat("Talking Heads", "Stop Making Sense"))
```

(Again, I emphasize that the name of this function is speculative—which is to say, purely a product of my imagination. Don't look for it in the XPath 2.0 spec!)

# CHAPTER 7

# XPointer Background

This chapter introduces the concepts and language of the XPointer 1.0 family of specifications. XPointer 1.0 Candidate Recommendation was a single document in September 2001 but was fragmented into a group of smaller specifications in July 2002. Most of these specifications were published as Last Call Working Drafts and are likely to move forward through the W3C process without significant changes, though the largest of them, the XPointer xpointer() Scheme, may have a longer process ahead.

To quickly rehash some of the material covered in Chapter 1, the purpose of the XPointer specifications is to provide a formal mechanism for identifying fragments of an XML document. This is accomplished, just as it was with (X)HTML, by appending to a standard URI a pound sign/hash character, #, followed by the fragment identifier itself—the XPointer, in this case. Just as with "regular" URIs, a URI including an XPointer may be relative instead of absolute even beginning with the #. In such cases, what precedes the # still exists after a fashion; it's implied, based on the context in which the URI is found.

The latest version of XPointer includes four specifications:

- XPointer Framework (*http://www.w3.org/TR/xptr-framework/*)
- XPointer xmlns() Scheme (*http://www.w3.org/TR/xptr-xmlns/*)
- XPointer element() Scheme (*http://www.w3.org/TR/xptr-element/*)
- XPointer xpointer() Scheme (*http://www.w3.org/TR/xptr-xpointer/*)

The Framework provides a foundation describing how XPointer works as a whole and defines the simplest kind of XPointer: a shorthand pointer. The other specifications define particular pieces of more complex XPointers, providing support for XML namespaces (xmlns), a simple element-structure pointer (element), and the full-strength XPath-based approach of the original XPointer work (xpointer).

Considering all the ground it has to cover, the XPath 1.0 Recommendation (the subject of the first part of this book) is a remarkably concise document (the hardcopy from my laser printer clocks it at a mere 29 pages). The XPointer 1.0 specifications, by contrast, seem on their face to be tackling a much simpler subject but in many more pages—42, to be exact, 22 of which cover just the xpointer( ) scheme. Why the disparity?

XPointer's subject matter is not self-contained but rather spills over into and from other areas of Internet technology. First, of course, there's the need to describe its relationship with XPath. Second, XPointers can be used in XLink documents, so that interface must also be satisfied. Third, there's some duplication of information. And finally, using XPointers requires considering certain standards that are the domain not of the W3C but of the Internet Engineering Task Force (IETF): media types.

## XPointer and Media types

The general purpose of any low-level hyperlinking standard, such as XPointer, is the location and retrieval of content to be found at some location other than that of the *reference* to the content. Most such standards confine themselves to content of a particular type; for instance, an XHTML document's a (anchor) elements can easily locate (X)HTML content but not a bookmark in a Microsoft Word document. XPointer is designed expressly to locate fragments of XML documents' content.

Now, over the Internet, content types—*media types*—are identified not by such more or less obvious cues as filename extensions or, for that matter, even the nature of the content itself (e.g., "This document begins with an XML declaration, therefore, it must be an XML document"). Rather, what determines the media type of a given resource is *how the resource is delivered over the network by its server*. If a server broadcasts a stream of what looks like XHTML but declares it to be mere text, an application receiving that stream is supposed to treat it as text.

Of course, nothing is ever that simple. In the first place, how a given data stream is served depends on the proper configuration—by an imperfect human server administrator—of the server itself. If that person hasn't instructed the server how to serve an XHTML document, for instance, it may be transmitted to the network not as XHTML but as plain text.

At the other end of the pipe, client applications bear the burden of interpreting media types "correctly," regardless of how "correctly" they're being served. A browser vendor's product, in theory, should recognize as (X)HTML only documents that are being served as such and not jump to conclusions based on possibly faulty guesswork about the filename extension, whether the first character is a left angle bracket, and so on. This kind of guesswork both contributes to the bloated size of client software and risks subverting the intention of the resource's nominal "owner," the server. (On the other hand, of course, it also makes clients such as web browsers seem more robust than they might otherwise.)

For details about working with XML media types, see the IETF Request for Comment (RFC) 3023 at *http://www.ietf.org/rfc/rfc3023*. Note that this RFC does not require the use of XPointers to locate XML fragments, although it does mention the W3C work in progress.

Media types are commonly identified in two parts, the top-level type and the subtype, separated by a slash. The top-level type is the general class of data being delivered; the subtype, the specific form of that class of data.

In the case of the XML resources that XPointer can locate, the XPointer Framework specification says that XPointer addresses documents of any of the following four media types: text/xml, application/xml, text/xml-external-parsed-entity, and application/xml-external-parsed-entity. As a general rule, the text top-level media types identify resources that in normal everyday use, would be readable by humans; application media types identify resources meant to be processed by software.

RFC 3023 recommends the use of application media types rather than text for serving XML, in the absence of reasons to the contrary. If the specific subtype—xml or xml-external-parsed-entity, in this case—is unknown to the client application, it will be treated in a generic manner. Thus, human readers of an XML document served as text over the Web, for example, might be treated to a stream of angle brackets, PIs, and the like. Not many such readers would welcome this kind of display.

(Note that the RFC also defines a fifth XML media type, application/xml-dtd, for serving and identifying DTD-type entities. XPointers into DTDs are not possible.)

# Some Definitions

The XPointer specifications, like most W3C documents, are very careful to use terminology in well-constrained ways. This can lead to confusion, ironically, because some of these terms are used in loose form in everyday English. That said, let's look at some of the most important such terms as they appear in the standard.

## Resource

Unlike some of the rest of the terms in this section, "resource" is not defined directly. Instead, under its definition of subresources, the previous version of the XPointer spec said, "...the whole resource being referred to is an XML document or external parsed entity."[*] That is, a resource is the entity within which some specific content resides.

---

[*] An "external parsed entity," unlike an XML document, need not be well-formed. In particular, it may lack a single root element. These quasi-documents are often used for such purposes as holding boilerplate text. They're meaningful—and parseable—only when included (using external entity references) within containing documents.

Note that XPointer uses "resource" rather differently than the way it's used in "Uniform Resource Identifier"—the familiar URI of the Web. The authoritative reference for URIs is IETF RFC 2396 ("Uniform Resource Identifiers (URI): Generic Syntax," located at *http://www.ietf.org/rfc/rfc2396.txt*), which defines the term in this way (emphasis added):

> A resource can be anything that has identity. Familiar examples include an electronic document, an image, a service (e.g., "today's weather report for Los Angeles"), and a collection of other resources. Not all resources are network "retrievable"; e.g., human beings, corporations, and bound books in a library can also be considered resources.
>
> The resource is *the conceptual mapping to an entity or set of entities, not necessarily the entity that corresponds to that mapping* at any particular instance in time. Thus, a resource can remain constant even when its content—the entities to which it currently corresponds—changes over time, provided that the conceptual mapping is not changed in the process.

Thus, in a URI such as *http://www.example.org/index.html*, the resource is not the document so pointed to but the address that points to it. In practice, XPointer works differently: if a given XPointer is to work at all, it must be applied to a portion of a *particular* XML document, not just to the address of whatever document happens to be there at the time. (On the other hand, one might be excused for wishing that a resource would always be a resource, regardless of the context in which she encounters the term.)

## Subresource

A subresource is the specific fragment of content identified by the XPointer. This may, but will almost never, be an entire document; it's far more likely, because XPointer uses XPath, that the subresource in question will be a single element, or an attribute, or some other (perhaps more complex) node-set. (As you'll see in a moment, however, XPointer expands on XPath's notion of node-sets, in the form of *location-sets*.)

## Location

If the subresource is the *what*—the content—identified by an XPointer, the location is the *where*.

(I wouldn't be surprised to see the terms subresource and location being used interchangeably, although this would make purists crazy. If I'm standing at a stove preparing a meal and ask you to "hand me that can," I of course hope you will not *empty* the can first—that you will deliver it to me contents and all. In the same way, people exchanging URIs often say that someone "sent me a web page"... even though, if anything, they are being sent *to* the page rather than the other way around.)

The spec makes an analogy between the term "node" as used in XPath and the term "location" as used in XPointer. Why then do we need a new term? Because XPointer can handle (via XPath) not only nodes, but two other forms of addressing: points and ranges. Both of these terms are discussed in the sections that follow.

## Location-set

As an XPointer location is to an XPath node, an XPointer location-set is to an XPath node-set. That is, a location-set is the complete list of locations identified by an XPointer. (And as in the XPath counterparts, if an XPointer has only a single location, it might just as well be considered a location-set containing only a single member.)

Note that the addition of the point and range location types requires enhancing the concept of document order established by XPath. This subject is addressed further in Chapter 9.

## Point

A *point* in XPointer terms is the abstract location between two adjacent chunks of text content. Figure 7-1 illustrates.

```
<phrase>

    <gerund>Being</gerund>
              ▲
    <preposition>in</preposition>

    <article>the</article>

    <noun><emph>prime</emph></noun>
              ▲
    <preposition>of</preposition>

    <possessive>my</possessive>
              ▲
    <noun>senility</noun>

</phrase>
```

*Figure 7-1. Point-type locations*

Ignoring the newline characters and other whitespace added for legibility, Figure 7-1 highlights the following point-type locations (among many others present in the document):

- Immediately following the gerund element's start tag (before the capital B)
- Immediately following the emph element's start tag (before the p in prime)
- Between the m and y in my

Point-type locations also exist at the interstices between the element boundaries. For instance, although not highlighted in Figure 7-1, there's a point-type location following the close of the gerund element. Just as important, though, are the places where there are no point-type locations at all. For instance, there is no point-type location between any adjacent characters in the name of an element in the element's start tag.

## Range

An XPointer range is the entire block of text content bounded by two points. In Figure 7-1, each individual word in the document exists in a range between the points immediately following and preceding the containing element's start and end tags, respectively. Each individual character also exists in its own range (the points in question immediately precede and follow the character). Note that a point alone doesn't "contain" anything; it must be paired in a range with another point first.

There's no particular requirement that a range be limited to a single containing element. For instance, you could establish a range by fixing one point before the p in prime and another point after the n in senility. The resulting range (again, ignoring whitespace) would be primeofmysen.

## Points and Ranges: Flattening the Logical Hierarchy

One interesting aspect of these two XPointer location types, as opposed to the node types available under XPath, is that points and ranges more closely reflect a document's physical characteristics, not its logical or structural ones. There's no hierarchical containment going on in a range (except in the limited sense of "text contained within two points").

This difference is reflected in the common applications to which ranges and points might be put to use. In particular, they're useful as a way of formally expressing the physical act of selecting text, such as with a mouse or with keyboard commands. XPath nodes, on the other hand—while they of course are defined by a given document's physical characteristics, sequences of characters, and such—are purely logical constructs with no physical user-interface counterparts.

On the other hand, because points can't be located within certain portions of the markup (such as in element names), a range can't span just *any* text physically present in the document—as if you had the source code open in a text editor. What you can select is still constrained by certain features of the logical node tree.

You'll learn much more about points and ranges in the rest of this chapter and the two that follow, especially Chapter 9.

# The Framework

The XPointer Framework provides a basic set of rules for creating fragment identifiers. The original XPointer specifications defined a single set of rules for processing XPointers, though later versions offered two levels of conformance. The new framework takes a different approach, defining a more extensible system with a tiny core and an extensible scheme mechanism.

Rather than having to conform to a particular set of rules about how to identify fragments, XPointer processors now have to identify which schemes they support, and then deal with conformance at the scheme level. Error handling has also been generalized, with some syntax errors defined at the Framework level and other errors defined in particular schemes.

The W3C has provided three schemes beyond the XPointer Framework. One of these schemes, xmlns( ), is designed to provide namespace context for other schemes, effectively declaring namespaces for use in other parts of the XPointer. The element( ) scheme can be used to describe locations inside documents by walking the document tree from the root element (or from an ID value in the document) to the desired location. The most ambitious of the schemes, the xpointer( ) scheme, builds on XPath to create a mechanism for locating content that extends XPath's node-based mechanisms to support locations that cross node boundaries.

An xpath( ) scheme that stuck to XPath 1.0 might also be useful, but the W3C hasn't defined such a scheme, preferring to use xpointer( ) for that.

All XPointer processors will have to support the shorthand pointer syntax, but beyond that, developers will have to know what kind of XPointer processor their documents are going to face.

# Error Types

Like any application working on information on the Web, XPointers face a number of potential error conditions. The XPointer specifications describe a variety of errors, but they all fall into the three rough categories.

## Syntax Errors

Syntax errors are to an XPointer processor what well-formedness errors are to an XML processor—or, indeed, what syntax errors are to the compiler of a traditional programming language: they violate the rules of the language itself. In XPointer as in other languages meant for machine processing, when the standard says "A given left parenthesis must be balanced by a right parenthesis and vice versa," it means just that. You can't "balance" a left parenthesis with a square bracket, an asterisk, or the digit 9. If an XPointer fails syntactically, it doesn't make any difference if it falls into one of the other error classifications—the processor won't even be able to figure it out. Thus, syntax errors might be considered the most "catastrophic" and unrecoverable sort of XPointer error.

## Resource Errors

Once an XPointer passes muster syntactically, it's still not out of the woods as a "valid" XPointer. At this point, considering the XPointer as a simple string of characters—which is, after all, what a processor does when it verifies an XPointer's syntax—gives way to determining its usefulness for XPointer's stated purpose: locating some portion(s) of an XML-based document. When the document in question—the resource itself—doesn't exist, the processor must report a resource error to the controlling application.

## Subresource Errors

A subresource error, on the other hand, must be reported when a given XPointer identifies a specific subresource that doesn't exist—even though the document itself does. For example, consider this document:

```
<villain>
    <name>Blofeld</name>
    <film>Thunderball</film>
</villain>
```

A syntactically correct XPointer (one passing the syntax-error check) could point, correctly, to this document itself (and therefore pass the resource-error check); but if the XPath expression built into the XPointer referred to some descendant of the root element named, say, evil_world_dominaton_plan, the processor would report a subresource error. That is, the resource as a whole exists but not the particular portion of the resource identified by the XPointer.

Note in particular that while an empty node-set is perfectly legitimate in pure XPath terms—XPath allows for such a thing—an empty node-set *is* an XPointer error, called a "failure" by the XPointer Framework.

# Encoding and Escaping Characters in XPointer

As you know, authoring any XML document requires care not to confuse the XML processor. Ampersands must be escaped using the &amp; entity reference, for instance, and greater-than symbols with &gt;. Documents containing XPointers have an additional burden imposed on them, even when the XPointers in question are used in some context other than an XML document: because an XPointer is meant to be included as a part of a URI, it must adhere to the special escaping rules that pertain to that Internet standard as well.

## Characters Significant to XPointer Itself

A couple of characters have special significance to the XPointer standard itself. The first of these is the parenthesis, which in XPointer (as in other languages) is always expected to appear in left/right pairs. Under certain (and probably extremely rare) circumstances, you may need to use a parenthesis as a literal character in an XPointer, unbalanced by the opposite parenthesis. In this case, you escape the parenthesis by prefixing it with a circumflex character, ^. Thus, a literal left or right parenthesis would be legally represented by ^( or ^), respectively.

The second XPointer-significant character, therefore, is the circumflex itself. To escape a circumflex—that is, to cause the processor to recognize the character as a literal, not as an escaping character—prefix it with *another* circumflex. Thus, a literal circumflex can appear in an XPointer as ^^. All other uses of the circumflex character in an XPointer are illegal, resulting in a syntax error.

This is not to say, of course, that a literal circumflex may not be used elsewhere in an instance document. Remember that this constraint applies only to a circumflex *within* an XPointer.

## URI-Significant Characters

It's common for an Internet address—a URI—to include somewhere within it certain special characters such as spaces, percent signs, and so on. Web browsers and other Internet applications may or may not choke on these special characters. But if they follow the URI standard, they're *supposed* to choke; this standard requires that such characters in a URI be escaped, using a percent sign and the Unicode value for the character.

For instance, consider the following URI:

```
http://my.dot.com/my documents/index.html
```

The space between my and documents is supposed to be escaped, using the hexadecimal Unicode value for the space character, so its correct form is:

```
http://my.dot.com/my%20documents/index.html
```

Like other standards built on the Internet's basic linking infrastructure, XPointer follows the rules established for URIs—including, in this case, the rules for escaping special characters. These rules (as well as the others for URIs) are laid out in two IETF RFCs, numbers 2396 and 2372, which you can find at *http://www.ietf.org/rfc/rfc2396.txt* and *http://www.ietf.org/rfc/rfc2732.txt*, respectively.

### URIs versus IURIs

The old XPointer 1.0 spec distinguished between plain-old garden-variety URIs and Internationalized URIs, (IURIs). An ordinary URI is limited to ASCII characters; an IURI may consist of *any* characters directly representable via Unicode. For instance, currently the official home page of the President of the French Republic (currently Jacques Chirac) is *http://www.elysee.fr/pres/*. All the characters in that URI are ASCII and so it's both a legal URI and a legal IURI. If we were using an IURI-aware application, though, it might be desirable to employ a more correctly French version of the URI: *http://www.elysee.fr/prés/*. The presence of the é character here is what makes the address both an illegal URI and a legal IURI.

In an IURI, the only difficulty occurs when the address itself includes a literal percent sign. In this case, escape the percent (%) with %25. (25 is the hexadecimal Unicode value for the percent sign.)

The current XPointer Framework doesn't mention IURIs, but this issue is likely to reappear.

## Characters in XML Documents

Finally, of course, XPointer—being often used in XML documents—is no exception to the general rules of XML well-formedness. If your XPointer appears in an XML document and includes special XML-significant literal characters, such as greater-than signs or ampersands, you must escape them with standard XML entity references (such as &gt; and &amp;, respectively). Also remember that you must escape, with character entity references, any character(s) in the XPointer that can't be expressed in your instance document's own encoding; if you're working in a U.S.-ASCII-encoded document, therefore, you have to escape additional characters in the ISO-8859 encoding. In this scenario, for example, you'd have to escape Á (capital A with an acute accent) as either &#xc1; (hexadecimal form) or &#193; (decimal form).

## Progressive Escaping

XPointer specifications often use syntax that cannot be used directly in a URL. To implement them, you must use a prodecure called *progressive escaping*. This term is defined nowhere in the spec; but from the context, it clearly refers to how you, an XPointer-using document author, might apply successive levels of the above escaping types to a XPointer.

1. Start with the completely unescaped form. You might consider this to be the plain-text, common-sense version.

2. Escape any XPointer-significant characters meant to be interpreted as literals— that is, any parentheses or circumflexes.

3. Escape any percent signs in the URI portion of the XPointer, to ensure a legal IURI. (This may not be necessary if XPointer specifications continue to ignore IURIs.)

4. If the XPointer appears in an XML document, escape any XML-significant characters meant to be interpreted as literals, such as ampersands, double quotation marks, and so on.

5. Escape the entity-reference XML escaping forms as URI escaping forms, for example, replace &quot; with %22.

To repeat, this progressive-escaping mechanism does *not* suggest that this stack of escaping sieves is to be implemented in an XPointer processor: it's meant to make an XPointer acceptable to such a processor in the first place. On the processing side, each successive application layer—XML, the HTTP-aware application, and XPointer itself—unescapes the XPointer in reverse order, from the outside in as it were.

### Progressive escaping: a (perverse) example

Showing you an example of progressive escaping in practice is, to put it mildly, a challenge at this point. In the first place, you don't yet know enough (if anything) about XPointer syntax. Second, you seldom will have to pass even a full-blown URI, including an XPointer, through all five steps.

Still, you do already know something about XPointers: they can include XPath expressions. So let's imagine you're working on some kind of text-processing application and need to construct an XPointer to be used in an XML document; the XPointer includes the following (unescaped) XPath expression:

```
translate(., "()%&^", "[]@v")
```

This function call scans the string-value of the context node (that's the . used as the first argument) for any of the characters in the second argument, if it finds any of those characters, the function replaces it with the corresponding character in the third argument. So a left parenthesis is replaced with a left square bracket, a percent sign with @, and so on.

In this form, the XPath expression has been subject only to step 1 of all those required above: it's in its "natural language" form (well, as such things go). Now let's walk through the expression and fix it up according to the remaining steps in progressive escaping, so it can be used in an XPointer included in a URI.

2. *Escaping XPointer-significant characters.* There are two parentheses and a single circumflex in the XPath expression. To avoid confusing the XPointer processor downstream somewhere, you have to escape these XPointer-significant characters. Do this by preceding them with circumflexes:

```
translate(., "^(^)%&^^", "[]@v")
```

Note, by the way, that the parentheses enclosing the translate() function's arguments do not require escaping, since these are used in a "natural" way.

3. *Escaping IURI-forbidden characters.* Our XPath expression has only one percent sign in it, but that's sufficient to choke a processor expecting a valid *Internationalized* URI. To be sure the processor treats the literal percent sign as such, it must be escaped using an entity reference:

```
translate(., "^(^)%25&^^", "[]@v")
```

4. *Escaping XML-significant characters.* The ampersand in the first argument and the quotation marks enclosing the function's arguments are the only characters requiring escaping for XML's purposes. Thus:

```
translate(., &quot;^(^)%25&amp;^^&quot;, &quot;[]@v&quot;)
```

5. *Escaping URI-forbidden characters.* Finally, all spaces and any remaining special characters need to be "entitized" in the URI to be acceptable to a URI-aware processor. The expression to this point includes two spaces and the &quot; and &amp; entity references, all of which must be escaped. Furthermore, the expression includes a number of other special characters that are illegal in URIs in their unescaped form: the very circumflexes we so carefully escaped, in step 3. Thus, after passing it through this last step in progressive escaping, we have our final, fully escaped (although, granted, completely incomprehensible) expression:

```
translate(.,%20%22%5E(%5E)%25%26%5E%5E%22,%20%22[]@v%22)
```

This is nearly as painful to look at as it was to construct. Just remember that when and if the XPointer specifications make it to full Recommendation status, the XPointer-constructing toolkit (source code editors, automatic code generators, etc.) will certainly obviate the need to build these monstrosities by hand.

(One final caveat: while this example has shown progressive escaping applied to the XPointer portion of a URI, remember that steps 2 through 5 must be taken for special characters in the rest of the URI as well.)

 The notion of progressive escaping was covered at some length in the previous version of the XPointer spec but removed in the versions published July 10, 2002. Nonetheless, its an important concept, and one that may find its way back into the final XPointer Recommendations.

# CHAPTER 8

# XPointer Syntax

Like XPath, XPointer is not in itself an XML vocabulary. Rather, it's meant to be used within the markup in XML documents—most often in XLink or XLink-like situations requiring a URI. This chapter covers the details of coding the various XPointer forms. There are two approaches to defining XPointers as described in the XPointer Framework. *Shorthand pointers* use a very brief syntax, while *scheme-based XPointers* use a more complex syntax composed of pointer parts.

## Shorthand Pointers

In XHTML hyperlinking, as you know, you can locate a subresource using a combination of a named anchor (the <a name="**mybookmark**"/> sort of tag) and a normal anchor (<a href="**#mybookmark**">...). Notwithstanding the limitations of XHTML subresource hyperlinking, the XPointer spec's authors recognized its principal value: simplicity. Thus, they carried it forward into XPointer, enhanced slightly for the new standard's use with XML documents of any vocabulary. This form of an XPointer is called a shorthand pointer; it includes neither scheme nor XPath expression, just the "name" of the target resource:

> *name*

In an XPointer, as in an XHTML fragment identifier, the pound sign/hash mark, #, is not itself part of the XPointer or other fragment identifier. It merely serves to delimit the fragment from the full URI preceding it. The section "Using XPointers in a URI" at the end of this chapter addresses this issue more fully.

The value of *name* is the value of an ID-type attribute assigned to some element in the target resource. Thus, the shorthand form is in essence a shortcut for the longer XPointer form:

> xpointer(id("*name*"))

Consider the following simple XML document:

```
<gaming_platforms currency="sadly-outdated">
  <gaming_platform id="A">Atari</gaming_platform>
```

```
        <gaming_platform id="S">Sega</gaming_platform>
        <gaming_platform id="SN">Super Nintendo</gaming_platform>
        <gaming_platform id="P">Pong</gaming_platform>
    </gaming_platforms>
```

Assuming the id attributes are in fact ID-*type* attributes, therefore, you could locate the Pong gaming_platform element with this simple XPointer:

```
    P
```

Chapter 4 described how the XPath id() function works, how it depends on ID attributes having been declared in DTDs, and how it depends on those DTDs having been processed. XPointer's shorthand pointers have the same set of issues, but the XPointer Framework specification adds one more: in addition to IDs defined in XML 1.0 DTDs, it recognizes IDs defined in the W3C's XML Schema vocabulary.

In DTDs, IDs are pretty simple. An ID is plainly identified as an attribute of type ID. The only real problem with IDs is the requirement that a DTD be provided and processed. XML Schema offers a number of different options, including IDs provided as child attributes. This means that, if XML Schema processing took place and a Post-Schema Validation Infoset (PSVI) is available, shorthand pointers must look for IDs in that PSVI.

> For more on how XML Schema defines and uses IDs, see *XML Schema*, by Eric van der Vlist (O'Reilly).

Schema-aware ID processing is also specified for the element() scheme, but is not required for the xpointer() scheme, most likely because it builds on XPath 1.0, which is not XML Schema-aware.

# Scheme-Based XPointer Syntax

Scheme-based XPointers follow this general form:

```
    scheme(schemedata)...
```

The ellipsis (...) indicates that XPointers can be chained together in sequence. Each scheme/schemedata item in the chain is referred to as a pointer part; thus, some XPointers consist of just a single pointer part and some consist of multiple pointer parts. When multiple pointer parts are used, they may be delimited from one another with optional whitespace. You'll see more information about these chains of pointers in the section "Multiple Pointer Parts."

## The Scheme

The *scheme* of a pointer part functions something like the protocol of a URI (such as http:, ftp:, gopher:, and so on). Its purpose, said the previous draft of the spec, is to

---

"[identify] the particular notation" used by the XPointer; you'll probably agree this isn't an especially descriptive definition. From the examples provided in the spec, though, we can come up with a simple definition like: the scheme tells us what kind of pointer part we're dealing with.

A pointer part is typically one of two predefined kinds, denoted by three predefined schemes:

- A scheme of xpointer—easily the most common scheme—says that this pointer part is to be used in XPointer's typical manner: to identify some portion of an XML document of interest.
- A scheme of element indicates that this pointer part will identify a portion of an XML document using a "child sequence" notation for walking the document tree.
- A scheme of xmlns marks this pointer part as a prelude to the pointer parts that follow. By itself, it doesn't locate any resource at all; it simply declares a namespace context in which succeeding pointer parts (within the same scheme-based XPointer) are to be evaluated. More information on xmlns-type schemes appears later in this chapter.

You may also use custom schemes instead of these three predefined kinds. More information on this option is found in the section "Custom Schemes" later in this chapter.

## The schemedata

The schemedata contents of pointer parts vary with their schemes, and the XPointer Framework itself does very little to constrain them. Each scheme specification provides its own set of rules describing how its schemedata is to be interpreted.

## Contents of the xmlns() Scheme

When the scheme of a pointer part is xmlns, the expr_or_decl declares the namespace associated with a particular namespace prefix used in subsequent pointer parts. This namespace declaration takes the form:

```
prefix=namespaceURI
```

For instance:

```
xmlns(xsl=http://www.w3.org/1999/XSL/Transform) [subsequent pointer parts]
```

asserts that the namespace prefix xsl: appearing in the rest of the multipart XPointer is to be associated with the indicated namespace URI (that is, in this case, the namespace for XSLT elements and attributes).

## Contents of the element( ) Scheme

You can locate content without knowing anything at all about the specific named nodes of a target resource. This XPointer form, which uses the element( ) scheme and schemedata known as child sequences, uses a conventional tree-navigation syntax to locate the *n*th child of each succeeding level in the document.

Consider the gaming-platform document again:

```
<gaming_platforms currency="sadly-outdated">
    <gaming_platform id="A">Atari</gaming_platform>
    <gaming_platform id="S">Sega</gaming_platform>
    <gaming_platform id="SN">Super Nintendo</gaming_platform>
    <gaming_platform id="P">Pong</gaming_platform>
</gaming_platforms>
```

To locate the Sega gaming_platform element, aside from any other options you can use the element( ) scheme:

```
element(/1/2)
```

This simply directs the processor to walk the tree, getting the first child (that is, the root gaming_platforms element) of the root node, and then selecting that child's second child (the Sega gaming_platform element).

Note a few things about XPointers built using the element( ) scheme. First, they can locate elements only; all other "children" (such as PIs contained within the element's start and end tags) are effectively invisible. Second—barring some way of resetting the context in which the child sequence is to be evaluated—the very first integer in a child sequence will nearly always be 1; this follows from XML's well-formedness requirement that a document have no more than one root element.

 As the XPointer spec mentions, while a well-formed XML document must have only one root element, XPointer can be used for locating content in possibly non-well-formed external unparsed entities as well. such entities may have multiple "root" elements, leading to the possibility of a child sequence such as:

```
/12/3/7
```

Third, although it may not be as obvious as with shorthand pointers, child sequences are also shortcuts for scheme-based XPointers. To locate the Sega gaming_platform element as described above, using element(/1/2) is effectively an abbreviated form of the scheme-based XPointer:

```
xpointer(/*[position()=1]/*[position( )=2])
```

or, more simply:

```
xpointer(/*[1]/*[2])
```

Finally, child sequences are both robust (the simplest ones won't break at all) and fragile (when they break, they're liable to break in more or less subtle and difficult-to-diagnose ways).

To understand this last point, consider an XML document such as the following:

```
<books>
  <book>
    <title>XML in a Nutshell</title>
    <author>Harold &amp; Means</author>
  </book>
  <book>
    <title>DocBook: The Definitive Guide</title>
    <author>Walsh &amp; Muellner</author>
  </book>
  <book>
    <title>Learning XML</title>
    <author>Ray</author>
  </book>
  <book>
    <title>HTML &amp; XHTML: The Definitive Guide</title>
    <author>Musciano &amp; Kennedy</author>
  </book>
  <book>
    <title>Building Oracle XML Applications</title>
    <author>Muench</author>
  </book>
</books>
```

Using a child sequence, we could construct an XPointer to the author of the last book, which would look as follows:

```
element(/1/5/2)
```

This locates the second child of the fifth child of the first child of the root node. Note the right-to-left reading of the child sequence. This is often the simplest way to express in everyday language what a child sequence points to. Thus, this child sequence is functionally equivalent to an XPointer using the more robust xpointer( ) scheme, such as:

```
xpointer(//author[../title = "Building Oracle XML Applications"])
```

If, however, the document changes—particularly with the addition or removal of book elements—the child sequence will now point to a different author element or, worse, return an empty location-set altogether. The xpointer( ) approach, on the other hand, continues to point to the author of that book as long as a book with that title exists in the document, regardless of where in the document it is.

(Whether this is desirable, of course, depends on your application's specific needs. Personally, I'm much more comfortable knowing *what* I'm pointing to than I am knowing *where* it's supposed to be.)

Potential fragility aside, child sequences feature what can be a killer advantage: a processor can simply read only as much of a document as it needs to locate the desired node. Relying on loading the entire document—as other kinds of XPointers must—can make processing very large documents practically infeasible.

## Combining Names and Child Sequences

Because shorthand pointers—at least, assuming liberal use of ID-type attributes—are so convenient and simple, XPointer provides an option that combines them with child sequences. These open using the same rules for connecting names to ID values as shorthand pointers, followed by a child sequence starting at the element so identified.

Assume the following XML fragment is coded in a vocabulary in which each attribute named id has been declared as an ID-type attribute:

```
...
<brewery id="petes">
   <brew>
      <name>Wicked Ale</name>
      <alc_pct>5.3</alc_pct>
      <calories>174</calories>
      <carbs>17.7</carbs>
      <plato>13.65</plato>
   </brew>
   <brew>
      <name>Strawberry Blonde</name>
      <alc_pct>5.0</alc_pct>
      <calories>160</calories>
      <carbs>13.6</carbs>
      <plato>12.05</plato>
   </brew>
   <brew>
      <name>Helles Lager</name>
      <alc_pct>5.0</alc_pct>
      <calories>163</calories>
      <carbs>14.6</carbs>
      <plato>12.30</plato>
   </brew>
</brewery>
...
```

Using the element( ) scheme, you could locate the carbs element corresponding to Helles Lager this way:

```
element(petes/3/4)
```

Note that this combines the content awareness of a shorthand pointer with the structure awareness of a child sequence and thus avoids some of the problems associated with each.

## Contents of the xpointer( ) Scheme

When the scheme is xpointer, what appears within the required parentheses of a scheme-based XPointer is based on an XPath expression, locating some subresource within a target resource.

The XPath expression in an xpointer-type pointer part is *not* set off from what surrounds it with quotation marks. This makes XPointer syntax notably different from that of XSLT, XPath's other big "client." XPath expressions in XSLT stylesheets always appear as attribute values and therefore must be enclosed in quotation marks. (On the other hand, remember that XPointer will almost never be used by itself; rather, it will be used to locate a subresource of a resource located by XLink or a similar standard. Just as in XHTML, these resources *as a whole*—URIs—will almost always appear within quotation marks, as attribute values.)

For example, consider the following simple XML document:

```
<gaming_platforms currency="sadly-outdated">
  <gaming_platform id="A">Atari</gaming_platform>
  <gaming_platform id="S">Sega</gaming_platform>
  <gaming_platform id="SN">Super Nintendo</gaming_platform>
  <gaming_platform id="P">Pong</gaming_platform>
</gaming_platforms>
```

You could locate all gaming_platform elements whose names begin with S using a scheme-based XPointer such as this:

```
xpointer(//gaming_platform[starts-with(., "S")])
```

Or you could locate any given gaming_platform simply by referring to its id attribute (assuming, of course, that the attribute by that name is explicitly declared as an ID-type attribute):

```
xpointer(id("P"))
```

This latter approach is very similar to the shorthand pointers described earlier. More detailed coverage and examples of the xpointer( ) scheme appear in Chapter 9.

## Custom Schemes

The XPointer Framework's mechanisms are generic enough that developers can extend XPointer by devising custom schemes beyond the predefined element, xpointer and xmlns. These schemes would be used in locating subresources in documents of a specific XML vocabulary.

For instance, assume a street-mapping vocabulary in which you might code a document like the following:

```
<map>
  <street name="Main" segment="1001_3498"
    xstart="34.3" ystart="679.2"
    xend="145.7" yend="1003.0"/>
  <street name="Main" segment="1001_3499"
    xstart="145.7" ystart="1003.0"
    xend="145.7" yend="1372.2"/>
</map>
```

The developers of this vocabulary could adopt the XPointer syntax to their own purposes, enabling an application to locate a particular street (consisting of all segments sharing the same name) with a scheme-based XPointer such as:

```
streetseg(name("Main"))
```

where streetseg is the custom scheme.

Note that what appears within the parentheses following such a custom scheme may or may not be an XPath expression or a namespace URI. The Framework doesn't constrain schemes or schemedata very much, leaving the meaning and significance of the expression up to the conventions of the application in question.

---

### Real-World Custom Schemes

I confess I don't fully know what to make of the XPointer spec's "generosity" in making its syntax freely extensible through custom schemes. Indeed, I'd argue that a custom-schemed XPointer isn't an XPointer at all—just a snippet of code that happens to use a string followed by a left parenthesis followed by another string followed by a right parenthesis. It can't be processed in any practical way by a generic XPointer-aware application (except that the XPointer processor can look at it and decide that it doesn't know how to deal with it, and move on to the next part of the XPointer).

That said, custom schemes are already making their way into the real world of XML-based applications. For example, the Scalable Vector Graphics (SVG) specification uses a custom scheme as one alternative to the xpointer scheme for linking to a particular "view" within an SVG document. Here, the custom scheme is svgView( ), as in this example from the spec:

```
MyDrawing.svg#svgView(viewBox(0,200,1000,1000))
```

(More information on using this form of SVG fragment identifiers is available at *http://www.w3.org/TR/SVG/linking.html#SVGFragmentIdentifiers*.)

An IETF Internet-Draft by Jonathan Borden ("A generic fragment identifier syntax for URI references," at *http://www.ietf.org/internet-drafts/draft-borden-frag-00.txt*) also singles out custom schemes as a valuable generic format for identifying fragments of any given resource. In this case, the custom scheme is associated with a namespace by way of a Resource Directory Description Language (RDDL) description. RDDL provides a formal mechanism for describing a namespace's characteristics; for more information about RDDL, see *http://www.rddl.org*.

---

## Multiple Pointer Parts

When an XPointer consists of more than one pointer part, the XPointer-aware processor evaluates the XPointer from left to right. This enables the XPointer to serve either or both of two purposes: failure-proofing the XPointer and/or using namespace contexts in the XPointer.

---

### "Failure-proofing" XPointers

If the first pointer part has an unrecognized scheme, or results in a resource or subresource error, the processor can fall back on the second; if the second fails, it can fall back on the third, and so on.

This makes XPointer much more robust than its simple XHTML counterpart. Assume the following XHTML hyperlink:

```
<a href="#speech-para2">
```

If the current document contains a named anchor whose value is speech-para2, all is well; the browser scrolls the document to place that named anchor at the top of the window. But if there is no named anchor, the only fallback possible for the browser is a rather crude one: to align the top of the document at the top of the window.

An XLink/XPointer solution to this problem might look like the following:

```
<anchor xlink:href="xpointer(id('speech-para2')) xpointer(id('speech-para3'))"
```

Thus, the processor would first try to locate an element whose ID-type attribute has a value of speech-para2; if no such element is located, the processor attempts to locate an element with an ID-type attribute of speech-para3; and if *that* attempt fails, the processor reports a subresource error.

### Declaring and using namespaces

The other principal reason for using a multipart XPointer is to establish namespace contexts for evaluating XPath expressions in other pointer parts. When an xmlns-schemed pointer part is encountered, any pointer parts to its right may freely use elements and attributes with the associated namespace prefix. Note that to declare multiple namespaces, you must use multiple xmlns pointer parts; you can't declare more than one namespace in a given pointer part.

Consider this example (taken directly from the XPointer xmlns() Scheme spec):

```
<doc>
  <x:a xmlns:x="http://example.com/foo">
    <x:a xmlns:x="http://example.org/bar">This element and its parent are in
    different namespaces."</x:a>
  </x:a>
</doc>
```

The following XPointer will fail, not because it fails to locate a (sub-)resource but because the reference to the x:a element can't be unambiguously evaluated by the processor:

```
xpointer(//x:a)
```

To get around this problem, you'd use a multipart scheme-based XPointer, such as:

```
xmlns(x=http://example.com/foo) xpointer(//x:a)
```

or:

```
xmlns(x=http://example.org/bar) xpointer(//x:a)
```

Note that you need to use an `xmlns` pointer part *every* time you need to use a namespace-qualified element or attribute name in a subsequent XPointer expression. Otherwise, the XPointer processor is unable to resolve namespace prefixes used in XPath expressions in the XPointer; the processor has no way, for example, to peek inside the target document to retrieve the namespace declarations that the latter makes.

One final note here: the spec explicitly says that the prefix used in your pointer parts needn't match the prefixes used in the resource. In effect, each occurrence of a namespace prefix—both in your XPointers and in a target resource as located by them—behaves as though it were physically replaced by the namespace URI prior to the act of locating the (sub-)resource. Thus, the preceding two examples might just as well be coded:

```
xmlns(abc=http://example.com/foo) xpointer(//abc:a)
```

and:

```
xmlns(fershlugginer=http://example.org/bar) xpointer(//fershlugginer:a)
```

For clarity of intent, though, it never hurts to use exactly the same prefixes in an XPointer as appear in the target.

### Mixing it up

When using multipart XPointers that declare namespaces, although it may seem natural to always begin with the `xmlns` pointer part, it's not a requirement. In fact, *not* starting off with the `xmlns` might be less confusing or otherwise desirable in certain circumstances. For instance:

```
xpointer(id("JSimpson")) xmlns(mydoc=http://mydoc.com) xpointer(/mydoc:root)
```

Here, the "fallback" convention for multipart XPointers says to attempt to locate the element whose ID-type attribute has a value of `JSimpson`; if that attempt fails, fall back to the alternative: locate the root `mydoc:root` element of the target resource. The only requirement is that a corresponding `xmlns` pointer part *must* appear to the left of any pointer part that uses a namespace prefix; the `xmlns` pointer parts need not, however, precede *all* other pointer parts.

Also note that succeeding `xmlns` parts for the same prefix override one another. Thus (this is a single complete XPointer broken over two lines for clarity):

```
xmlns(w=http://wexample1.com) xpointer(//w:bush)
    xmlns(w=http//wexample2.com) xpointer(//w:bush)
```

This attempts to return a location set consisting of all bush elements in the `http://wexample1.com` namespace; failing that, the XPointer falls back and attempts to return a location-set consisting of all bush elements in the `http://wexample2.com` namespace. (Remember not to be confused by the `w:` prefix, which may or may not actually be used in the target document. What counts is the namespace URI, regardless of the prefix associated with it.)

# Using XPointers in a URI

You may already have concluded how to do this, based on a handful of examples in this chapter. Syntactically, including an XPointer fragment identifier in a URI is the same as doing so in XHTML: separate the XPointer from what precedes it using a hash/pound character, #, as in these examples (using scheme-based XPointer, shorthand pointer, and two flavors of the element( ) scheme, respectively):

```
http://www.example.com/lucy.xml#xpointer(//character[@castmember="arnaz"])
http://www.example.com/lucy.xml#ricky
http://www.example.com/lucy.xml#element(/1/2/4/3)
http://www.example.com/lucy.xml#element(cast/3)
```

If the XPointer is locating content in the same document in which the XPointer itself appears, simply prefix the XPointer with a hash, as in:

```
#xpointer(//character[@castmember="arnaz"])
```

As a final note, remember a couple of additional considerations when using XPointer in URIs, which I've pointed out in this and the previous chapter:

- Escape special characters as needed, both to comply with XPointer's own constraints and those of the standards with which XPointer must interoperate. These special characters include the circumflex (^) for escaping unbalanced parentheses, the percent sign (%), markup-significant characters such as the less-than sign (left angle bracket, <), and spaces, as well as other characters in non-ASCII encodings.

- While XPointer itself does not require the use of quotation marks, XPath expressions used in scheme-based XPointers frequently do. Furthermore, because XPointers in XLink and other hyperlinking contexts are used in attribute values, you need to remain aware of nested-quotation-mark issues in the event that your scheme-based XPointers do use quotation marks of their own (such as in embedded XPath expressions).

# CHAPTER 9

# XPointer Beyond XPath

Using XPath, in conjunction with XPointer, provides a wide (seemingly infinite) variety of ways to locate XML content. But it stops short of being able to "locate" everything. This chapter covers XPointer extensions to XPath's already rich facilities, extensions that plug the gap between what XPath does and what users might expect of a full-fledged "point to some XML-based content" standard.

In this chapter, when I refer to "XPointer" or "the XPointer spec," I'm referring to the XPointer xpointer( ) Scheme Working Draft dated July 10, 2002.

## Why Extend XPath?

After you've worked with XPath for a while—especially in XSLT—you may start to get a little cocky. It seems impossible that something in an XML document might be *un*locatable. From everything in the document down to individual PIs, comments, even individual characters (in the sense of using functions such as substring( ) and translate( ))—what's left? The reason your cockiness may be unjustified is that you've overlooked a small but disproportionately significant class of activities for which XPointer would be useful, but for which XPath provides absolutely no support.

Consider XPointer's unintelligent counterpart in XHTML: simple fragment identifiers that use named anchors; then consider the activity XHTML supports: web browsing. The Web is already driven by content authors and browser capabilities, no? What could possibly be missing?

What's missing is the third party in a web-based transaction: the user. The web site visitor. The human sitting at her PC, mouse, or other pointing device probably at the ready. Ready, in short, to select content in ways that cannot be anticipated by a document author or browser vendor.

Imagine this hypothetical user sees something like Figure 9-1 on her screen. For one reason or another, she decides to select the portion of this document depicted in Figure 9-2.

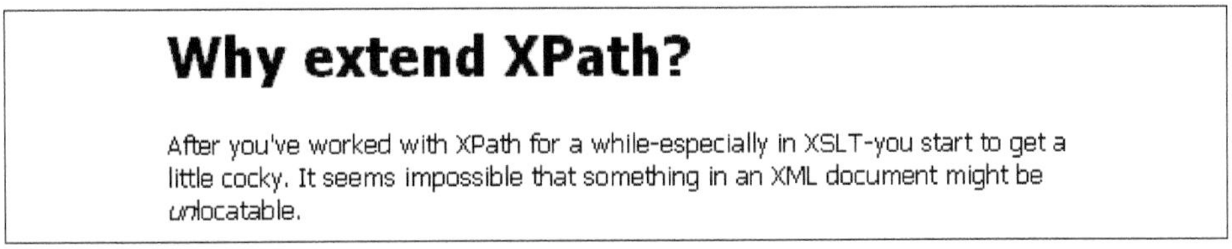

## Why extend XPath?

After you've worked with XPath for a while-especially in XSLT-you start to get a little cocky. It seems impossible that something in an XML document might be *un*locatable.

Figure 9-1. Hypothetical web document (as displayed)

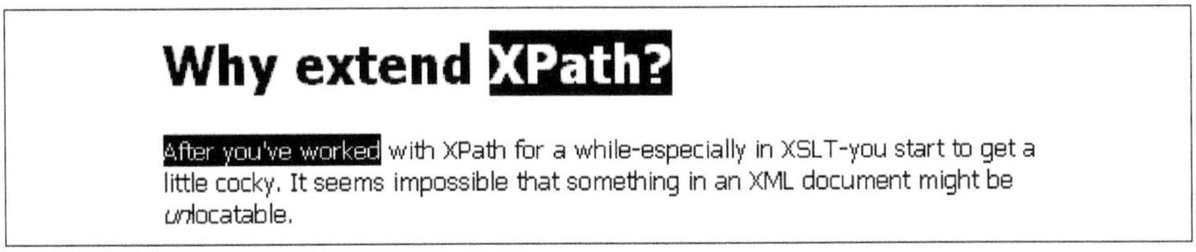

## Why extend XPath?

After you've worked with XPath for a while-especially in XSLT-you start to get a little cocky. It seems impossible that something in an XML document might be *un*locatable.

Figure 9-2. Hypothetical web document (with selection)

Now ask yourself: How do I construct an XPath-based XPointer that corresponds to the selected text? To answer this question, you'll need to examine the XHTML code behind the page, the relevant portion of which may look something like the following:

```
<h1>Why extend XPath?</h1>
<!-- Intro paragraph -->
<p>After you've worked with XPath for a while-especially in XSLT-you
start to get a little cocky. It seems impossible that something in an
XML document might be <em>un</em>locatable.</p>
```

You *can* construct such an XPointer, but it will be extremely ad hoc and ungainly, involving, first, acquiring all text in the document and then sub-stringing it from the "X" in the level-1 heading through the "d" in "worked." And somehow you'd need to grab that comment, too, and ensure—to preserve the source's integrity—that the comment was somehow placed where it belonged: smack in the middle of the two partial text nodes. The resulting mutant XPointer might look something like this:

```
xpointer(substring(//h1[1], 12, 6) | //comment()[1] |
    substring(//p[1], 1, 19))
```

And you'd really be frustrated when the XPointer processor fails (because the result of this XPointer is a simple string).

XPointer would be much more natural and easy-to-use if there were an XPointer analog to the real-world practice of selecting text with a pointing device: starting at one point in the document and continuing over a contiguous range of content to a second point. That's the function of XPointer's handful of extensions to XPath.

## Points and Ranges

I mentioned these extensions to XPath's basic node types first in Chapter 7 (elements, attributes, and so on). Now let's look at them in detail.

## Holes in the Analogy

The analogy between XPointer's "selecting" mechanism and the real world has a number of seemingly loose ends.

The most important of these, I think, is: why do you need an XPointer to handle selection? Isn't this why we have user interfaces (UIs) in the first place? Yes, as long as the UI in question actually supports visual text selection. Selecting text is meant to communicate something to the operating system, in a way that feeds back to the user "this is what I've selected" prior to his actually *doing* anything with the selection. In a purely graphical UI, the feedback is in the form of highlighted, reverse-video, or similar text-representation device. If the UI isn't graphical, though, how to provide feedback—let alone how to communicate the selection to the underlying operating system—is a much murkier problem.

Such non-graphical UIs include text-to-speech interpreters and other interfaces for visually impaired users. They're likely to become more important to the non-disabled as well, with the prospect of making content available to users who simply need their eyes for other things at the moment: cooks, automobile drivers, jet pilots, and so on.

And then there's a whole class of potential applications for which the use of human eyes isn't an option anyway—because the principal "consumers" of such applications aren't human but machine. Imagine an application, for example, that selects a paragraph from a target document using plain-old XPath-based XPointer, then within that paragraph, selects a sentence or phrase for highlighting of some kind, regardless of the underlying markup or node tree.

## Points

A point is simply a location in a document—a location between two characters of interest. Like a point in plane geometry, a point in XPointer has no dimension at all: a single point "contains" nothing at all, not even a single character. There's also a point at the start of the string-value and at its end (and, as you will see, before and after each node in the document).

Note that points are found not only in text nodes, but in *any* string-value. An attribute's value, a comment, a PI, indeed the root node itself—all have string-values as well and are thus potential targets in which to locate points.

Each point has two properties, a container node and an index. The container node, obviously, is the point's parent—the context in which the point is located. The index is a positive integer ranging from 0 through the number of points (less 1) in that container node.

Consider the following fragment:

```
<storage>disk</storage>
```

The storage element's string-value—its text node child—consists of four characters; within the text node, the interstice between each pair of characters (d and i, i and s, and s and k) is one point, and there's also a point before the d and after the k—a total of five points. The container node for the points (indexes 0 through 4) before and after each character is the text node; the container node for the two points (indexes 0 and 1) before and after the text node is the storage element. Figure 9-3 illustrates.

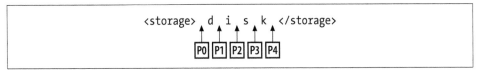

*Figure 9-3. Point locations in an element with a text-node child*

An important implication of Figure 9-3 is that the node tree as understood by XPath is not the same as the "location tree" as understood by XPointer (although naturally there are overlaps). See Figure 9-4.

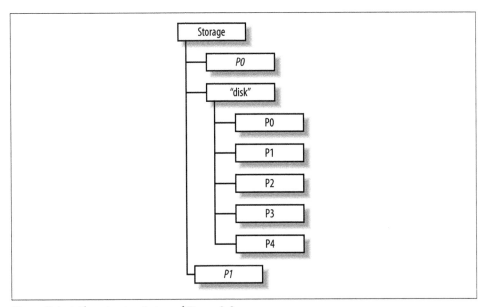

*Figure 9-4. A "location tree" view of Figure 9-3*

As you can see, the storage element now has not just one child (the text node), but three children (the text node plus the points before and after it). Furthermore, while a text node can have no children from XPath's perspective, it *does* from XPointer's; the number of child points always equals the length of the text node, plus 1.

One effect of a point's being defined by its container and its index within that container is that *there are no identical points in a document*, at least within a given container. However, there will be points indistinguishable from one another. For instance, in the above example, point P0 within the storage element is indistinguishable from the "separate" point P0 within the text node.

This might seem disconcerting at first. It makes sense, though, when you remember that XPath, too, often provides several ways of locating a given "thing"; a given node might be visible along more than one axis, for example.

### Node points versus character points

A given point can be classified as either a *node point* or a *character point*.

- A node point is any point in the document occurring between adjacent nodes; there's also a node point immediately before and after each child of a given node. In the above example, there's a node point immediately preceding and following the text node.

- A character point is any point in the document occurring between adjacent characters in a text node, before the first character in a text node or following the text node's last character. The storage element as described above has five character-point children.

### Point syntax

To address a point with an XPointer, use the point( ) node (or location) type in the XPath expression used by a full XPointer, especially with a predicate. For example, assume the simple storage element we've been using so far is part of a larger document:

```
<media>
    <storage>microform</storage>
    <storage>CD-ROM</storage>
    <storage>DVD</storage>
    <storage>disk</storage>
</media>
```

To locate the character point between the m and i in "microform"—that is, the *second* point within the *first* storage element—you could use the following:

```
xpointer(//storage[1]/point( )[1])
```

While the numbering of the storage elements starts at 1, the numbering for the points is zero-based.

### Points as "nodes"

Like other node types, the XPointer point node-type extension can be followed in an XPath expression by further location steps that shift the context up, down, or sideways in the document as a whole. These shifts in context—accomplished here as elsewhere using axes—behave a little differently for a point-type "node," however; Table 9-1 breaks it down for you.

*Table 9-1. Axes and points*

| Axes | Node-set locatable from a point |
| --- | --- |
| child, descendant, preceding-sibling, following-sibling, preceding, following, attribute, namespace | None (node-set is empty) |
| self, descendant-or-self | The point itself |
| parent | The point's container node |
| ancestor | The point's container node, that container's parent, and so on (up the tree to the root node) |
| ancestor-or-self | The point itself, its container node, and the container node's ancestors |

Unlike standard XPath node types, points do not have an expanded-name; their string-values are empty.

### Points and general entities

Consider the following document:

```
<!DOCTYPE gadget [
<!ENTITY R "Ronco" >
]>
<gadget>
    <name>Veg-O-Matic</name>
    <company>&R;</company>
</gadget>
```

How many character points are there within the company element, and where are they?

There are six character points there—four between each pair of characters in the entity's replacement text "Ronco," and one point before and after the replacement text. There is no point, for instance, between the & and the R in the &R; entity reference itself. This is consistent with XPath, with XML, and for that matter with common sense: by the time an XPointer-aware application gets its hands on a document's content, the document has already been parsed—entity substitutions made, attribute values defaulted, and so on. In short, the entity *reference* itself might just as well not exist.

# Ranges

A range, as you might expect, is whatever lies in a given document between any two given points, not surprisingly referred to as the start and end points. The start and end points may be equal (in which case the range is called a *collapsed range*); if they are not equal, the end point must follow the start point, in document order.

A reminder: I'm using the term "document" loosely in the preceding sentence. In this sense, it comprises not only well-formed XML documents, but also non-well-formed external parsed entities. The spec asserts that the start and end point must be within the same document or external parsed entity; nonetheless, it's safe to assume that a document containing a reference to an external parsed entity may have ranges that overlap the "border" between document and entity. Consider the case of the following document:

```
<!DOCTYPE speechinfo [
<!ENTITY getty SYSTEM "gettysburg.xml">
]>
<speechinfo>
    <speaker>Abraham Lincoln</speaker>
    <text>&getty;</text>
</speechinfo>
```

where the *gettysburg.xml* document contains the text (marked up or otherwise) of Lincoln's famous address.

A start point/end point for a legitimate range might be, respectively, the point just before the L in Lincoln (in the main document) and following the o in and seven years ago (in the external parsed entity). As I discussed at the end of the section about points, for all intents and purposes, an entity reference can be assumed to have been expanded by the time the XPointer application sees a document. What the spec really means by restricting the start and end point to the same document or external parsed entity is, for example, that you can't set the start point to just before the L in Lincoln and the end point in some *other* document (or in some unreferenced external parsed entity).

## What can be in a range

There's one important restriction to the kinds of content a legitimate range may contain, a restriction based on the container nodes for the start and end points. If the container for one point is *anything other* than the root node, an element, or a text node, the two points must lie within the same node.

At the beginning of this chapter, following Figure 9-2, I showed some hypothetical source code behind a user's selection of text on a web page. The range in question looked like this:

```
XPath?</h1><!-- Intro paragraph --><p>After you've worked
```

Although it looks a little nonsensical (and certainly not well-formed!), this is a legitimate range. Both start and end points lie within element nodes (more precisely, *within text nodes* within element nodes), and they need not lie within the *same* node for the range to be valid. On the other hand, the boldfaced portion of the following fragment does not constitute a valid range:

```
XPath?</h1><!-- Intro paragraph --><p>After you've worked
```

The end point is still within a text node, true. But the start point lies within the comment. The only legitimate end point for such a start point would be a point within the same comment (and equal to or following the start point, of course).

## Range syntax

Like points, ranges have their own node type, range( ) in this case, which may be referred to in the expression portion of a full XPointer. Therefore, the following is presumably a legitimate XPointer:

```
xpointer(//range( )[4])
```

I say "presumably" because although syntactically correct—translated, this would mean something like "locate the fourth range in the document"—it's not practically useful. If a range is delimited by its start and end points, where does the range in question start and end? (The start point, obviously, is the one corresponding to index 0; it's the end point that's not clear.)

More likely, you'll use the range( ) node type with any of several XPointer functions in the predicate. You will see examples of this use in a moment.

## Ranges as "nodes"

Like points, ranges have no expanded names. Unlike points, though, ranges do have string-values: "the characters that are in text nodes and that are between the start point and end point of the range."

So says the spec, anyhow. But this is a bit ambiguous, and in the absence of examples, we're left to conjecture what might be the string-value of a range such as the following:

```
<front_matter>
   <epigraph id="GIRA001">
      <author born="1882-10-29" died="1944-01-31">Giraudoux, Jean</author>
      <source year="1942">The Apollo of Bellac</source>
      <text>When you see a woman who can go nowhere without
      a staff of admirers, it is not so much because they think
      she is beautiful, it is because she has told them they
      are handsome.</text>
   </epigraph>
</front_matter>
```

The start point of this range immediately precedes the epigraph element's start tag; the end point follows the period at the end of the text element. A literal reading of the spec might seem to indicate that the string value of this range is:

```
GIRA0011882-10-291944-01-31Giradoux, Jean1942The Apollo of BellacWhen you see a woman
who can [...] handsome.
```

That is, not only the text nodes but also the attribute values might seem to make up the string-value. After all, the latter are indeed "between the start point and end point," aren't they? Don't be deceived, though; this literal reading is *too* literal. The key word in the excerpt from the spec is "and"—that is, the range's string-value consists of *those portions of all text nodes that lie between the start and end points.* Thus, the true string-value of this range is:

```
Giradoux, JeanThe Apollo of BellacWhen you see a woman who can [...] handsome.
```

That said, there *is* a problem with the wording of this portion of the spec, in the phrase "text nodes." But text nodes exist only as children of elements. Given that a legitimate range in the above example might be, for instance, the 1882 portion of the born attribute's value, I think the spec's authors might have tinkered with the wording of the paragraph a little more.

The other XPath-related question we might ask about ranges is how they behave when included in a location step followed by others that use axes. This is easy: navigating through a document from a range-type "context node" is identical to navigating through it from the range's start point. Refer back to Table 9-1 for this information, remembering that only the start point "counts" when orienting yourself along an axis from a range.

### Covering ranges

An important concept in understanding ranges as described in the XPointer spec is that of *covering ranges*. As the name implies, a covering range is the range that spans the entirety of some location. (And remember that locations in XPointer are basically the same as nodes in XPath, extended to include points and ranges.) Covering ranges are defined in terms of the location type in question; this may involve implicit start and end points, with their respective container nodes and indexes. Table 9-2 summarizes.

*Table 9-2. Covering ranges*

| Location type | Container of start and end points | Covering range's start point index | Covering range's end point index | Notes |
|---|---|---|---|---|
| Range | — | — | — | Identical to the range itself |
| Point | — | — | — | Start and end points of covering range are identical: the point itself |
| Attribute and namespace | Attribute or namespace location itself | 0 | Length of attribute or namespace location's string-value | |
| Root | Root location itself | 0 | Number of children of root location | |
| All others | Parent of the location in question | Number of preceding siblings of the location | Index of the start point, plus 1 | |

Determining the covering range of a point or range location, obviously, is pretty trivial. (Note, by the way, that the covering range of a point is a collapsed range, as defined earlier in the chapter.) The covering ranges of other location types might be more easy to understand by way of an example. Here's a simple but complete document including at least one of all other location types:

```
<?xml-stylesheet type="text/xsl" href="maginfo.xsl"?>
<mag:magazine id="NY"
    xmlns:mag="http://www.example.com/magml">
    <mag:name>The New Yorker</mag:name>
    <!-- Update: Brown hasn't been the editor for years. -->
    <mag:editor>Brown, Tina</mag:editor>
</mag:magazine>
```

Table 9-3 breaks down the covering ranges for various locations in this document.

*Table 9-3. Covering range examples*

| Location | Container of start and end points | Index of start point | Index of end point |
|---|---|---|---|
| id attribute | The id attribute itself | 0 | 2 (length of string-value "NY") |
| mag: namespace location | The namespace location itself | 0 | 28 (length of string-value "http://www.example.com/magml") |
| Root | The root location itself | 0 | 2 (number of children of root location—don't forget the PI!) |
| xml-stylesheet PI | Root (parent of the PI) | 0 (the PI has no preceding siblings) | 1 (index of the start point, plus 1) |
| Comment | The mag:magazine element | 1 (there's one preceding sibling of the comment, the mag:name element) | 2 (index of the start point, plus 1) |
| Text node, "The New Yorker" | The mag:name element | 0 (no preceding siblings) | 1 (index of the start point, plus 1) |
| mag:editor element | The mag:magazine element | 2 (mag:name element and the comment are preceding siblings) | 3 (index of the start point, plus 1) |

If you refer back to the document's source code, you should see that all this follows not only the spec's definition of a covering range, but also a common-sense version of that definition. For example, *within its container*—the root—the xml:stylesheet PI is "covered" by a range that starts at point 0 (that is, the start point's index) through point 1 (the end point's index, immediately following the PI).

Remember that we're talking here about covering ranges. The PI's covering range isn't the only range possible for it; any number of ranges could be set within its string-value, from the whole thing (type="text/xsl" href="maginfo.xsl") down to individual characters—indeed, individual points—within that string-value.

# XPointer Extensions to Document Order

The XPointer specification extends XPath's concept of document order to accommodate the point and range location types. The need to do so might not be obvious; after all, "document order" seems to be one of those terms describing a physical, unambiguous reality. What could be more *un*ambiguous than that a bit of document content appears before or after another bit?

But XPointer points and ranges toss a big handful of mud into these formerly transparent waters, even in the simplest documents. Consider an example:

```
<employee emp_id="73519">
    <start_date type="probationary">1979-03-12</start_date>
    <start_date type="full_perm">1979-09-12</start_date>
</employee>
```

The possible locations in this document number in the dozens, from individual character and node points through all the various ranges, attribute and text locations, on up to the full root location. The problem in determining the "order" of these locations is that some XPointer locations can be found *within* others. It's like you're looking at a wooden crate, filled with freshly picked corn: does a kernel on this ear of corn come before or after the husk on the same ear? does a slat of wood on one side of the crate precede or follow the crate as a whole? In the case of the above document, does the character point location between the b and a in probationary precede or follow the type attribute location for which probationary is the value? Does the range of characters from 03-12 through 1979-09 precede or follow the second start_date element location?

The questions seem absurd, yet they go to the heart of what is meant by document order in the first place. The XPointer xpointer() Scheme spec tries to put them to rest by carefully mapping out the various combinations of location types and how to determine which of a given pair of locations precedes or follows the other. To do so, it first defines a new term, *immediately preceding node*, which applies to any point location (either node or character type) in a document or external parsed entity. The immediately preceding node depends on the type of point location and its index value:

- If the point is a character point, the immediately preceding node is the point's container.
- If the point is a node point:
  - When the index, *n*, is greater than 0, the immediately preceding node is the *n*th child of the node point's container.
  - When the index equals 0, the immediately preceding node is the container itself—unless the container also has one or more attribute or namespace nodes. In the latter case, the immediately preceding node is the *last* such attribute or namespace node.

Note that determining the immediately preceding node for the first node point (index 0) in a container rather overturns a central principle of XML itself, which is that the order of attributes and namespaces cannot be relied on. For example, take a look at the following code fragment:

```
<place longitude="84.259337W"
    latitude="30.428563N">
    <name>Tallahassee</name>
</place>
```

What is the immediately preceding node of the node point between the place and name element's start tags (that is, the node point identified by the expression place/point( )[0])? Common sense might indicate that it's the latitude attribute—that is, the last attribute of the node point's container (the place element). This isn't necessarily true, though, because an XML parser is free to order an element's attributes in any way it wishes. A parser can be expected to impose some kind of order (e.g., alphabetical) on attributes, which might simplify constructing a lookup index for the document. If the parser does use alphabetical rather than document ordering of attributes, the immediately preceding node for this node point will be the longitude attribute.

The XPointer spec gets around this point by noting, parenthetically, "the order of attribute and namespace nodes is implementation dependent." The lesson here: if you need to determine the immediately preceding node of a 0-indexed node point, you'd better be sure you understand the behavior of any parser accessing the document to which you're pointing. It's unlikely that you'd know for sure about the parser's ordering of attribute and namespace nodes. The spec's authors needed to codify the immediately preceding node concept somehow; and the XML Recommendation painted them into something of a corner. In this case, though—for 0-indexed node points—it's a shame that the codification seems to imply a practical impossibility. (On the other hand, unless you're trying to work out for some reason the order of nodes within a document, you don't need to worry about the immediately preceding node at all.)

Table 9-4 summarizes how to determine if a location of a given type—node, point, or range—is "before" or "after" another according to XPointer's definition of document order.

*Table 9-4. Document order and location types*

| When comparing locations of type... | Their document order is equal if... | Location 1 is before location 2 if... | Location 1 follows location 2 if... |
| --- | --- | --- | --- |
| Node and node | (Per XPath) | (Per XPath) | (Per XPath) |
| Node and point | (N/A: never equal) | The node is before or equal to the point's immediately preceding node | The node follows the point's immediately preceding node |

*Table 9-4. Document order and location types (continued)*

| When comparing locations of type... | Their document order is equal if... | Location 1 is before location 2 if... | Location 1 follows location 2 if... |
|---|---|---|---|
| Node and range | (N/A: never equal) | The node is before the range's start point | The node follows the range's start point |
| Point and point | Their immediately preceding nodes are equal *and* their indexes are equal | The first point's immediately preceding node is before the second's, *or* if they share the same immediately preceding node and the first point's index is less than the second's | The first point's immediately preceding node follows the second's, *or* if they share the same immediately preceding node and the first point's index is equal to or greater than the second's |
| Point and range | The point, and the range's start and end points, are equal | The point is before or equal to the range's start point | The point is after the range's start point |
| Range and range | The two ranges' start points are equal and their end points are equal | The first range's start point is before the second's, *or* if they have the same start point but the first range's end point precedes the second's | The first range's start point follows the second's, *or* if they have the same start point but the first range's end point follows the second's |

# XPointer Document Order Extensions: Examples

Let's look at how these extensions to XPath's definition of document order work in practice. I won't reconsider the node-versus-node case (corresponding to the first row in Table 9-4); if you need a refresher, refer back to Chapter 2.

Here is a brief sample document from which I'll pick arbitrary locations and show how to apply Table 9-4 to a real-world example.

```
<dictionary source="Welsh" target="English">
    <word>
        <in>ffwlbart</in>
        <out>polecat</out>
    </word>
    <word>
        <in>rhaglaw</in>
        <out>governor</out>
        <out>lieutenant</out>
    </word>
    <word>
        <in>ymyl</in>
        <out>edge</out>
        <out>border</out>
    </word>
</dictionary>
```

Here are the locations to be considered:

1. Nodes:
   a. The root node
   b. The target attribute
   c. The first out child of the second word element (corresponding to the string-value "governor")

2. Points:
   a. The node point between the dictionary element's start tag and the first word element's start tag
   b. The node point between the last two out elements (string-values "edge" and "border")
   c. The character point between the r and h in rhaglaw

3. Ranges:
   a. Extending from points 2a to 2b, above
   b. Extending from points 2c to 2b, above

Table 9-5 illustrates how an XPointer processor would interpret the document order of various combinations of these locations.

*Table 9-5. XPointer document order examples*

| Location 1 | Location 2 | Row in Table 9-4 | Interpretation |
|---|---|---|---|
| Node 1a | Point 2a | Node and point | The node point's index within its container (the dictionary element) is 0. Therefore, the immediately preceding node—assuming simple document order is used by the parser—is the target attribute. Because the root node "precedes" the target attribute, the root node is considered to be before this point, in document order. |
| Node 1b | Range 3a | Node and range | Because the target attribute node is the range's start point, the target attribute is before the range, in document order. |
| Node 1c | Range 3b | Node and range | The range encompasses the out element node in question. The range's start point occurs before the out element, so the range is assumed to precede the node. |
| Point 2a | Point 2b | Point and point | As above, the immediately preceding node of Point 2a is the target attribute. The immediately preceding node of Point 2b is the next-to-last out element ("edge"). Therefore, Point 2a precedes Point 2b. |
| Point 2c | Range 3b | Point and range | The point and the range's start point are equal. Therefore, either the point and range are equal, or the point is before the range. The determining factor in this case is the range's *end* point, which follows the point; therefore, the point precedes the range. |
| Range 3a | Range 3b | Range and range | The two ranges overlap, sharing the same end point but with different start points. In this case, look at their start points. Whichever range has the first start point—3a, here—is assumed to precede the other. |

Similar logic applies for any combination of nodes, points, and ranges.

# XPointer Functions

Unsurprisingly—given the extensions to XPath elsewhere provided by XPointer—the XPointer spec defines a handful of additional functions for processing the two new location types (points and ranges). Any application claiming XPointer xpointer() Scheme conformance must make these functions available.

> The word "must," although it seems to carry the force of law, is a notoriously slippery concept in practice. For starters, just consider what it might denote in the context of a W3C document whose final status can never be greater than "Recommendation."

As in Chapter 4, covering XPath functions, in this section I'll first present these functions briefly in Table 9-6, then examine each in greater detail. In that earlier chapter, each table included a column for the type of value the function returns; this column isn't needed in this case, because all eight functions return a location-set. (Most of them are passed a location-set as well, designated locset in their prototypes.)

*Table 9-6. XPointer functions*

| Function prototype | Description |
| --- | --- |
| start-point(locset) | Returns a location-set consisting of the start points for all locations in locset |
| end-point(locset) | Returns a location-set consisting of the end points for all locations in locset |
| range-to(locset) | Returns a range for each location in locset |
| string-range(locset, string, number1?, number2?) | Returns a range for each location in locset, based on a search for the string argument in each location's string-value |
| range(locset) | Returns a covering range for each location in locset |
| range-inside(locset) | Returns a range for the *contents* of each location in locset |
| here( ) | Establishes the document in which the XPointer appears as the context for further location steps |
| origin( ) | Used with XPointer-based XLinks to identify the location from which the link traversal began |

## start-point(locset)

Exactly how the start-point( ) function behaves varies according to the type of each location in locset.

> A reminder: the term "location-set" is the same as XPath's "node-set," extended to cover points and ranges. As with XPath functions, a passed location-set may include one or more locations, or even be empty. In the latter case, of course, the XPointer using the function will fail.

Not very surprisingly, if a given location is a point or range, start-point( ) returns that point or the range's start point, respectively. If a given location is the root location, an element, text, comment, or PI, the point returned is the one whose index is 0 within that container.

Surprisingly (to me, anyway), if a given location is an attribute or namespace location, "the pointer part in which the function appears fails." What this probably refers to is just that you can't identify the start point of an attribute or namespace location; still, it seems to fly in the face of examples elsewhere in the spec, which assert (for example) that a substring of an attribute value can constitute a range.

Here's a document fragment as an example:

```
<transaction type="deposit">
    <account>1234-0987-65</account>
    <amount currency="USD">1009.46</amount>
    <source>cash</source>
</transaction>
```

We could construct an XPointer into this source such as the following:

```
xpointer(start-point(//account))
```

This XPointer locates the point within the account element whose index is 0—that is, the node point immediately preceding the text node whose value is "1234-0987-65." We could also pass to the start-point( ) function a multimember location-set, as in:

```
xpointer(start-point(/transaction/*))
```

The value returned would be a series of points, representing the start points of each child of the root transaction element. Because there are three such children—the account, amount, and source elements—we'd get back a location-set, in this case, of three node points: the points immediately following each child element's start tag. On the other hand:

```
xpointer(start-point(/transaction))
```

locates the node point between the transaction and account element's start tags.

## end-point(locset)

As you might expect, the end-point( ) function is the flip-side of start-point( ), returning—for each location in the passed location-set—an end point determined according to the location's type.

For point and range locations, the function returns that point or the range's end point, respectively. For attribute and namespace locations, as with start-point( ), the XPointer part containing the function call fails. How end-point( ) treats the other location types, though, is a little less generic.

- For the root and each element location, end-point() returns a point whose container is the root or that element, respectively, and whose index equals the number of children of the root or that element.
- For each text, comment, or PI location, end-point() returns a point whose container is that location, and whose index equals the length of the location's string-value.

Referring back to the previous XML code example, this XPointer:

```
xpointer(end-point(/))
```

locates the node point following the root transaction element's end tag. (The container is the root node. The 0-index point within that container is the node point preceding transaction's start tag; there's only one child of the root location, which is the transaction element, therefore the index of the point returned by end-point() is 1.)

Similarly:

```
xpointer(end-point(//text()))
```

returns a location-set consisting of three points: the character point at the very end of each of the source's three text locations. For example, the first text location's string-value is 1234-0987-65, 12 characters long; the point within that text location whose index is 12 is the character point following the digit 5.

## range-to(locset)

To understand how this function works, you need to understand the start-point() and end-point() functions as well. (If you're not sure about them, check the descriptions above.) Its behavior also depends on the context location at the point of the call to range-to(). The function returns a range whose start point is calculated as if you'd passed the *context* location to start-point(), and whose end point is calculated as if you'd passed the locset argument to end-point(). The effect, therefore, is to locate everything from the context location through that end point, inclusively.

Returning to the banking-transaction document, consider this XPointer:

```
xpointer(//account/range-to(account))
```

At the time of the call to range-to(), the context location is the account element. Its start point (as if calculated using start-point(//account)) is the node point immediately following that element's start tag (just before the digit 1). Thus, this XPointer returns everything between that start point and the end point of the amount element—that is, the node point just before amount's end tag. The result is a location-set (containing a single range) whose string-value is the concatenated string-values of the account and amount elements:

```
1234-0987-651009.46
```

Note the similarity in behavior of the range-to( ) location to a user's selection of text in a GUI environment (at least insofar as selection of complete text nodes is concerned). If for no other reason, I suspect this similarity will make range-to( ) a very popular XPointer function.

As the spec points out, the range-to( ) function puts an additional spin on XPath's definition of a location step. XPath says that a location step can consist of either the full or abbreviated form of the axis-node test-predicate combination. In the XPointer universe, this definition is broadened to include one or more optional calls to range-to( ), each perhaps with a predicate of its own. Thus, with XPointer we may now see location paths such as the one highlighted here:

```
xpointer(//lawn[@type = 'zoysia']/sowing[@time = 'earliest']/range-to(following-
sibling::sowing[@time = 'latest']))
```

The location steps preceding the call to range-to( ) locate a node-set restricted to all sowing elements with a time attribute of "earliest" that are children of lawn elements with a type of "zoysia"; this node-set thus establishes the context for the call to range-to( ) (which establishes a range from the "earliest" sowing through the "latest"). This call to range-to( ) thus excludes from the final range any text within the selected lawn element except the text that appears in that range of its child sowing elements.

In the examples above—as in the XPointer spec itself—the location-set passed to range-to( ) always consists of a single location. I've tried to wrap my mind around what happens if the passed location-set contains more than one location, but confess that it seems too complex to put into words (assuming that it's even a possible, let alone reasonable or desirable, thing to do).

## string-range(locset, string, number1?, number2?)

This odd-looking beast of a function searches all locations passed as the first argument; each location's string-value is matched against the second argument, and if a match is found, a location-set consisting of a number of ranges is returned, one range for each discrete match for the string argument found within the range's string-values. By default, a range starts just before the matched string, and ends just after it, so the string-value of each range returned is the matched string, wherever they occur within the location-set. However, you can override these defaults using the optional third and fourth arguments. The number1 argument fixes the start point of the range (offset from the first character in the match); the number2 argument specifies the length of the returned range, in characters.

For instance, given a document such as this:

```
<people>
  <person>
    <name>Simpson,John</name>
  </person>
```

```
<person>
    <name>Kirby,John</name>
</person>
<person>
    <name>Simpson,Mike</name>
</person>
</people>
```

You could use the string-range() function as in the following XPointer to return just those name elements whose string-values contained the string "Simpson":

```
xpointer(string-range(//name[contains(., "Simpson")], "Simpson")
```

This locates two ranges; both ranges consist of the string "Simpson" because by default—in the absence of the third and fourth arguments—the range(s) returned match the sought-for string exactly. You could also include the optional third and fourth arguments to return (for example) ranges consisting of the four characters following the comma:

```
xpointer(string-range(//name[contains(., "Simpson")], "Simpson", 8, 4))
```

This returns two ranges, comprising the strings "John" and "Mike."

## range(locset)

Use the range() function when you want not a location-set of ranges per se, but of their *covering* ranges. For each location in locset, the function returns its covering range. Refer back to "Covering ranges" to see how covering ranges are determined for the various location types.

## range-inside(locset)

The range-inside() function works similarly to the range() function, in that it may return a range for each location in locset. But range-inside() may also return non-range-type locations. Table 9-7 summarizes.

*Table 9-7. range-inside() behavior, by location type*

| When location is... | Location itself returned? | Container of range returned | Index of start point of range returned | Index of end point of range returned |
|---|---|---|---|---|
| Point | Yes | (N/A) | (N/A) | (N/A) |
| Range | Yes | (N/A) | (N/A) | (N/A) |
| Any other type | No | Location itself | 0 | If the location is a node that can have children (that is, the root node or an element node), then the number of children of that node; otherwise, the length of the location's string-value |

As always, this behavior will be easier to understand using a concrete example. So consider the following:

```
<neighborhood>
   <street>
      <name>Post Avenue</name>
      <address>101</address>
      <address>103</address>
      <address>109</address>
   </street>
   <street>
      <name>Mercy Lane</name>
      <address>1424A</address>
      <address>1424B</address>
   </street>
</neighborhood>
```

And now consider the following XPointer:

```
xpointer(range-inside(//address))
```

Because the location-set passed to the function includes five members—the address elements—each of which is neither a point nor a range, we should expect this function to return a set of five range-type locations. The container for each of these locations is an address element, and the start point of each location within its container is at index 0 (that is, immediately following the element's start tag). The end point is the length of the corresponding address element's string-value—immediately following the 1, 3, 9, A, and B characters in the address elements. Thus, the function call returns the five ranges with the following string-values:

```
101
103
109
1424A
1424B
```

Now let's look at a different XPointer that uses range-inside( ):

```
xpointer(range-inside(//street[2]))
```

Only one location is passed to range-inside( ) here—the second street element—so we'll get back a single range. The container for the range is that street element itself, and the start point is set at index 0 (the node point immediately following the second street element's start tag). The end point of this street element location is a node point—the one preceding that street element's end tag. Therefore, the index of the returned range's end point is set to the number of children of the street element, or 3 (one name element and two address elements)—setting the end point to the node point immediately preceding the second street element's end tag. Thus, the returned range is:

```
<name>Mercy Lane</name>
<address>1424A</address>
<address>1424B</address>
```

# here( )

The here( ) function provides a convenient means to refer to the XML document or external parsed entity in which the XPointer itself appears. The location-set returned by the function has a single member, determined as follows:

- If the XPointer is in a text node inside an element node, the function returns that element node.
- Otherwise, the function returns whatever node directly contains the XPointer.

 The spec is careful to say that an XPointer using the here( ) function must appear in an XML document or external parsed entity, other- wise, the XPointer fails.

Here's a sample XML document using two XPointers:

```
<code>
    <navel-gazing>xpointer(here( )/..)</navel-gazing>
    <looking-elsewhere xlink:href="xpointer(here( )/..)"/>
</code>
```

The first XPointer, of course, appears in an element node—as the text node contained by the navel-gazing element. Therefore, the first XPointer locates the code element. The second XPointer occurs in the xlink:href attribute of the looking-elsewhere element; thus, this XPointer locates the parent of that attribute, or the looking-elsewhere element.

# origin( )

The only application in which you'll make use of the origin( ) function is when constructing an XPointer in an XLink context—specifically, when you need to identify the location at which a particular XLink's traversal begins. Complete coverage of XLink lies well outside this book's scope. In general, though, XLink provides for so-called "third party" and inbound links, in addition to the more familiar outbound-only links (such as XHTML's a elements with href attributes).

The particular problem that the origin( ) function addresses has to do with a series of XLinks in which succeeding links need to be *relative* to preceding ones. Without getting into the details of how the XLinks themselves are effected (syntactically or conceptually), an example of such a situation might be depicted something like the following pseudocode:

```
XLinkToChapter(xpointer([XPointer to a resource in some other document]))
XLinkToChapter(xpointer(origin( )/following-sibling::*))
```

Again, I stress that this is *not* the way these XLinks are actually constructed. The point is that the second link (the one with the call to the origin( ) function) need not "know" what the first one located; by using a relative XPath expression starting with the location designated by origin( ), it automatically gets (in this case) the next sibling of whatever was located by the first link. (If the target resources of the two XPointers were in the same document where the XLinks themselves were located, you could replace the call to origin( ) with a call to here( ) to achieve the same effect.)

Note that the origin( ) function depends for its operation not just on an XPointer-aware processor, but also on some level of XLink awareness. At the time of this writing, the XML landscape is not yet exactly littered with XLink-aware applications.

# Extension Functions for XPath in XSLT

While XPath includes a powerful set of basic functions, some applications of XPath need to support capabilities that go beyond that core. Currently, the most widely used XPath-based application is, of course, XSLT; aside from proprietary extensions offered through the various XSLT processors, it acquires these extra capabilities by way of two commonly used sets of extension functions. (Don't count on their availability in other XPath-based contexts, although because of their usefulness they may be adopted elsewhere as well.)

The first set of functions comes from XSLT itself, providing access to path, node, and string-value handling facilities necessary for XSLT processing. The second set of functions comes from the independent Extensions to XSLT (EXSLT) project, providing support for a variety of tasks that weren't addressed in either XPath 1.0 or XSLT 1.0.

## Additional Functions in XSLT 1.0

When XPath and XSLT were separated into two specifications, it was clear that there were some functions that relied on information available only through an understanding of the current XSLT processing context. These functions were kept in XSLT rather than in XPath, and (to repeat) may or may not be available in XPath processing in other contexts. You will see these functions used frequently in XSLT processing. Table A-1 lists the additional functions provided by XSLT 1.0.

*Table A-1. Additional functions provided by XSLT 1.0*

| Function prototype | Description |
| --- | --- |
| current() | Returns a node-set containing only the current node of the document being processed. |
| document(object, node-set?) | Returns a node-set containing either a document representing the union of the arguments (if the node-set argument is present) or, more typically, the document identified by the URI in the argument (if the first and only argument is a string containing a URI pointing to XML content.) |

*Table A-1. Additional functions provided by XSLT 1.0 (continued)*

| Function prototype | Description |
|---|---|
| `format-number(number, string, string?)` | Returns a string representing the number as formatted according to rules provided in the format pattern in the second argument, as well as the rules in an `xsl:decimal-format` element named by the optional third argument. Formatting patterns use the syntax of the Java JDK 1.1 DecimalFormat class. |
| `function-available(string)` | Returns a Boolean true or false, indicating whether the function named in the argument is available for use in the current XSLT processing environment. This is especially important in testing for the availability of EXSLT functions,, as well as extension functions that may be provided only by a given XSLT processor. |
| `generate-id(node-set?)` | Returns a string that can be used as a unique identifier for the first node in the node-set. Returns the empty string if the node-set is empty. |
| `key(string, object)` | Returns a node-set representing the content of a key created in the stylesheet using the `xsl:key` element. |
| `system-property(string)` | The string argument for this function must be a QName. Returns an object that represents the value of the system property identified by that name. All XSLT implementations must support `xsl:version`, `xsl:vendor`, and `xsl:vendor-url`. |
| `unparsed-entity-uri (string)` | Returns a string containing the URI of an unparsed entity declared using the string provided as the argument. If there is no entity declared using that name, it returns the empty string. |

Again, these functions should be used *only in the context of XSLT stylesheets*. While some non-XSLT implementations of XPath may provide more general support for them, the functions' behavior in those other contexts might only more or less correspond to their behavior according to the XSLT specification.

 The XSLT additional functions (and the XSLT features that provide the extra support they need) are all documented in the XSLT specification at *http://www.w3.org/TR/xslt#add-func*.

# EXSLT Extensions

EXSLT is a community project that provides extra functionality for XSLT and XPath. While not a product of the W3C, the EXSLT foundation is implemented across a variety of XSLT and XPath processors. Some EXSLT extensions require support for elements in XSLT stylesheets and are thus tightly bound to XSLT; others are relatively free standing and *may* be usable in other XPath contexts. The EXSLT extensions can be supported either through direct implementation in XSLT processors or through the use of XSLT modules, which themselves provide support for EXSLT functions using scripting or XSLT. EXSLT extensions may be implemented either as XSLT templates or as functions. In XPath terms, only the functions approach is easily available.

EXSLT is divided into eight modules, each containing its own group of functions (and possibly elements) and using its own namespace to identify the module. Within those modules reside "Core" functionality, which all EXSLT implementations *must* support, as well as "Other" functionality, which EXSLT implementations *may* support. The following sections explain each module and its contents.

 For additional information on EXSLT, including pointers to implementations and information on how to participate in creating or implementing EXSLT, see *http://www.exslt.org*.

## EXSLT Functions Module

Despite its name, the EXSLT Functions module doesn't contain any functions. Instead, it contains three elements that may be used to define extension functions. All these elements are in the http://exslt.org/functions namespace, typically mapped to the func prefix. Table A-2 lists these elements and their uses.

*Table A-2. EXSLT Functions module elements*

| Element name | Description | Status |
|---|---|---|
| func:function | Defines a named function visible throughout the XSLT stylesheet. Must appear in the top level of the XSLT stylesheet (that is, as a child of the root xsl:stylesheet element). Arguments are specified using xsl:param, while the return value is specified using func:result. | Core |
| func:result | Used inside of func:function to specify the value returned by the function. Its select attribute identifies the value to return. | Core |
| func:script | Used to define functions with scripting languages (such as ECMA-Script). Not all processors support all scripting languages, so this is useful primarily when the particular implementation that will be used for processing is known in advance. | Other |

Using these elements, you can create new functions for a wide variety of processing tasks, if the rest of the EXSLT library proves insufficient.

## EXSLT Dates-and-Times Module

The EXSLT Dates-and-times module provides a wide variety of tools for processing dates and times. All these elements and functions are in the http://exslt.org/dates-and-times namespace, typically mapped to the date prefix. Most of the module is simply functions, but there is also a date:date-format element for defining alternative formats to the ISO 8601 dates used by W3C XML Schema. Table A-3 lists this element and its use.

*Table A-3. Table A-3: EXSLT Dates-and-times module element*

| Element name | Description | Status |
|---|---|---|
| date:date-format | Permits the use of date formats other than ISO 8601's Gregorian format. The name attribute identifies a QName for the format, the calendar attribute identifies the calendar type (gregorian is the default), lang identifies the language used, and first-day-of-week provides a named value (i.e., sunday) to be used for the first day of the week. | Other |

The date:date-format element hasn't yet been implemented as of June 2002. Most of the rest of the Dates-and-times module is widely implemented, so working with ISO 8601 dates using EXSLT is not very difficult. ISO 8601 dates use the general format:

```
CCYY-MM-DDThh:mm:ss(Z|((+|-)hh:mm))
```

XML Schema Part 2: Datatypes provides more information on date and time formats at *http://www.w3.org/TR/xmlschema-2/*.

The EXSLT Dates-and-times module offers the wide variety of functions listed in Table A-4.

*Table A-4. EXSLT Dates-and-times module functions*

| Function prototype | Description | Status |
|---|---|---|
| date:date-time() | Returns a string containing the current date and time in ISO 8601 format. | Core |
| date:date(string?) | If the string argument is present, it returns a string containing the date portion of that ISO 8601 string. If the argument is not present, it returns the current date. | Core |
| date:time(string?) | If the string argument is present, it returns a string containing the time portion of that ISO 8601 string. If the argument is not present, it returns the current time. | Core |
| date:year(string?) | If the string argument is present, it returns a number containing the year portion of that ISO 8601 string. If the argument is not present, it returns the current year. | Core |
| date:leap-year(string?) | If the string argument is present, it returns a Boolean identifying whether the date in that ISO 8601 string occurs in a leap year. If the argument is not present, it returns whether the current year is a leap year. | Core |
| date:month-in-year(string?) | If the string argument is present, it returns a number containing the month portion of that ISO 8601 string. If the argument is not present, it returns the current month. | Core |
| date:month-name(string?) | If the string argument is present, it returns a string containing the name of the month identified by that ISO 8601 string. If the argument is not present, it returns the current month name. | Core |
| date:month-abbreviation(string?) | If the string argument is present, it returns a string containing an abbreviation for the name of the month identified by that ISO 8601 string. If the argument is not present, it returns the current month abbreviation. | Core |

*Table A-4. EXSLT Dates-and-times module functions (continued)*

| Function prototype | Description | Status |
|---|---|---|
| `date:week-in-year(string?)` | If the string argument is present, it returns a number identifying the week of the year of the date in that ISO 8601 string. If the argument is not present, it returns the current week of the year. | Core |
| `date:day-in-year(string?)` | If the string argument is present, it returns a number identifying the day of the year of the date in that ISO 8601 string. If the argument is not present, it returns the current day of the year. | Core |
| `date:day-in-month(string?)` | If the string argument is present, it returns a number containing the day portion of that ISO 8601 string. If the argument is not present, it returns the current day. | Core |
| `date:day-of-week-in-month(string?)` | If the string argument is present, it returns a number identifying which iteration of the current day of the week within the month for the date in that ISO 8601 string. If a date represents the second Friday in a month, the value is 2. If the argument is not present, it returns the value for the current date. | Core |
| `date:day-in-week(string?)` | If the string argument is present, it returns a number identifying which iteration of the current day of the week within the month for the date in that ISO 8601 string. If a date represents the second Friday in a month, the value is 2. If the argument is not present, it returns the value for the current date. | Core |
| `date:day-name(string?)` | If the string argument is present, it returns a string containing the name of the weekday identified by that ISO 8601 string. If the argument is not present, it returns the current weekday name. | Core |
| `date:day-abbreviation(string?)` | If the string argument is present, it returns a string containing an abbreviation for the name of the weekday identified by that ISO 8601 string. If the argument is not present, it returns the current weekday abbreviation. | Core |
| `date:hour-in-day(string?)` | If the string argument is present, it returns a number containing the hour portion of that ISO 8601 string. If the argument is not present, it returns the current hour. | Core |
| `date:minute-in-hour(string?)` | If the string argument is present, it returns a number containing the minute portion of that ISO 8601 string. If the argument is not present, it returns the current minute. | Core |
| `date:second-in-minute(string?)` | If the string argument is present, it returns a number containing the second portion of that ISO 8601 string. If the argument is not present, it returns the current second. | Core |
| `date:format-date(string, string)` | Formats a date (given as the first string argument) according to the pattern identified by the second string argument and returns it as a string. Permitted patterns are `xs:dateTime`, `xs:date`, `xs:time`, `xs:gYearMonth`, `xs:gYear`, `xs:gMonthDay`, `xs:gMonth`, and `xs:gDay`. | Other |
| `date:parse-date(string, string)` | The inverse of `date:format-date`, this function takes a string containing the date information and a pattern from the list above and returns a date in ISO 8601 format. | Other |
| `date:week-in-month(string?)` | If the string argument is present, it returns a number identifying the week of the month into which the date specified by the ISO 8601 string falls. If the argument is not present, it returns the week for the current date. | Other |

| Function prototype | Description | Status |
|---|---|---|
| `date:difference(string, string)` | Returns a string representation of the duration between the two dates passed as string arguments. | Other |
| `date:add(string, string)` | Returns a string representation of the date produced by adding the date in the first string argument to the duration in the second string argument. | Other |
| `date:add-duration(string, string)` | Returns a string representation of the duration produced by adding the duration in the first string argument to the duration in the second string argument. | Other |
| `date:sum(node-set)` | Returns a string representation of the duration produced by adding the durations stored in the node-set argument. | Other |
| `date:seconds(string?)` | Returns the number of seconds specified by the duration passed as a string. | Other |
| `date:duration(number?)` | Returns a duration string corresponding to the number of seconds passed as an argument. | Other |

The Dates-and-times module largely provides functionality that may eventually be provided by XPath 2.0.

(Note that day and month names returned by various of the functions listed in Table A-4, such as `date:day-name()` and `date:month-abbreviation()`, are the English-language forms, such as "Sunday" and "Jan." Also note that the abbreviation functions return the three-letter abbreviations for day and month names, e.g., "Thu" and "Sep" for Thursday and September, respectively.)

# EXSLT Dynamic Module

The EXSLT Dynamic module provides support for the dynamic evalution of XPath expressions created during XSLT or other processing. All these functions are in the http://exslt.org/dynamic namespace, typically mapped to the dyn prefix. This module contains only functions.

None of the Dynamic module has been implemented as of June 2002. The functions it provides are listed in Table A-5, and you should check the documentation of your implementation to find out if any of this is supported.

*Table A-5. EXSLT Dynamic module functions*

| Function prototype | Description | Status |
|---|---|---|
| `dyn:evaluate(string)` | Evaluates the string argument as an XPath expression and returns the result as an object. | Other |
| `dyn:min(node-set, string)` | Returns a number representing the minimum value produced by applying the XPath expression passed as the second argument to the node-set passed as the first argument. | Other |

*Table A-5. EXSLT Dynamic module functions (continued)*

| Function prototype | Description | Status |
|---|---|---|
| dyn:max(node-set, string) | Returns a number representing the maximum value produced by applying the XPath expression passed as the second argument to the node-set passed as the first argument. | Other |
| dyn:sum(node-set, string) | Returns a number representing the sum of the values produced by applying the XPath expression passed as the second argument to the node-set passed as the first argument. | Other |
| dyn:map(node-set, string) | Returns a node-set containing all the results produced by applying the XPath expression passed as the second argument to the node-set passed as the first argument. | Other |
| dyn:closure(node-set, string) | Returns a node-set containing all the results produced by applying the XPath expression passed as the second argument to the node-set passed as the first argument, after those results are processed using the XPath expression repetitively until no results are left. | Other |

# EXSLT Common Module

The EXSLT Common module provides one element for creating multiple output documents from a given transformation and two functions that address minor structural limitations of XSLT. The element and functions are in the http://exslt.org/common namespace, typically mapped to the exsl prefix. Table A-6 lists the one element and its use.

*Table A-6. EXSLT Common module element*

| Element name | Description | Status |
|---|---|---|
| exsl:document | Provides support for the creation of multiple output documents in XSLT processing. | Other |

The exsl:document element is widely implemented in EXSLT-compliant processors. It has no effect on XPath processing.

The EXSLT Common module offers the functions listed in Table A-7.

*Table A-7. EXSLT Common module functions*

| Function prototype | Description | Status |
|---|---|---|
| exsl:node-set(object) | Creates an XSLT node-set from an XSLT result tree fragment, permitting further processing of that information. Also converts strings into text nodes. | Core |
| exsl:object-type(object) | Returns the type of the object as string, number, boolean, node-set, RTF, or external. | Core |

Some of this functionality will be provided in XSLT 2.0 or XPath 2.0.

# EXSLT Math Module

The EXSLT Math module provides a variety of common mathematical functions and is easily used with XPath. All these functions are in the http://exslt.org/math namespace, typically mapped to the math prefix. With this module, you can use XPath to perform mathematical calculations on the contents of your documents, in ways far beyond the reach of XPath's own numeric functions and operators.

The EXSLT Math module offers the functions listed in Table A-8.

*Table A-8. EXSLT Math module functions*

| Function prototype | Description | Status |
|---|---|---|
| math:min(node-set) | Returns a number representing the minimum numeric value contained in the node-set. | Core |
| math:max(node-set) | Returns a number representing the maximum numeric value contained in the node-set. | Core |
| math:highest(node-set) | Returns a node-set containing the nodes whose value is the maximum numeric value contained in the node-set. | Core |
| math:lowest(node-set) | Returns a node-set containing the nodes whose value is the minimum numeric value contained in the node-set. | Core |
| math:abs(number) | Returns a number containing the absolute value of the number passed as an argument. | Other |
| math:sqrt(number) | Returns a number containing the square root of the number passed as an argument. | Other |
| math:power(number, number) | Returns a number representing the value of the first number argument raised to the power of the second number argument. | Other |
| math:constant(string, number) | Returns a constant specified by the string argument (PI, E, SQRRT2, LN2, LN10, LOG2E, SQRT1_2) to the precision specified by the number. | Other |
| math:log(number) | Returns a number containing the natural logarithm (base e) of the number passed as an argument. | Other |
| math:random() | Returns a random value between 0 and 1. | Other |
| math:sin(number) | Returns a number containing the sine of the number (in radians) passed as an argument. | Other |
| math:cos(number) | Returns a number containing the cosine of the number (in radians) passed as an argument. | Other |
| math:tan(number) | Returns a number containing the tangent of the number (in radians) passed as an argument. | Other |
| math:asin(number) | Returns a number containing the arcsine of the number passed as an argument. | Other |
| math:acos(number) | Returns a number containing the arccosine of the number passed as an argument. | Other |
| math:atan(number) | Returns a number containing the arctangent of the number passed as an argument. | Other |

*Table A-8. EXSLT Math module functions (continued)*

| Function prototype | Description | Status |
|---|---|---|
| `math:atan2(number, number)` | Returns the angle (in radians) from the X axis to the point where X is the first number and Y is the second. | Other |
| `math:exp(number)` | Returns a number containing the exponential of the number passed as an argument. | Other |

Various implementations provide different levels of support for the Math module.

## EXSLT Regular Expressions Module

The EXSLT Regular Expressions module provides regular expression functionality through three functions. All these functions are in the http://exslt.org/regular-expressions namespace, typically mapped to the regexp prefix. With this module, you can use XPath to break down or lexically analyze the contents of your documents. The EXSLT Regular Expressions module offers the functions listed in Table A-9.

*Table A-9. EXSLT Regular Expressions module functions*

| Function prototype | Description | Status |
|---|---|---|
| `regexp:test(string, string, string?)` | Returns a Boolean indicating whether the first string matches the regular expression identified by the second string. The third argument may contain flags for case sensitivity. | Other |
| `regexp:match(string, string, string?)` | Returns a node-set containing the pieces from the first string as returned from the match against the second string. The third argument may contain flags for case sensitivity or requirements for a global match. | Other |
| `regexp:replace(string, string, string, string)` | Returns a string containing a value produced by matching pieces of the first string against the regular expression in the second string and replacing those pieces with the string in the fourth argument. The third argument may contain flags for case sensitivity or requirements for a global match. | Other |

A variety of implementations for the Regular Expression module is available, though no processors support it natively.

## EXSLT Sets Module

The EXSLT Sets module provides six functions for working with node-sets. All these functions are in the http://exslt.org/sets namespace, typically mapped to the set prefix. With this module, you can use XPath to compare node-sets. The EXSLT Sets module offers the functions listed in Table A-10.

*Table A-10. EXSLT Sets module functions*

| Function prototype | Description | Status |
|---|---|---|
| `set:difference(node-set, node-set)` | Returns a node-set containing nodes that are in the first node-set argument but not in the second. | Core |
| `set:intersection(node-set, node-set)` | Returns a node-set containing nodes that are in both the first node-set argument and the second. | Core |
| `set:distinct(node-set)` | Returns a node-set containing a subset of nodes whose string values are unique within the node-set passed as an argument. | Core |
| `set:has-same-node(node-set, node-set)` | Returns a Boolean value indicating whether the two node-sets have any nodes in common. | Core |
| `set:leading(node-set, node-set)` | Returns a node-set containing the nodes in the first node-set that precede (in document order) those in the second node-set. | Core |
| `set:trailing(node-set, node-set)` | Returns a node-set containing the nodes in the first node-set that follow (in document order) those in the second node-set. | Core |

The Sets module is built into every processor that supports EXSLT, and implementations are available for other processors as well.

## EXSLT Strings Module

The EXSLT Strings module provides string-processing functionality through three functions. All these functions are in the http://exslt.org/strings namespace, typically mapped to the str prefix. With this module, you can use XPath to process the text contents of your documents using common string tools not otherwise provided by the XPath string functions. The EXSLT Strings module offers the functions listed in Table A-11.

*Table A-11. EXSLT Strings module functions*

| Function prototype | Description | Status |
|---|---|---|
| `str:tokenize(string, string?)` | Returns a node-set of token elements, containing fragments from the first string argument as broken down at boundaries established by the second. If the second argument is empty, the first argument is tokenized into individual characters. | Other |
| `str:replace(string, object, object)` | Returns a node-set. The first string argument is matched against the contents of the second argument, and those matches are replaced with the content of the third. | Other |
| `str:padding(number, string)` | Returns a string containing characters of the string argument repeated to create the length the number argument specifies. | Other |
| `str:align(string, string, string?)` | Returns the first string aligned to match the second string. The third argument specifies left, right, or center alignment. | Other |
| `str:encode-uri(string)` | Returns a string that reflects the value of the string argument URI-encoded for use in web documents. | Other |

*Table A-11. EXSLT Strings module functions (continued)*

| Function prototype | Description | Status |
|---|---|---|
| str:decode-uri(string) | Returns a string that reflects the value of the string argument URI-deoded for conversion from web documents. | Other |
| str:concat(node-set) | Returns a string containing the values of all the nodes in the node-set argument concatentated as a single string. | Other |
| str:split(string, string?) | Returns a node-set of token elements, containing fragments from the first string argument as broken down at boundaries established by the second. If the second argument is empty, the first argument is tokenized into individual characters. | Other |

A variety of implementations for the Strings module is available, though no processors support it natively.

# Index

We'd like to hear your suggestions for improving our indexes. Send email to *index@oreilly.com*.

## About the Author

**John E. Simpson's** forte is taking obscure bits of technical information and making them accessible. He is the author of *Just XML*, now in its second edition, and *Just XSL* (Prentice Hall), as well as XML.com's monthly XML Q&A column. John has been working with XML, XSL, and XPath since the technologies first emerged.

## Colophon

Our look is the result of reader comments, our own experimentation, and feedback from distribution channels. Distinctive covers complement our distinctive approach to technical topics, breathing personality and life into potentially dry subjects.

The birds on the cover of *XPath and XPointer* are bee-eaters. Bee-eaters can be found in tropical parts of Africa and Asia. Bee-eaters are brightly colored birds, often with a black stripe running from their eyes to the base of their long, sharp bills. They measure 6 to 14 inches in length.

Bee-eaters feed mostly on bees and wasps, hence their name. They catch the flying insects and bring them back to a perch, where the insects are devenomized. This is accomplished by pounding and rubbing the insect until all the venom is gone. Only one type of bee-eater eats vegetable matter. This type of bee-eater will also only feed on things it's caught in motion: it snatches nutshells dropped by squirrels out of the air and eats them.

Bee-eaters are gregarious birds. They often travel in flocks of hundreds or thousands, and they nest together in large colonies on riverbanks or along roads. Some species migrate between mating seasons.

Linley Dolby was the production editor and copyeditor, and Sarah Sherman was the proofreader for *XPath and XPointer*. Matt Hutchinson and Claire Cloutier provided quality control. Johnna VanHoose Dinse wrote the index. Kimo Carter and Judy Hoer provided production assistance.

Ellie Volckhausen designed the cover of this book, based on a series design by Edie Freedman. The cover image is a 19th-century engraving from the Dover Pictorial Archive. Emma Colby produced the cover layout with QuarkXPress 4.1 using Adobe's ITC Garamond font.

David Futato designed the interior layout. This book was converted to FrameMaker 5.5.6 with a format conversion tool created by Erik Ray, Jason McIntosh, Neil Walls, and Mike Sierra that uses Perl and XML technologies. Joe Wizda provided additional Tools support. The text font is Linotype Birka; the heading font is Adobe Myriad Condensed; and the code font is LucasFont's TheSans Mono Condensed. The illustrations that appear in the book were produced by Robert Romano and Jessamyn Read using Macromedia FreeHand 9 and Adobe Photoshop 6. The tip and warning icons were drawn by Christopher Bing. This colophon was written by Linley Dolby.